ADVANCED
STM32
MICROCONTROLLERS

A Step-by-Step Mastery for STM32 Hardware and Firmware Engineers

ETHAN COLE MARSTON

Dedication

To the engineers, developers, and makers who stay up late solving problems,
debugging lines of code, and sketching out designs on scraps of paper.
May this book fuel your journey and remind you that every challenge is an opportunity to innovate.

Table of Contents

Preface

About This Book

The STM32 family of microcontrollers has evolved into one of the most versatile and widely adopted platforms in embedded systems development. From industrial automation to consumer electronics, from robotics to IoT, STM32 has become a cornerstone for engineers who demand flexibility, performance, and reliability. Yet, despite its popularity, many developers find themselves trapped at the beginner or intermediate level—comfortable with GPIO toggling, UART communication, or simple timers, but hesitant to dive into advanced features, hardware optimization, or firmware scalability.

This book was written to change that.

ADVANCED STM32 MICROCONTROLLER: A Step-by-Step Mastery for STM32 Hardware and Firmware Engineers is not a beginner's guide. Instead, it's designed as a **deep technical roadmap** that transitions you from a capable developer into a master-level engineer. The focus is not just on *how* to program an STM32, but on *why* design decisions matter, *what trade-offs* to consider, and *how to future-proof* your projects in real-world applications.

Throughout the chapters, you'll find a balance of **hardware design considerations**, **firmware engineering techniques**, **scalability strategies**, and **professional workflows** including version control, testing, and compliance. The book mirrors the natural evolution of a project: from idea to prototype, to productization, and finally to long-term support.

At its core, this book is about **building confidence and mastery** with the STM32 platform—equipping you with the mindset and skills needed to design systems that don't just "work," but excel.

Who Should Read This Book

This book is written with a clear audience in mind:

- **Intermediate Engineers Ready to Advance**
  If you already have experience with STM32 basics—such as blinking LEDs, simple peripheral drivers, or using STM32CubeMX—but want to move toward more professional engineering practices, this book is for you.

- **Professional Firmware and Hardware Engineers**
  If you are actively working in embedded systems, robotics, or IoT, this book will help sharpen your design thinking, debugging techniques, and optimization strategies to meet production-grade standards.

- **Students and Researchers**
  If you're a graduate student, researcher, or technical enthusiast aiming to push STM32 applications into advanced domains like machine learning, signal processing, or real-time control, this text provides the tools and frameworks to expand your scope.

- **Product Developers and Entrepreneurs**
  If you're building commercial devices, this book highlights not just engineering techniques but also **scalability, compliance, and supply chain considerations**—critical elements for moving from prototype to mass production.

In short: whether you're an **engineer sharpening your skills**, a **student building expertise**, or an **entrepreneur scaling a product**, this book speaks to you.

How to Use This Book

This book has been structured with a **progressive workflow** that mirrors how projects evolve in the real world. You don't need to read it linearly, but doing so provides a full picture of advanced STM32 development.

- **Start with the Foundations** – Early chapters cover project workflows, design considerations, and core firmware practices. Even if you're experienced, revisiting these with an advanced lens will sharpen your approach.

- **Dive into Hardware and Firmware Mastery** – The central chapters explore peripheral optimization, memory management, real-time systems, debugging strategies, and advanced STM32 features such as FPU, DSP, and low-power modes.

- **Transition to Scalability and Productization** – Later chapters address critical professional aspects such as migration between STM32 series, certification, compliance, production programming, and test fixtures.

- **Stay Future-Ready** – The final chapters explore long-term support strategies, supply chain challenges, and emerging trends like AI at the edge, security frameworks, and energy-aware computing.

Practical Tip: Don't just read this book—*use it*. Revisit chapters during your projects, reference workflows while debugging, and apply techniques directly into your firmware and hardware design. This book is meant to be a **hands-on companion**, not just a reference manual.

What's New in STM32 Microcontroller and Beyond

The STM32 ecosystem continues to evolve rapidly, with STMicroelectronics expanding its lineup to meet emerging challenges in edge computing, AI integration, and ultra-low-power applications. In writing this book, I've incorporated the **latest advancements and shifts in the STM32 landscape**, including:

- **STM32H7 and STM32MP1 Families** – High-performance series with dual-core Cortex-M7/M4 and microprocessor-class capabilities, enabling more complex applications.

- **TrustZone and Security Features** – Newer STM32 devices emphasize **hardware-based security**, secure boot, and cryptographic accelerators to support IoT security standards.

- **AI at the Edge** – STM32Cube.AI and related frameworks now allow machine learning models to be deployed directly onto STM32 devices, opening doors for edge AI applications.

- **Ultra-Low Power Innovations** – Families like STM32L4 and STM32U5 continue to push the limits of battery-powered designs with advanced sleep modes and optimized power domains.

- **Enhanced Development Ecosystem** – Tools such as STM32CubeIDE, STM32CubeProgrammer, and STM32CubeMX now integrate more seamlessly with version control systems and CI/CD pipelines, supporting professional-grade workflows.

Looking beyond STM32 itself, the trends in embedded systems point toward:

- **Greater Integration of AI and ML** into resource-constrained devices.

- **More robust real-time and safety-critical frameworks** as embedded devices penetrate medical, automotive, and aerospace sectors.

- **Growing emphasis on energy efficiency, supply chain resilience, and long-term support**, all of which shape how we design today for tomorrow's constraints.

This book doesn't just focus on what STM32 *is* today—it prepares you for **where it is heading** and ensures you stay ahead of the curve.

Chapter 1: Introduction to STM32 Microcontrollers

STM32 is STMicroelectronics' family of 32-bit microcontrollers built on Arm® Cortex-M cores. It spans tiny, cost-sensitive devices through ultra-high-performance parts with rich connectivity, security, and advanced analog. Because the software ecosystem is mature (HAL/LL drivers, CubeMX/CubeIDE, FreeRTOS integrations, and extensive middleware) and the hardware lineup is broad, STM32 has become a default choice for learning embedded systems and for shipping commercial products at scale

This chapter gives you a working mental model of the STM32 universe: what the families are, how the Arm Cortex-M architecture works in practice, how to choose the right series for a project, and where these devices show up in real products and research.

Overview of the STM32 Family

Big picture. STM32 devices are grouped by series, each targeting a performance/power/cost niche. Within a series you'll find many part numbers that vary in core, clock speed, flash/RAM sizes, packages, peripherals, temperature range, and qualification level.

Common architectural ingredients across series

- **Arm Cortex-M cores** (M0/M0+, M3, M4, M7, M33; occasionally dual-core combinations).

- **Hierarchical bus and clocking** (AHB & APB buses; multiple domains and prescalers).

- **Rich timers** (basic, general-purpose, advanced; PWM, encoder, input capture/compare).

- **Analog** (ADC(s), comparators, op-amps in some series, DAC(s)).

- **Digital comms** (UART/USART, I²C, SPI; many series add CAN FD, USB, SDMMC, QSPI, Ethernet).

- **Direct Memory Access (DMA/DMAMUX)** to move data without CPU intervention.

- **Security** (from basic read-out protection to TrustZone®, secure boot, crypto accelerators on newer lines).

- **Low-power modes** (Sleep/Stop/Standby + retention options).

- **Development stack** (CMSIS + HAL/LL drivers, CubeMX configuration, middleware such as USB, TCP/IP, file systems, RTOS).

Representative STM32 series (conceptual map)

- **Entry / Cost-Optimized: C0, G0, F0** – simple control/IO, small memory, aggressive pricing.

- **Mainstream: F1, F3, G4** – balanced performance, robust analog/control (F3/G4 popular for motor control).

- **High Performance: F4, F7, H7** – DSP/FPU, large memory, external memory interfaces, rich connectivity; H7 at the top end with very high CPU throughput and dual-core options (M7+M4 on some parts).

- **Ultra-Low-Power: L0, L1, L4, L4+, L5, U5** – optimized for battery life; newer L5/U5 bring Cortex-M33 with TrustZone and advanced power features.

- **Security- and Connectivity-Centric**: **H5 (M33)** with modern security, **W series (WB/WBA/WL)** for Bluetooth LE or sub-GHz LoRa® radios integrated on-chip.

(STM32MP1 is an MPU family with Cortex-A cores; powerful but outside "microcontroller" scope.)

ARM Cortex-M Architecture Fundamentals

Understanding the Cortex-M substrate helps you write efficient, predictable firmware that ports across STM32 series.

Core and Instruction Set

- **Thumb-2 ISA**: 16/32-bit mixed-width instruction encoding for code density + performance.

- **Cores**:

  - **M0/M0+**: smallest, no hardware divide (M0), baseline microcontroller feature set.

  - **M3**: adds richer instructions and better exception handling.

  - **M4**: optional single-precision **FPU** and **DSP** (SIMD) instructions (many STM32F4/G4 include these).

  - **M7**: high-performance pipeline, caches, tightly coupled memories; ideal for control + signal processing + UI.

  - **M33**: Armv8-M with **TrustZone** for hardware-enforced separation; optional FPU & DSP; modern low-power.

Privilege, Exceptions, and Real Time

- **NVIC (Nested Vectored Interrupt Controller)**: fixed vector table at reset, configurable priority levels and sub-priority groupings, tail-chaining to reduce interrupt latency.

- **SysTick**: 24-bit down counter commonly used for OS ticks or simple timing.

- **MPU (Memory Protection Unit)**: present on many cores; enforces region-based access control and aids RTOS isolation.

- **Determinism**: With caches (e.g., M7), understand instruction/data cache effects and TCM/AXI SRAM placement for real-time critical code and ISRs.

Memory Map and Buses

- **Unified 4 GB map** with regions for code/flash, SRAM, peripherals, external memories, and system control.

- **AHB/APB domains**: peripherals live on APB; high-bandwidth blocks (DMA, FMC/QSPI, Ethernet) sit on AHB/AXI.

- **Wait states & latency**: flash wait states at higher clocks are hidden by prefetch and cache; locate hot loops or ISR data in fast SRAM/TCM when available.

Low-Power Model

- **Clock gating** per domain and peripheral.

- **Sleep/Stop/Standby**: progressively deeper modes; SRAM/reg retention options vary by series; wakeup sources include EXTI, RTC, LPTIM, and communication events.

- **Measure & verify**: use IDD measurement pins or on-chip monitors where provided; design firmware around event-driven operation.

Acceleration and Peripherals

- **DMA/DMAMUX**: chain transfers, circular buffering for ADC/UART, double-buffer for continuous streaming.

- **Math & DSP**: utilize CMSIS-DSP for filters/FFTs; single-precision FPU accelerates control/signal algorithms.

- **Security** (newer series): true RNG, AES/PKA, secure boot/firmware update, immutable root of trust, TrustZone partitioning.

STM32 Series Comparison and Selection Guide

Choosing the "right" MCU is an engineering trade-off. Use the checklist below, then narrow to 2–3 candidate series.

ADVANCED STM32 MICROCONTROLLERS

Selection Checklist

1. **Workload & Performance**

   - Control-oriented, signal processing, or UI/graphics?

   - Estimated MIPS/MFLOPS; ISR latency requirements; use of DSP/FPU.

   - Need caches/TCM (e.g., M7) or is deterministic SRAM sufficient?

2. **Power Budget**

   - Duty cycle (active vs sleep), battery capacity/chemistry, peak vs average current.

   - Required wake-up sources and resume latency; RTC accuracy.

3. **Memory**

   - Code size now + 2× headroom; data buffers; RTOS/middleware footprint.

   - External memory? (QSPI/XIP, FMC SDRAM/PSRAM).

4. **Peripherals**

   - **Comms**: # of UART/I²C/SPI; USB FS/HS; Ethernet; CAN FD; SDMMC; QSPI/OSPI.

   - **Analog**: # channels, sampling rate, resolution, internal op-amps/comp, DAC.

   - **Timers**: advanced PWM for motor control (complementary outputs, dead-time), encoder inputs.

   - **Special**: touch sensing, camera DCMI, graphics accelerators, cryptography, hardware radio.

5. **Security / Safety**

   - TrustZone, secure boot, crypto accelerators, tamper detection.

   - Functional safety (documentation and diagnostics support), AUTOSAR needs.

6. **Cost, Availability, Lifecycle**

o   Package constraints and PCB complexity; temperature rating; AEC-Q100/industrial variants.

o   Long-term availability and multi-sourcing strategy.

7. **Ecosystem & Reuse**

o   Middleware requirements (USB, TCP/IP, file system).

o   Internal team familiarity; reuse of drivers/boards.

Series-at-a-Glance (qualitative)

- **C0/G0/F0 (Entry)**

    o   **Use when**: minimal cost, simple control, modest memory, few comms.

    o   **Notes**: great for glue logic, basic sensors/actuators, simple IoT endpoints with external radios.

- **F1 (Classic Mainstream)**

    o   **Use when**: proven ecosystem, many examples, general control tasks.

    o   **Notes**: legacy-friendly; not the lowest power or highest performance today.

- **F3 / G4 (Control & Mixed-Signal)**

    o   **Use when**: motor control, PFC, fast ADCs, comparators, internal op-amps, high-resolution timers.

    o   **Notes**: G4 adds modern features and performance uplift over F3.

- **F4 (High-Perf M4)**

    o   **Use when**: DSP/FPU needed, substantial middleware, but you don't require M7 speed.

    o   **Notes**: rich connectivity; mature libraries and community content.

- **F7 (Early M7)**

- o **Use when**: higher throughput than F4, external memory interfaces, advanced graphics/UIs.

- o **Notes**: instruction/data caches; be mindful of cache coherency with DMA.

- **H7 (Top-End Performance)**

  - o **Use when**: maximum MCU performance, dual-core options (M7+M4), high-speed peripherals, external memory/graphics.

  - o **Notes**: excellent for complex gateways, audio, vision preprocessing, industrial control with networking.

- **L0/L1 (Legacy ULP)**

  - o **Use when**: very low cost + low power with modest performance.

  - o **Notes**: superseded in many cases by L4/L5/U5.

- **L4/L4+ (Modern ULP M4)**

  - o **Use when**: excellent energy efficiency, decent performance, rich analog.

  - o **Notes**: sweet spot for battery IoT and data logging.

- **L5 / U5 (ULP with Security, M33)**

  - o **Use when**: low energy + **TrustZone**, modern crypto, secure boot, more memory.

  - o **Notes**: good for medical/wearable/enterprise IoT where security is a must.

- **H5 (Secure Mainstream, M33)**

  - o **Use when**: mainstream cost with modern security features and solid performance.

  - o **Notes**: bridge between ULP-secure and high-performance families.

- **WB/WBA (Bluetooth LE) & WL (Sub-GHz)**

  - o **Use when**: integrated radios reduce BOM and size; you need certified stacks.

  - o **Notes**: plan PCB/radio design carefully (RF layout, antennas, coexistence).

Tip: If you're unsure, prototype on **Nucleo** boards for 2–3 candidate series (e.g., ULP vs performance-oriented) and measure real-world current, throughput, and peripheral behavior before freezing the design.

Example Decision Patterns

- **Battery sensor node** (years of life): U5/L5/L4; use STOP modes, RTC, LPTIM, DMA-driven ADC bursts.

- **Field-oriented motor controller**: G4/F3 or H7 for multi-motor/high-bandwidth; leverage op-amps/comp and high-res timers.

- **Secure connected gateway**: H5/U5/H7 with crypto, TrustZone (M33), Ethernet/USB HS/QSPI for OTA + external storage.

- **High-end UI (TFT, touch, audio)**: F7/H7 with external SDRAM and graphics acceleration; consider parallel RGB/DSI and SAI.

Key Applications in Industry and Research

STM32 devices power everything from disposable sensors to industrial automation lines. Below are representative domains and the MCU features they lean on.

Industrial & Motor Control

- **Use cases**: servo drives, robotics joints, CNC, power factor correction, digital power supplies.

- **Key features**: advanced timers (center-aligned PWM, dead-time insertion), fast ADCs synchronized to PWM, comparators/op-amps (G4/F3), encoder interfaces, CAN FD, Ethernet for real-time comms, high-temperature grades.

- **Why STM32**: deterministic peripherals, DMA pipelines, mature motor-control libraries.

IoT Endpoints & Gateways

- **Use cases**: environmental sensors, asset tracking, home/office automation, industrial telemetry.

- **Key features**: ULP modes (L4/L5/U5), RTC, LPTIM, hardware crypto, secure boot/OTA, integrated radios (WB/WBA/WL) or external modules over SPI/UART, TLS stacks.

ADVANCED STM32 MICROCONTROLLERS

- **Why STM32**: comprehensive low-power toolkit, TrustZone (M33), long-lived ecosystem and middleware.

Consumer Electronics & Wearables

- **Use cases**: smartwatches, audio accessories, toys, small appliances.

- **Key features**: ULP + decent performance (L4/U5), USB audio/MIDI, SAI/I²S for sound, capacitive touch, display interfaces, Bluetooth LE (WB/WBA).

- **Why STM32**: balance of energy efficiency, peripherals, and small packages.

Medical and Laboratory Devices (non-diagnostic discussion)

- **Use cases**: patient monitors, handheld analyzers, lab instruments, infusion controllers.

- **Key features**: high-resolution ADCs, reliable timers, secure firmware update, event logging with RTC, USB/HS for data, Ethernet for integration, safety diagnostics.

- **Why STM32**: wide range of analog and security options; documentation suited to regulated environments (with appropriate system-level compliance).

Networking, HMI, and Audio

- **Use cases**: human-machine interfaces with TFTs, touch, and audio feedback; PoE panels; intercoms.

- **Key features**: external SDRAM via FMC, QSPI/XIP for large code/assets, LTDC/DSI display, Chrom-ART/graphics acceleration (on select series), SAI, USB HS, Ethernet MAC with DMA.

- **Why STM32**: high-bandwidth peripherals, caches/TCM (M7), robust middleware.

Research & Education

- **Use cases**: algorithm prototyping (control, DSP, ML inference), sensor fusion, custom instrumentation.

- **Key features**: FPU/DSP (M4/M7/M33), CMSIS-DSP/NN libraries, fast ADCs and timers, easy inline assembly and cycle-accurate profiling via DWT counters.

- **Why STM32**: affordable dev kits, consistent toolchain, reproducible timing behavior.

Practical Notes: Tools, Code Style, and Reuse

- **CubeMX/CubeIDE** accelerates pin/peripheral configuration and generates HAL/LL scaffolding. Use **HAL** for portability and quick bring-up; drop to **LL** or **register-level** for time-critical paths.

- **RTOS**: FreeRTOS and ThreadX are commonly used; pair with DMA and event-driven drivers to keep ISRs short.

- **Testing & CI**: abstract hardware access behind interfaces so you can host-test business logic; on-target testing via semihosting/serial; capture power/throughput metrics as part of regression.

- **Security hygiene**: set **RDP** level appropriately, enable **secure boot**/authenticity checks on capable parts, partition code/data with **TrustZone** where available, and plan **OTA** with rollback and monotonic counters.

- **Documentation habit**: keep a "clock tree" and "pin/peripheral map" page per project, plus a power-modes table with measured currents and wake latencies.

Quick Start: Mapping Needs to Series (cheat sheet)

- **Lowest cost control** → C0/G0/F0

- **Analog + motor control** → G4/F3

- **General purpose, rich examples** → F4

- **Max performance / heavy middleware / UI** → H7 (or F7 if legacy)

- **Battery IoT with security** → U5/L5 (M33 TrustZone)

- **Integrated Bluetooth LE or sub-GHz** → WB/WBA or WL

- **Modern security with mainstream perf** → H5

Chapter 2: Understanding the STM32 Ecosystem

The STM32 ecosystem is more than microcontrollers—it is a coordinated stack of **hardware platforms (boards and probes), software tools (IDEs, code generators, debuggers, programmers),** and **reference assets (firmware packages, middleware, application notes, and community examples).** Learning how these pieces fit together lets you move from idea to working prototype—and then to production—rapidly and reliably.

STM32 Nucleo, Discovery, and Eval Boards

STM32 development boards fall into three broad families, each optimized for a different phase of the design journey: **Nucleo** for general prototyping, **Discovery** for feature-rich demonstrations and hands-on learning, and **Evaluation (Eval)** for product-level validation of interfaces and performance.

Nucleo Boards (Rapid Prototyping and Education)

Purpose. A low-cost, general-purpose platform that exposes most MCU pins and makes it easy to stack add-on shields.

Defining traits

- **On-board ST-LINK debugger/programmer** (typically STLINK-V2-1 or V3E), so you can flash and debug over USB without extra tools.

- **Standard expansion headers**: most Nucleo-64 and -144 boards provide Arduino Uno R3–compatible headers; many also include **ST morpho** headers that break out nearly every MCU pin.

- **Variants by size**:

  - **Nucleo-32**: compact, breadboard-friendly; often with Arduino Nano-style header spacing.

  - **Nucleo-64**: common "sweet spot" for learning and prototyping.

  - **Nucleo-144**: high-pin-count MCUs with more peripherals, often including Ethernet or HS USB on certain models.

- **Breadth across families**: available for entry-level (G0/C0), mainstream (F1/F3/G4), ultra-low-power (L4/L5/U5), and high-performance (F7/H7) MCUs.

When to choose Nucleo

- You need fast bring-up, flexible IO access, and compatibility with popular shields and sensor boards.

- You want a board whose **schematics and BOM** are public, aiding custom PCB design.

Typical workflow

1. Create/initialize a project with STM32CubeMX/CubeIDE.

2. Verify pin muxing against Arduino and morpho headers.

3. Debug via the on-board ST-LINK; monitor logs over the virtual COM port.

Discovery Kits (Feature Demonstrations and Thematic Learning)

Purpose. To showcase a device family's **key peripherals** through on-board sensors, displays, audio, radios, and connectors—ideal for learning and for reference designs.

Defining traits

- Populated with **peripheral hardware** matched to the MCU's strengths: TFT displays, MEMS microphones, audio codecs, motion sensors, environmental sensors, radios (BLE/sub-GHz), PMICs, and sometimes cameras.

- Provided **demo firmwares** and application notes that show best practices (graphics pipelines, DSP chains, connectivity stacks, security boot flows).

- Still include **on-board ST-LINK** for one-cable bring-up.

When to choose Discovery

- You want to study a **complete subsystem** (e.g., graphics on H7 with external SDRAM and LTDC; IoT node with sensors + Wi-Fi/BLE).

- You value **reference schematics/layouts** that demonstrate high-speed or analog design techniques you can replicate.

Evaluation Boards (Comprehensive Connectivity and Validation)

Purpose. High-end, fully loaded platforms that expose **every major interface** of a device for performance and compliance validation.

Defining traits

- External memory (QSPI/OSPI, SDRAM/PSRAM), multiple PHYs (Ethernet HS, USB HS with ULPI), camera connectors, high-power stages, expansion sites.

- Often larger, costlier, and targeted at professional validation, benchmarking, and pre-certification work.

- Rich documentation: schematics, layout files, power trees, and sometimes IBIS or simulation models.

When to choose Eval

- You are architecting a product that will use **external memories**, **HS connectivity**, or complex **graphics/vision** pipelines.

- You need to de-risk bandwidth, latency, and signal integrity **before** spinning custom hardware.

Blue Pill, Black Pill, and Third-Party Boards

Beyond ST's official boards, the community and third-party ecosystem provide compact, inexpensive modules. These are excellent for learning and small deployments, but require informed choices.

"Blue Pill"

- Typically built around **STM32F103C8/C8T6** (Cortex-M3, 72 MHz), though clones and variants abound.

- Extremely low-cost; common for hobby projects, basic control, and educational use.

- **Caveats**

  - Quality varies. Some boards use non-ST chips or mislabeled parts.

  - Early batches famously shipped with an **incorrect USB pull-up resistor** value that breaks native USB—verify or be prepared to rework.

  - Schematic consistency is not guaranteed; always inspect the specific board's pinout and components.

"Black Pill"

- Popular modern variants (e.g., WeAct) use **STM32F411CE** or **F401** (Cortex-M4 + FPU, up to ~100–120 MHz), offering **more Flash/RAM** and better performance than Blue Pill.

- Often include **USB (FS)**, onboard oscillator, and convenient pin headers in a compact layout.

- Better suited to **DSP, control loops, and moderately complex middleware** than the F103.

Other Third-Party Options

- **Pyboard** (STM32F405): reference MicroPython board—rock-solid build, great for rapid scripting.

- **Feather/Express-style boards** (e.g., STM32F405 variants): integrate well with Adafruit's Feather ecosystem (sensors, radios).

- **Arduino Pro/Portenta boards** (e.g., Portenta H7 with STM32H747): dual-core M7+M4 with rich connectivity and commercial-grade modules.

- **Specialist modules**: STM32WB/WBA (BLE) or WL (sub-GHz) modules pre-certified for RF, saving time on regulatory approvals.

Best practices with third-party boards

- Confirm **exact MCU part number**, **Flash/RAM size**, and **crystals**; update your CubeMX settings accordingly.

- Check **boot configuration** (BOOT0/BOOT1) and any **DFU** or **UART boot** access method the board supports.

- Keep an **ST-LINK** handy: even if a board ships with a USB bootloader, ST-LINK gives you reliable debug and recovery.

- For production, prefer boards with **published schematics** and predictable sourcing.

ST-LINK Debugger and Programmer Options

ST-LINK is the default path for flashing and debugging STM32. It speaks **SWD** (and sometimes JTAG) and often exposes a **virtual COM port** and **bridge interfaces** to help during development.

Embedded vs External

- **Embedded ST-LINK**: present on most Nucleo/Discovery/Eval boards. Convenient for that board and can often be **broken out** to program external targets via a small header.

- **External ST-LINK**: a standalone probe you can use with any board that exposes SWD signals.

ST-LINK Variants (capabilities you should know)

- **STLINK-V2-1** (legacy on-board): SWD + VCP; recognized by CubeIDE/CubeProgrammer; adequate for most tasks.

- **STLINK-V3 family** (current generation):

  ○ **V3MINI**: compact, affordable external probe; SWD/SWO, VCP, and high-speed operation in a pocket form factor.

  ○ **V3SET / V3MODS**: modular probes with **bridge features** (I²C/SPI/UART/GPIO) for scripting and testing, and standardized **STDC14/MIPI-10** connectors and adapters.

  ○ **V3E**: commonly embedded on newer Nucleo/Discovery boards.

  ○ **V3PWR**: adds **precision power measurement and power supply** capabilities so you can profile current consumption while debugging firmware.

- **Signal considerations**: connect **SWDIO, SWCLK, NRST, GND**, and **VTref** (target voltage sense). Keep cables short to avoid signal integrity issues.

SWD, SWO, and ETM

- **SWD (Serial Wire Debug)**: two wires plus reset and ground—standard for STM32.

- **SWO (Serial Wire Output)**: enables **ITM "printf"-style tracing**, RTOS awareness, and live variable views with minimal CPU overhead.

- **ETM instruction trace**: requires additional trace pins and typically a **dedicated high-end probe** (e.g., ULINKpro / J-Trace). ST-LINK supports SWO; for full ETM streaming, plan appropriate hardware and probe.

Alternatives and Interoperability

- **SEGGER J-Link** and **Keil ULINK** probes work well with STM32 and may offer advanced trace.

- **CMSIS-DAP/DAPLink** works with open tools and VS Code environments.

- **OpenOCD** and **pyOCD** provide open-source debug servers that integrate with GDB, VS Code, and PlatformIO.

Practical tips

- Always share **ground** between probe and target, and ensure **VTref** is connected so the probe detects IO voltage.

- If the target won't connect, try **Recovery**: hold the MCU in **bootloader** or **reset**, lower SWD speed, or connect under reset via CubeProgrammer.

- For low-power validation, consider **V3PWR** to log current while stepping through code.

STMicroelectronics Support Tools and Resources

ST's software stack and documentation are extensive. The following tools cover 95% of day-to-day development, testing, and productization.

Core Development

- **STM32CubeMX**: graphical configuration tool for **pin muxing**, **clock trees**, and **peripheral initialization**. Generates HAL/LL scaffolding and middleware hooks.

- **STM32CubeIDE**: Eclipse-based IDE integrating MX, GCC/Clang toolchains, debugging, RTOS awareness, and code analysis in one environment.

- **STM32CubeProgrammer (GUI + CLI)**: universal programmer for **ST-LINK, UART, SPI/I²C, and USB DFU** interfaces. Replaces older ST-LINK Utility/DFuSe. Automate production flashes with STM32_Programmer_CLI.

Firmware and Middleware

- **STM32Cube MCU Firmware Packages** (e.g., **STM32CubeF4, STM32CubeH7**): HAL/LL drivers, BSPs for official boards, examples, and middleware (USB Device/Host, **FATFS**, **LwIP**, **FreeRTOS** integration).

- **X-CUBE / I-CUBE expansions**: add-on stacks for **BLE, LoRaWAN, Matter/Thread**, motor control, graphics, security, and more.

- **CMSIS-DSP and CMSIS-NN**: optimized math, filters, FFTs, and neural-network kernels for Cortex-M.

Graphics and HMI

- **TouchGFX Designer**: WYSIWYG tool and code framework for creating **hardware-accelerated UIs** on MCUs with LTDC/Chrom-ART™. Includes simulators, resource management, and BSPs for Discovery/Eval boards.

Connectivity, Sensing, and Control

- **STM32 Motor Control SDK + Workbench**: model-based configuration and code generation for **FOC**, PFC, and multi-motor control using G4/F3/H7 families.

- **STM32CubeMonitor**: live variable visualization and dashboards over ST-LINK/VCP—great for tuning control loops and calibrations.

- **STM32CubeMonitor-RF**: RF testing/monitoring for **Bluetooth LE** devices (WB/WBA).

- **STM32CubeMonUCPD**: USB Type-C / Power Delivery monitoring and tuning.

AI and Data Processing

- **STM32Cube.AI**: converts trained ML models (TensorFlow/Keras, ONNX) into optimized C inference code for STM32; supports quantization and memory/performance trade-offs.

- **NanoEdge AI Studio**: on-device tinyML (often anomaly detection/classification) with automated feature generation; particularly useful for **predictive maintenance** on vibration sensors.

Documentation and Knowledge Base

- **Datasheets** (electrical characteristics, pinouts), **Reference Manuals** (peripheral registers), **Programming Manuals** (core and instruction set), and **Errata** (silicon limitations and workarounds).

- **Application Notes**: deep dives on bootloaders, low power, memory protection, USB, Ethernet, security, and motor control. A must-read example is the system-memory bootloader overview used to select DFU/UART/CAN boot interfaces for each series.

- **Board User Manuals** and **Altium/GERBERs** for official kits—excellent for learning proper power, clock, and high-speed layout practices.

- **ST Community Forum** and **ST Wiki**: searchable answers, example projects, and clarifications straight from ST engineers and users.

- **MCU Finder** (desktop/mobile): filters MCUs by peripherals, memory, power, package, and availability; links directly to documentation and eval kits.

Production and Test

- **CubeProgrammer CLI** scripting for **factory programming** (option bytes, readout protection levels, unique ID serialization).

- **STLINK-V3PWR** or external SMUs for **current profiling** in test fixtures.

- **Hardware expansion packs** and **BSP drivers** to create repeatable **manufacturing tests** for IOs, memories, and senso

---

Putting It All Together: A Practical On-Ramp

1. **Pick a board** that matches your learning goal:

   ○ General embedded fundamentals → **Nucleo-64** in the series you plan to use.

   ○ Graphics or audio → a **Discovery** kit with a TFT and codec.

   ○ High-speed networking or external memories → the relevant **Eval** board.

2. **Create the project** in **STM32CubeIDE**:

   ○ Configure **clocks**, **pins**, and **peripherals** in **CubeMX**.

   ○ Generate **HAL/LL** scaffolding with DMA-friendly data paths.

3. **Flash and debug** using the **on-board ST-LINK**:

   ○ Use **SWO/ITM** for non-intrusive runtime logs.

   ○ Keep ISRs short and push work to DMA and tasks (if using an RTOS).

4. **Iterate with measurement**:

   ○ Validate **latency** (scope/logic analyzer on timer/comms pins).

     ○   Profile **power** (STLINK-V3PWR or shunt + DMM) and adjust sleep strategies.

5. **Scale your design**:

     ○   Migrate the same project to another Nucleo (e.g., G4 → H5) by re-pinning in MX.

     ○   When ready, transfer pinout, clocks, and power design from the Nucleo/Discovery **schematics** into your custom board CAD.

Common Pitfalls and How to Avoid Them

- **Assuming all Blue/Black Pills are identical**: verify the exact MCU and crystal values; adjust clock configuration accordingly.

- **Ignoring Option Bytes and RDP**: set **readout protection** and boot configuration early; document them for production.

- **Overlooking cache/DMAs on M7/H7**: manage cache coherency (clean/invalidate) when DMA touches buffers that the CPU also accesses.

- **Not planning for low power**: measure early; use STOP modes, LPTIM, and DMA to keep the core asleep; disable unused clocks.

- **Using long, noisy SWD cables**: keep the probe close; if connection is unreliable, slow the SWD clock and connect under reset.

Quick Reference: What to Use When

- **First project, fast learning** → Nucleo board + CubeIDE + on-board ST-LINK

- **Hands-on with graphics/IoT/audio** → Discovery kit with matching peripherals

- **Performance and interface validation** → Evaluation board with external memories and HS interfaces

- **Tiny budget or breadboard build** → Black Pill (F411/F401) with an external ST-LINK

- **Factory and scaling** → CubeProgrammer CLI + STLINK-V3PWR for power profiling and production programming

Chapter 3: Hardware Fundamentals and Pinout Mastery

This chapter gives you the practical hardware knowledge you need to design reliable STM32-based systems and to select and assign pins with confidence. It covers GPIO architecture and alternate-function mapping, power-supply and voltage-domain considerations, clocking and oscillators, and reset & boot modes. Wherever STM32 families differ, I'll flag the variation and point you to the exact place to verify (datasheet / reference manual).

---

1. GPIO Architecture and Alternate-Function Mapping

1.1 What a GPIO really is

A GPIO pin on an STM32 is more than "a wire you drive high/low." It's a programmable I/O cell with configurable:

- direction (input / output),

- input stage (floating / pull-up / pull-down),

- output type (push-pull / open-drain),

- output speed (drive/slew control),

- analog mode (disables input buffer for ADC),

- alternate function (peripheral mapping),

- external interrupt/event capability (EXTI).

The programmable cell is backed by:

- a **port** register set (GPIOA, GPIOB, ...),

- an **I/O clock** gate (enable with RCC before using),

- multiplexing hardware that connects the pin to a peripheral AF line.

1.2 Pin configuration fields (what to set and why)

- **Mode**

    o   GPIO_MODE_INPUT: digital input

    o   GPIO_MODE_OUTPUT_PP / OD: push-pull or open-drain output

    o   GPIO_MODE_AF_PP / AF_OD: alternate function for peripherals

    o   GPIO_MODE_ANALOG: for ADC/low power

    o   GPIO_MODE_IT_RISING/FALLING/RT or GPIO_MODE_EVT_...: for EXTI

- **Pull**: NOPULL, PULLUP, PULLDOWN. Use internal pulls only when acceptable for power and reliability; external resistors are preferable for defined power-up states.

- **Speed**: LOW → VERY_HIGH. Higher speed = faster edges, more EMI and power. Choose the lowest speed that meets timing.

- **Output type**: Push-Pull (default) for strong driven levels; Open-Drain for wired-AND buses (I2C, certain multi-master lines) or level shifting with pull-ups.

- **Alternate Function (AF)**: numeric mapping (AFx) that routes a peripheral (USART, SPI, TIM, etc.) to that pin.

1.3 Alternate-Function mapping and pin selection

Each pin supports a subset of alternate functions. Key steps to pick pins correctly:

1. **Consult the datasheet package pinout** and the "Alternate functions" table in the datasheet/reference manual. The AF number for USART1_TX on PA9 may not be the same AF number for the same peripheral on a different pin or device.

2. **Watch for conflicts**: many peripherals want the same pin. Resolve by choosing alternate pins (if available) or moving another peripheral.

3. **Prefer native pins**: use the hardware AF that requires fewer internal multiplexers—this reduces the likelihood of conflicts and timing issues.

4. **Avoid pins with special roles** (BOOT pins, NRST, SWD) unless you are certain you won't need the special function.

CubeMX is extremely useful: it highlights conflicts and shows available AFs visually. Still, double-check the datasheet.

1.4 External interrupts (EXTI)

EXTI lines can be mapped to specific pins (often any pin in a port can map to an EXTI line through a SYSCFG multiplexer). Use EXTI for push-button wakes and event handling. Key tips:

- Configure **debouncing** in software or use RC filter hardware.

- Set appropriate NVIC priorities and keep ISRs short; delegate work to tasks or DMA.

- Remember that some EXTI lines are shared — monitor pending flags carefully.

1.5 Analog pins and ADC/DAC considerations

- **Analog mode** disables digital input buffers to reduce leakage and noise.

- Avoid enabling internal pull resistors on analog input pins.

- Pay attention to sampling time and ADC input impedance. If your source has high impedance, add a buffer op-amp or increase sampling time.

- Keep analog traces away from digital switching lines and place VREF+/VREF- decoupling close to the device.

1.6 Electrical limits and practical constraints

- **Absolute max voltage** on IO is typically 0–VDD + 0.3V (often 3.6V if VDD=3.3V). Never exceed the device's IO voltage rating.

- **I/O current limits**: each pin and port has max source/sink ratings. Heavy loads should be driven by drivers or use multiple pins carefully. Check datasheet for per-pin and per-port maximums.

- **ESD & surge**: add series resistors, TVS diodes, and consider input clamps for exposed pins (USB, UART, sensor lines).

- **Level shifting**: for interfacing 5V logic or other domains, use proper level shifters or ensure IO is 5V tolerant (not all are).

---

2. Power Supply Considerations and Voltage Domains

Power design is the most critical PCB subsystem. A marginal power design produces mysterious bugs.

2.1 Basic power rails

- **VDD / VSS**: main MCU supply and ground. Typically 3.3V.

- **VDDA / VSSA**: analog supply/ground for ADC/DAC/opamps; on many parts must be tied to VDD/VSS through low-impedance connection but decoupled separately.

- **VBAT**: backup domain supply for RTC and backup registers (if present).

- **VDDIOx**: some modern STM32 have separate I/O banks that accept different voltage rails (1.8V/3.3V). Check datasheet—mixing levels incorrectly can damage the MCU.

2.2 Regulators: LDO vs switching

- **LDO**: simple, low noise, low ripple — good for sensitive analog circuits and ADC rails (VDDA). Higher dissipation for big voltage drop.

- **DC-DC (switching)**: high efficiency, good for battery operation. Must be followed by LC filters and careful layout to control EMI. Use a dedicated LDO or filter for analog VDDA if needed.

2.3 Decoupling and layout

- Place **0.1 µF (100 nF)** ceramic decoupling capacitors as close as possible to each VDD pin (between VDD and VSS). Add **one 10 µF** bulk cap near the regulator output. For VDDA use dedicated decoupling and a ferrite if needed.

- Use **multiple vias** to connect decoupling to the power plane. Keep traces short and wide.

- Establish a **solid ground plane**; avoid splitting little ground islands that cause return-current loops.

- For mixed-signal boards, consider **analog ground (AGND)** and **digital ground (DGND)** with a controlled single point tie (or keep AGND and DGND on the same plane and separate with star routing depending on complexity).

2.4 Power sequencing and brown-out

- Some STM32 devices require specific **power sequencing** for certain supplies (VDD before VDDA or VBAT). Check datasheet for sequence and recommended ramp rates.

- **BOR (Brown-Out Reset)** / PVD (Programmable Voltage Detector) should be configured to avoid operation at undervoltage which can corrupt flash or peripherals.

- For battery systems include reverse-polarity protection, input TVS, and an inrush limiting resistor or NTC if needed.

2.5 Measuring power

- Use a small series shunt resistor on the 3.3V rail and a differential amplifier or a precision current meter to measure active and sleep currents.

- For accurate low-current measurement (<10 µA) use a high-resolution SMU or a specialized current logger and minimize leakage paths during measurement.

3. Clock System and Internal/External Oscillators

Clocking decisions affect performance, power, USB/Ethernet functionality, and ADC accuracy. The clock tree on STM32 is powerful but complex.

3.1 Typical clock sources

- **HSI**: internal high-speed oscillator (fast startup, less precise).

- **HSE**: external crystal or oscillator (preferred for accurate system clocks and USB/ethernet).

- **LSI**: internal low-speed RC (for watchdogs and RTC backup, less accurate).

- **LSE**: 32.768 kHz external crystal for RTC — essential for accurate timekeeping and low-power RTC wakeups.

- **PLL**: multiplies/divides clock sources to create SYSCLK and peripheral clocks.

3.2 PLL basics and constraints

- PLL takes an input (HSI/HSE) and produces higher-frequency system clocks; typical parameters are dividers/multipliers (named M/N/P/Q/R on many families). Key constraints:

    - **VCO input range** and **VCO output range** must be met (check RM).

    - **Flash latency** must be configured to support resulting SYSCLK frequency.

    - **USB/SDMMC** clocks often require a specific derived frequency (e.g., 48 MHz).

- For multi-core or high-perf MCUs (M7/H7), the PLL and clock domains are more advanced—use CubeMX or RM calculations.

3.3 Clock domains and prescalers

- **AHB / APB** prescalers route SYSCLK to peripheral buses. Some timers run at APB×2 (when APB prescaler > 1) — verify in RM since behavior varies by family.

- **Flash wait states**: increase flash latency as SYSCLK increases. Forgetting this causes random faults.

- **Peripheral clocks**: many peripherals (USART, SPI) have independent clock sources or prescalers—ensure they get a suitable clock for your baudrates and sample rates.

3.4 Clock integrity & layout

- External crystals require proper layout: short traces, recommended load capacitors, no vias under crystal, ground plane reference. Follow the crystal manufacturer's and STM32 application note layouts.

- If using an external oscillator module, feed the oscillator buffer input and bypass the crystal pins per the datasheet.

- Use **LSE** for RTC when timekeeping accuracy and low-power wakeups are essential.

3.5 Clock monitoring and safety

- Enable **Clock Security System (CSS)** where available to detect HSE failure and switch to safe clock (HSI) automatically.

- Implement software checks for PLL lock and clock stability at startup and be prepared for fallback behavior.

---

4. Reset and Boot Modes

Understanding resets and boot modes lets you design reliable recovery paths and secure firmware update flows.

4.1 Reset sources

Common reset sources include:

- **POR/PDR** (power on/power down reset)

- **NRST** (external reset pin)

- **Software reset** (system request SYSRESETREQ)

- **IWDG / WWDG** (independent / window watchdog)

- **Option byte reset** (after option byte update)

- **Pin reset circuits** (brown-out / BOR)
  You can read reset flags (RCC_CSR or equivalent) after reset to determine cause.

4.2 Boot configuration and bootloader

- Boot mode is typically controlled by **BOOT0/BOOT1** (or option bytes) which select boot from:

  - **User flash** (normal application),

  - **System memory** (built-in bootloader),

  - **SRAM** (for special debugging).

- The **system bootloader** (in system memory) supports various interfaces depending on the MCU (UART, USB DFU, I2C, CAN, SPI). The exact supported media varies across STM32 families — check the AN and RM for your MCU.

- **Option bytes** can also remap vector table or enable/disable bootloader behavior. Use CubeProgrammer to set option bytes in production.

4.3 Secure boot and readout protection

- **RDP (Readout Protection)** prevents external reading of flash via ST-LINK or other probes. Use with care — entering higher RDP levels may lock you out permanently without special procedures.

- On TrustZone-capable parts (M33), system-level secure boot can be enforced. Plan keys, monotonic counters, and rollback prevention in your OTA design.

4.4 NRST and hardware reset best practices

- Tie NRST to a push-button (active low) for manual reset and to the programmer header for recovery.

- Add RC filtering so spurious resets are avoided but ensure reset pulse width meets the datasheet minimum.

- Drive NRST with an open-drain reset supervisor if you need external reset supervision or POR thresholds.

4.5 Boot troubleshooting tips

- If the MCU doesn't boot after programming:

  - Check BOOT0 state (pull-downs/up).

  - Confirm option bytes and readout protection status.

  - Connect with ST-LINK and try "connect under reset" or "connect under halt".

  - If code uses external SDRAM/OSPI XIP at early startup, check initialization order (FMC/QUADSPI must be ready before using those areas).

5. Practical checklists & quick reference

PCB & bring-up checklist (hardware)

- All VDD, VDDA, VBAT rails connected and decoupled per datasheet.

- VREF+ / VREF- and ADC best-practice layout placed.

- RESET button + resistor + optional supervisor.

- SWD header with GND, SWDIO, SWCLK, NRST, VTref.

- Boot pins labeled and accessible (strap resistors or pads).

- Crystal footprints & loads placed correctly.

- ESD protection on exposed interfaces; series resistors on high-speed IOs.

Pin selection checklist (schematics)

- Pick peripherals → list required signals.

- Use CubeMX to find candidate pins → cross-check datasheet AF table.

- Avoid SWD pins unless you don't need debug.

- Reserve pins for future use (I2C, UART, or debug) and document.

- Check IO voltage domain compatibility before connecting external sensors.

Layout & measurement checklist (layout)

- Decoupling caps close to power pins, short traces.

- Ground plane under MCU, no splits under crystal unless recommended.

- High-speed traces impedance-controlled, differential pairs length-matched.

- Measurement shunt or test pads for power profiling near regulator output.

Chapter 4: Programming Basics for STM32

This chapter covers the essential programming concepts you need to move from "power-on →
blinking LED" to robust, real-world firmware: C language patterns and constraints used in
embedded systems, how to use ST's HAL and LL libraries, how startup and the interrupt vector table
work, and practical techniques for writing safe, fast, and maintainable STM32 code.

---

1. C Language Essentials for Embedded Systems

Embedded C is standard C plus a few pragmatic idioms and attributes to interface with hardware and
constrained environments. Below are the features and practices you will use constantly.

1.1 Fixed-width types and headers

Always use the types in <stdint.h> and device headers in CMSIS:

- uint8_t, uint16_t, uint32_t, int32_t, etc.

- CMSIS device header (stm32f4xx.h, etc.) provides peripheral register structs and SCB, NVIC, etc.

Why: portability and exact byte widths matter for register access, protocol structures, and memory layout.

1.2 volatile is your friend (and sometimes foe)

volatile tells the compiler a value can change outside normal program flow:

- Use for memory-mapped peripheral registers (volatile uint32_t *) or shared variables modified by ISRs or DMA.

- Missing volatile leads to optimized-away reads/writes; over-using volatile can obscure real concurrency bugs.

Example:

volatile uint32_t *const RCC_AHB1ENR = (uint32_t*)(0x40023830UL);

*RCC_AHB1ENR |= (1<<0); // enable GPIOA clock

1.3 const and placement in FLASH

const data typically goes to .rodata (flash). Use const for lookup tables and string literals to save RAM.

1.4 static, inline, and scope

- static at file scope limits visibility (good encapsulation).

- static inline is useful for small peripheral helper functions where you want zero overhead and no external symbol.

- Limit global variables; prefer module-level static state with accessor functions.

1.5 Attributes and pragmas (GCC-style)

Useful attributes you will encounter:

- __attribute__((weak)) — make a symbol overridable (used for default IRQ handlers).

- __attribute__((packed)) — pack struct fields (use carefully: may cause unaligned accesses).

- __attribute__((aligned(n))) — control alignment, useful for DMA buffers that require 4/8/32-byte alignment.

- __attribute__((section(".noinit"))) — place variables in a section not initialized at reset (useful for retaining values across software resets).

Example: weak symbol for default IRQ:

void Default_Handler(void);

void __attribute__((weak, alias("Default_Handler"))) SysTick_Handler(void);

1.6 Bitfields — use with caution

Bitfields can be convenient but are compiler- and endianness-sensitive. For register definitions, prefer the vendor-provided CMSIS structs or explicit masks and shifts.

1.7 Atomicity, critical sections, and race conditions

- Use __disable_irq() / __enable_irq() (CMSIS) for short critical sections where single-core code must prevent ISR preemption.

- For multi-register updates or 64-bit variables on 32-bit cores, protect with critical sections.

- Use __atomic builtins or CMSIS functions for lock-free atomic ops when supported.

1.8 Memory usage: stack and heap

- Embedded systems have limited RAM. Track stack usage (compile-time heuristics + runtime tests).

- Avoid deep recursion and large stack-allocated arrays; prefer static buffers.

- If you use dynamic memory (malloc), adopt pool allocators or deterministic allocators—don't rely on general-purpose heap in production-critical embedded firmware.

1.9 Reentrancy and interrupts

- Keep ISRs minimal: set flags / copy small data then return.

- Long processing should run in a task or background context.

- If an ISR calls a library function that isn't reentrant (e.g., stdio), you'll have data corruption.

1.10 Floating point and FPU considerations

- If using FPU instructions in ISRs, ensure the interrupt stack frame and compiler options save/restore floating-point registers (this costs cycles).

- Prefer to avoid heavy FP math inside ISRs; do conversions in tasks.

2. Understanding HAL (Hardware Abstraction Layer)

The STM32 HAL (provided in the STM32Cube packages) is a consistent, higher-level C API that hides register-level details and accelerates bring-up. It is widely used in examples, CubeMX-generated code, and quick prototyping.

2.1 HAL architecture and components

- **HAL drivers**: stm32xx_hal_*.c — provide initialization and runtime APIs for peripherals (GPIO, UART, ADC, TIM, etc.).

- **Board Support Package (BSP)**: convenience functions for kit-specific peripherals (LCDs, sensors).

- **Middleware**: USB stacks, FATFS, LwIP, FreeRTOS integrations provided in Cube packages.

2.2 Typical HAL workflow

1. Generate MX_* initializer functions with CubeMX/CubeIDE (e.g., MX_GPIO_Init(), MX_USART2_UART_Init()).

2. HAL_Init() to initialize HAL library (SysTick config, NVIC priority grouping, etc.).

3. Call the MX_..._Init() functions in main() before using peripherals.

4. Use HAL APIs for peripheral operations and register callbacks.

Basic example (blinking LED):

```
int main(void) {

 HAL_Init();

 SystemClock_Config();

 MX_GPIO_Init();


 while (1) {

  HAL_GPIO_TogglePin(GPIOA, GPIO_PIN_5);

  HAL_Delay(500); // uses SysTick

 }

}
```

Example UART transmit:

```
HAL_UART_Transmit(&huart2, (uint8_t*)"Hello\n", 6, HAL_MAX_DELAY);
```

2.3 HAL interrupt and callback model

HAL IRQ handlers are thin wrappers called from the vector table:

```
void USART2_IRQHandler(void) {

 HAL_UART_IRQHandler(&huart2);

}
```

-
- The HAL layer calls user callbacks like:

- ○ void HAL_UART_RxCpltCallback(UART_HandleTypeDef *huart) when reception completes.

- ○ void HAL_TIM_PeriodElapsedCallback(TIM_HandleTypeDef *htim).

- Implement callbacks in your application code (not in the generated HAL files) — CubeMX provides /* USER CODE BEGIN */ blocks.

2.4 HAL pros and cons

Pros

- Fast development and portability across STM32 series.

- Cortex/series-agnostic API (same function names across families).

- Extensive examples and middleware integration.

Cons

- Larger code size and some runtime overhead compared to LL or direct register access.

- Less deterministic timing in some cases.

- Some advanced features or optimal performance patterns are easier with LL/reg-level code.

2.5 Best practices with HAL

- Use HAL for initial bring-up and medium-complexity applications.

- Use DMA and interrupt-based HAL APIs (e.g., HAL_UART_Receive_DMA) to keep CPU idle.

- For timing-critical loops, use LL or register-level code.

- Keep user code in separate files or user-blocks to preserve changes across CubeMX regenerations.

3. LL (Low-Layer) APIs for High-Performance Control

The LL API is a thin, register-level wrapper provided by ST that trades portability for speed and smaller code size. LL functions map closely to hardware registers and are designed for real-time, high-performance needs.

3.1 When to use LL

- Time-critical control loops (motor control, control law loops).

- Minimizing code size and overhead in ISR hot-paths.

- Precise peripheral configuration where you need exact register control.

3.2 LL vs HAL: philosophy

- **HAL**: abstraction, convenience, cross-family portability.

- **LL**: minimal overhead, direct control, manual configuration.

- You may **mix HAL and LL** in a project, but never let both configure the same peripheral concurrently. Example: use HAL for system and peripherals you don't touch in tight loops, and LL for the timing-critical peripheral.

3.3 Example: toggling a GPIO with LL

```
/* Enable GPIOA clock (example for STM32F4 family) */

LL_AHB1_GRP1_EnableClock(LL_AHB1_GRP1_PERIPH_GPIOA);


/* Configure PA5 as output */

LL_GPIO_SetPinMode(GPIOA, LL_GPIO_PIN_5, LL_GPIO_MODE_OUTPUT);

LL_GPIO_SetPinOutputType(GPIOA, LL_GPIO_PIN_5, LL_GPIO_OUTPUT_PUSHPULL);

LL_GPIO_SetPinSpeed(GPIOA, LL_GPIO_PIN_5, LL_GPIO_SPEED_FREQ_LOW);

LL_GPIO_SetPinPull(GPIOA, LL_GPIO_PIN_5, LL_GPIO_PULL_NO);


/* Toggle loop */
```

```
while (1) {

  LL_GPIO_TogglePin(GPIOA, LL_GPIO_PIN_5);

  for (volatile int i=0; i<100000; ++i); // crude delay

}
```

3.4 Example: configuring a timer for PWM (LL)

LL has a more verbose but deterministic flow: enable clocks, configure prescaler/ARR/CCR, configure channels, enable capture/compare, enable counter. The resulting code runs with minimal overhead.

3.5 LL pros and cons

Pros

- Faster in both execution and init time.

- Smaller generated code.

- Gives exact control over timing and registers.

Cons

- Less portable across series if register layouts differ.

- More verbose and lower-level; steeper learning curve.

4. Startup Code and Interrupt Vector Table

Understanding what happens before main() and how interrupts map to handlers is crucial for boot issues, bootloader design, and ISRs.

4.1 What happens at reset (high-level)

1. Hardware reset sets the stack pointer and loads the address of the Reset Handler from the vector table.

2. The **Reset Handler** (in the startup code) runs:

- ○ Optionally calls early system initialization (SystemInit() in system_stm32xx.c), which typically configures the clock and Flash prefetch/cache settings.

- ○ Copies .data section from flash to RAM.

- ○ Zeroes the .bss section.

- ○ Optionally sets up FPU or MPU if needed.

- ○ Calls main().

This flow is implemented in startup assembly (startup_stm32xxxx.s) and a system file (system_stm32xxxx.c) that defines SystemInit() and SystemCoreClock.

4.2 Vector table layout

The vector table is an array of pointers placed at a well-known address (FLASH base or can be relocated to RAM). Its first entries are:

Index	Description
0	Initial Main Stack Pointer value (_estack)
1	Reset Handler (Reset_Handler)
2	NMI Handler
3	HardFault Handler
...	Other core exceptions (MemManage, BusFault, UsageFault, etc.)

15+   External interrupt handlers (IRQ0, IRQ1, ...)

Example vector table in C (simplified):

extern uint32_t _estack;

void Reset_Handler(void);

void NMI_Handler(void)   __attribute__ ((weak, alias("Default_Handler")));

void HardFault_Handler(void)__attribute__ ((weak, alias("Default_Handler")));

// More handlers...

__attribute__ ((section(".isr_vector")))

const void *vector_table[] = {

 &_estack,

 Reset_Handler,

 NMI_Handler,

 HardFault_Handler,

 // ... other handlers ...

};

4.3 Default handlers and weak aliases

Startup code commonly declares IRQ handlers as weak aliases to a Default_Handler. If your application defines a symbol with the same name (e.g., void SysTick_Handler(void)), it overrides the weak symbol automatically through the linker.

4.4 Relocating the vector table (bootloader patterns)

A bootloader often resides at the start of flash and must jump to an application whose vector table is at a different offset. The application must:

1. Validate the application (checksum or signature).

2. Set the vector table offset: SCB->VTOR = application_address;

3. Set MSP (Main Stack Pointer) from the first word of the application vector table and jump to the Reset Handler (second word).

Relocation example:

```
#define APP_START_ADDR 0x08004000

uint32_t app_stack = *((uint32_t*)APP_START_ADDR);

uint32_t app_reset = *((uint32_t*)(APP_START_ADDR + 4));

SCB->VTOR = APP_START_ADDR;

__set_MSP(app_stack);

typedef void (*pFunction)(void);

pFunction start = (pFunction)app_reset;

start();
```

4.5 SystemInit and SystemCoreClock

- SystemInit() (called from Reset Handler) sets up early clock and power configuration (often controlled by Cube-generated code).

- SystemCoreClock is a global variable that holds the current CPU frequency; update it whenever you change clock settings (SystemCoreClockUpdate()).

Many HAL functions assume SystemCoreClock is accurate for delay loops and peripheral timing.

4.6 Exception handlers and debugging HardFaults

HardFaults and faults like MemManage, BusFault, UsageFault can be decoded by inspecting the stacked registers saved at the time of the fault. A common debug pattern is to implement a HardFault handler that retrieves stacked PC/LR/PSR:

Minimal HardFault handler that extracts stacked registers (example):

```c
void HardFault_Handler(void) {

  __asm volatile (

  "tst lr, #4        \n"

  "ite eq            \n"

  "mrseq r0, msp     \n"

  "mrsne r0, psp     \n"

  "b HardFault_Handler_C \n"

  );

}
```

```c
void HardFault_Handler_C(uint32_t *stack) {

  uint32_t r0  = stack[0];

  uint32_t r1  = stack[1];

  uint32_t r2  = stack[2];

  uint32_t r3  = stack[3];

  uint32_t r12 = stack[4];

  uint32_t lr  = stack[5];

  uint32_t pc  = stack[6];

  uint32_t psr = stack[7];

  // Optionally log values via ITM, UART, or store to RAM for post-mortem

  for(;;);

}
```

This yields the PC and LR at the time of the fault for post-mortem inspection.

4.7 NVIC, priorities, and priority grouping

- Each interrupt has a configurable priority (NVIC_SetPriority(IRQn, priority)).

- **Lower numerical priority = higher actual priority** (0 is highest).

- Priority granularity is implementation dependent (__NVIC_PRIO_BITS).

- CMSIS provides NVIC_SetPriorityGrouping() to control how many bits are preempt priority vs subpriority.

Best practices:

- Reserve highest priorities for critical ISRs (fault handlers, emergency shutoff).

- Keep ISRs short; offload heavy work to threads/tasks.

- Use __disable_irq() sparingly and for short intervals only.

4.8 SysTick and HAL tick

By default, HAL uses SysTick to implement HAL_GetTick() and HAL_Delay(). If you use an RTOS, map HAL tick to the RTOS tick or provide suitable hooks to avoid conflicts.

---

5. Putting It Together — Practical Examples & Patterns

5.1 Typical project skeleton

- startup_stm32xxx.s — startup vectors and Reset_Handler.

- system_stm32xxx.c — SystemInit() and clock helpers.

- main.c — main() with HAL_Init() and MX_*_Init() calls.

- peripherals.c/h — your peripheral usage, separated from generated HAL code.

- Makefile / project file — correctly references CMSIS, startup, and linker script.

5.2 Example: UART RX via HAL + callback

```c
/* global handle generated by CubeMX */

extern UART_HandleTypeDef huart2;

uint8_t rx_buf[64];


int main(void) {

  HAL_Init();

  SystemClock_Config();

  MX_GPIO_Init();

  MX_USART2_UART_Init();


  HAL_UART_Receive_IT(&huart2, rx_buf, sizeof(rx_buf));


  while (1) {

    // main loop: do processing on data flagged by callback

  }

}


void HAL_UART_RxCpltCallback(UART_HandleTypeDef *huart) {

  if (huart == &huart2) {

    // process rx_buf

    HAL_UART_Receive_IT(&huart2, rx_buf, sizeof(rx_buf)); // re-arm

  }

}
```

5.3 Example: ADC with DMA (HAL)

- Configure ADC in CubeMX for DMA circular mode.

- Use HAL_ADC_Start_DMA(&hadc1, (uint32_t*)adc_buf, N);

- When new data arrive, HAL or DMA complete callback notified and processing occurs in background context.

5.4 Example: Critical timing with LL (PWM control)

When you need deterministic timer update or DMA triggering, use LL to configure timer registers precisely, avoiding HAL overhead and function calls in tight loops.

---

6. Debugging & Best Practices

6.1 Useful debug hooks

- **SWO/ITM** for lightweight printf-like debugging (low overhead).

- **Semihosting** for small tests (but it is intrusive and slows execution).

- **Trace/ETM** for cycle-accurate analysis (requires trace probe).

- **Saving crash info**: store a small diagnostics structure in battery-backed SRAM or retention RAM before while(1) on HardFault to diagnose post-mortem.

6.2 Coding & maintenance recommendations

- Use a layered architecture: HAL/LL access isolated in driver modules; application logic independent.

- Encapsulate hardware access behind an API so unit testing of logic is possible on host machine.

- Avoid mixing automatic and manual initialization of the same peripheral. Use CubeMX consistently or commit to a full manual setup.

- Document interrupt priorities and resources per peripheral in a design doc.

- Keep a clock-tree diagram and update SystemCoreClock correctly after clock changes.

6.3 Safety & robustness

- Configure watchdog timers (IWDG/WWDG) with safe timeouts.

- Implement software validation for firmware image updates (CRC/signature).

- Plan RDP and option byte policies carefully; document how to recover development boards if locked.

---

7. Further Learning and Sample Labs

If you want hands-on practice, work through these labs in order:

1. Basic bring-up: blink LED via HAL and then via LL.

2. UART: synchronous transmit and asynchronous receive with HAL callbacks.

3. Timer: configure a TIM to toggle a pin (compare) and then to generate PWM for LED dimming.

4. ADC + DMA: sample a potentiometer at 1 kHz and log values over UART.

5. FreeRTOS: port a simple app with two tasks (logger and control) and map HAL tick to RTOS tick.

6. Bootloader: build a minimal bootloader that can receive a firmware image over UART and jump to application code with VTOR relocation.

Chapter 5: Digital I/O and Peripheral Control in STM32

Digital I/O (Input/Output) operations form the backbone of embedded system design. For the STM32 family of microcontrollers, mastering GPIO (General Purpose Input/Output) configuration and peripheral control is essential for controlling LEDs, reading switches, communicating with sensors, and interfacing with other logic devices. This chapter explores in depth how to configure, optimize, and use digital I/O features, as well as practical considerations for robust signal handling.

Configuring and Using GPIO Pins

GPIO pins in STM32 microcontrollers are highly versatile. Each pin can be configured as an input, output, or connected to an alternate peripheral function.

1. GPIO Modes
STM32 GPIO pins support multiple modes, selectable via registers or STM32CubeMX:

- **Input Mode** – Reads digital signals from an external device or sensor.

- **Output Mode (Push-Pull)** – Drives a pin high or low actively.

- **Output Mode (Open-Drain)** – Allows multiple devices to share the line; external pull-up is required.

- **Alternate Function Mode** – Connects the pin to a peripheral (UART, SPI, I2C, etc.).

- **Analog Mode** – Used for ADC inputs to avoid digital interference.

2. Pin Configuration Parameters

When setting up a pin in **STM32CubeMX** or directly through code, you define:

- **Mode** (Input, Output, Alternate Function, Analog)

- **Output Type** (Push-Pull or Open-Drain)

- **Pull-up/Pull-down Resistors**

- **Speed** (Low, Medium, High, Very High) – Determines slew rate for signal integrity.

3. Example: Configuring GPIO as Output for LED Control

Using HAL in C:

```c
GPIO_InitTypeDef GPIO_InitStruct = {0};


__HAL_RCC_GPIOA_CLK_ENABLE();  // Enable GPIOA clock


GPIO_InitStruct.Pin = GPIO_PIN_5;  // Example pin

GPIO_InitStruct.Mode = GPIO_MODE_OUTPUT_PP;  // Push-pull output

GPIO_InitStruct.Pull = GPIO_NOPULL;  // No pull-up/down

GPIO_InitStruct.Speed = GPIO_SPEED_FREQ_LOW;  // Low speed

HAL_GPIO_Init(GPIOA, &GPIO_InitStruct);
```

// Toggle LED

HAL_GPIO_TogglePin(GPIOA, GPIO_PIN_5);

Driving LEDs and Reading Buttons

1. Driving LEDs
Driving an LED is one of the most basic tasks in embedded systems, but it introduces key concepts:

- **Forward voltage drop**: LEDs require current-limiting resistors (typically 220–470Ω for 3.3V logic).

- **GPIO current limits**: Most STM32 GPIO pins can source/sink 8–25 mA; exceeding this risks damage.

- **Active-high vs. active-low**: Depending on wiring, logic HIGH may turn LED ON or OFF.

2. Reading Buttons (Switches)
Buttons are mechanical contacts that connect/disconnect a circuit. When reading a button:

- Configure GPIO pin as input.

- Use internal pull-up or pull-down resistors to define a stable logic level when the button is unpressed.

- Monitor pin state in the main loop or via an interrupt for event-driven behavior.

Example: Reading a Button Input

GPIO_InitStruct.Pin = GPIO_PIN_0; // Button on PA0

GPIO_InitStruct.Mode = GPIO_MODE_INPUT;

GPIO_InitStruct.Pull = GPIO_PULLUP; // Use internal pull-up

HAL_GPIO_Init(GPIOA, &GPIO_InitStruct);

if (HAL_GPIO_ReadPin(GPIOA, GPIO_PIN_0) == GPIO_PIN_RESET) {

  // Button pressed (active low)

}

Debouncing and Signal Conditioning

Mechanical switches introduce **contact bounce**—rapid on/off fluctuations when toggled. Without debouncing, your microcontroller may register multiple false presses.

1. Software Debouncing

- Delay after detecting a press (e.g., 10–50 ms) before checking again.

- Use a **state machine** to handle stable transitions.

2. Hardware Debouncing

- Use an **RC (resistor-capacitor) filter** to smooth the signal.

- Employ **Schmitt-trigger buffers** to clean up transitions.

Example: Software Debounce with HAL Delay

```
if (HAL_GPIO_ReadPin(GPIOA, GPIO_PIN_0) == GPIO_PIN_RESET) {

  HAL_Delay(20);  // Wait 20 ms

  if (HAL_GPIO_ReadPin(GPIOA, GPIO_PIN_0) == GPIO_PIN_RESET) {

    // Confirmed press

  }

}
```

Interfacing with External Logic Devices

GPIO pins are also used to interface with digital ICs, displays, and sensors.

1. Voltage Level Matching

ADVANCED STM32 MICROCONTROLLERS

- STM32 MCUs usually operate at 3.3V logic.

- For 5V devices, use **level shifters** (e.g., TXB0108) or voltage dividers.

2. Driving External Loads

- For high-current loads (motors, relays), use **transistors or MOSFETs** as drivers.

- Protect outputs with **flyback diodes** when driving inductive loads.

3. Handshaking and Control

- Digital outputs can trigger enable/disable lines.

- Inputs can monitor **status signals** from peripherals.

Example: Interfacing with a Shift Register (74HC595)
Shift registers expand GPIO outputs using SPI-like communication:

```
// Send byte to shift register controlling LEDs

HAL_SPI_Transmit(&hspi1, &dataByte, 1, HAL_MAX_DELAY);
```

Chapter 6: Timers and PWM — Comprehensive Guide

Timers are among the most powerful and versatile peripherals on any STM32. They provide deterministic timing and hardware-driven waveform generation, capture, synchronization, and event routing — everything from a simple millisecond tick to complex motor-control PWM with complementary outputs, dead-time, and ADC synchronization. This chapter explains timer concepts, shows how to calculate and configure timers and PWM, and gives code examples and best practices for real-world use.

Overview: what timers provide on STM32

STM32 timers are broadly split into:

- **General-purpose timers (TIMx)** — flexible, good for PWM, input capture, output compare, encoder interface, basic synchronization.

- **Advanced-control timers (TIM1, TIM8, etc.)** — include complementary outputs, dead-time insertion, break input, and are designed for motor control / power stages.

- **Basic timers (TIM6, TIM7)** — simple time base and DAC/triggering helpers.

- **Low-power timers (LPTIM)** — capable of running in low-power modes for ultra-low-power applications.

Common timer resources and terminology you'll see in every STM32 reference manual:

- **Prescaler (PSC)**: divides the timer input clock.

- **Auto-Reload Register (ARR)**: top value for counting (timer period).

- **Counter (CNT)**: current counter value.

- **Capture/Compare registers (CCR1..CCR4)**: channel compare values (PWM duty) or capture targets.

- **Channels**: per-timer compare/capture channels (usually up to 4).

- **Update Event (UEV)**: occurs when counter overflows (or underflows in center-aligned modes).

- **Triggers (TRGO, TRGI, ITRx)**: hardware trigger outputs/inputs used for synchronization.

- **Shadow registers / preload**: ARR/CCR often use buffered writes; new values take effect on an update event.

- **Counter modes**: up, down, up-down (center-aligned).

- **Clock domain**: timer clock derived from APB bus — important for frequency calculation.

1. General-Purpose Timers and Advanced Timers

1.1 Timer hardware summary

A typical general-purpose timer includes:

- 16-bit or 32-bit counter width (family dependent).

- Several channels that can operate in input-capture, output-compare, or PWM modes.

- DMA request capability on update / capture / compare events.

- Internal routing to other peripherals via triggers (TRGO).
  Advanced timers add:

- Complementary outputs (CHx / CHxN).

- Dead-time generator (DTG).

- Break input (synchronous and asynchronous).

- Main output enable (MOE) control (BDTR register).

1.2 Timer clocking (important gotcha)

Timer frequency depends on the APB clock it is attached to. On many STM32 families:

- If APB prescaler = 1, TIM_clk = PCLKx.

- If APB prescaler > 1, TIM_clk = 2 × PCLKx.

Always check your device reference manual for the exact rule for your part — it's critical for correct frequency math.

1.3 Timer resolution and size

- If counter is 16-bit, CNT spans 0..65,535. For higher resolution or lower PSC needs, choose a 32-bit timer where available.

- Timer resolution (steps per period) is ARR + 1 (the number of distinct counter values).

- **PWM resolution in bits** $\approx \log2(ARR + 1)$ (e.g., ARR=3599 → ~11.8 bits → effectively 11 bits of integer resolution).

2. Generating Pulse Width Modulation for Motor Control

A PWM waveform is defined by two parameters: **frequency** and **duty cycle**. For motor control, additional concerns include center-aligned waveform, complementary outputs, dead-time, break handling, and synchronization with ADC (for current sensing).

2.1 PWM basics (formulae)

Given:

- TIM_clk = timer input clock (Hz),

- PSC = prescaler register value (0..),

- ARR = auto-reload register (0..),

Edge-aligned PWM frequency:

f_pwm = TIM_clk / ((PSC + 1) * (ARR + 1))

Center-aligned (up-down) PWM frequency (counts up then down):

f_pwm_center = TIM_clk / (2 * (PSC + 1) * (ARR + 1))

(important: center-aligned halves the frequency for the same PSC/ARR.)

Duty cycle (for PWM1, active high):

duty = CCRx / (ARR + 1)

Numeric example (step-by-step)

Goal: f_pwm = 20 kHz with TIM_clk = 72 MHz (common on many STM32 lines).

1. Compute ARR + 1 = TIM_clk / f_pwm = 72,000,000 / 20,000 = 3,600.

2. So ARR = 3,600 − 1 = 3,599.

3. If we choose PSC = 0, then f_pwm = 72 MHz / (1 * 3,600) = 20 kHz. **ARR fits in 16 bits.**

4. For 50% duty: $CCR = (ARR + 1) * 0.5 = 3,600 * 0.5 = 1,800 \rightarrow CCR = 1,800$.

Resolution: $\log 2(3600) \approx 11.81$ so you have ~11 bits of resolution (2048 steps = 11 bits, 4096 = 12 bits). Practically, you get 3600 distinct steps.

2.2 Choosing PSC and ARR

- Aim to keep ARR within the natural counter width (16 or 32 bits).

- Prefer PSC as small as possible to maximize resolution, unless you need a very low frequency requiring a larger product.

- If you need exact frequency and resolution, solve the equation for integers (PSC and ARR). This is often a trade-off; real systems pick a near match and accept small frequency error.

2.3 Center-aligned vs edge-aligned PWM

- **Edge-aligned**: counter resets at ARR. Good for simple control.

- **Center-aligned** (up-down): symmetric switching edges — reduces even harmonics and torque ripple in motor control and helps with balanced switching losses. Use center-aligned for FOC and high-performance out-of-phase waveforms.

2.4 Complementary outputs, dead-time, and break input (advanced timers)

For half-bridge/full-bridge motor drivers:

- Use **complementary outputs** (CHx and CHxN) to drive high-side and low-side MOSFET gates via gate drivers.

- **Dead-time** prevents shoot-through: set via BDTR (break & dead-time register) on advanced timers or via CubeMX. Dead-time is specified in timer clock cycles using DTG fields; the exact scaling depends on device family.

- **Break input**: hardware emergency stop that forces outputs inactive upon fault (overcurrent, fault pin). Configure break polarity, automatic output disable, and fault recovery.

Example HAL snippet — configure PWM with dead-time (conceptual):

TIM_HandleTypeDef htim1;

```
TIM_BreakDeadTimeConfigTypeDef sBDTR = {0};


/* After TIM PWM init and channel config */

sBDTR.OffStateRunMode = TIM_OSSR_ENABLE;

sBDTR.OffStateIDLEMode = TIM_OSSI_ENABLE;

sBDTR.LockLevel = TIM_LOCKLEVEL_OFF;

sBDTR.DeadTime = desired_deadtime_ticks; // set based on datasheet calculation

sBDTR.BreakState = TIM_BREAK_ENABLE;

sBDTR.BreakPolarity = TIM_BREAKPOLARITY_LOW;

sBDTR.AutomaticOutput = TIM_AUTOMATICOUTPUT_ENABLE;


HAL_TIMEx_ConfigBreakDeadTime(&htim1, &sBDTR);

HAL_TIM_PWM_Start(&htim1, TIM_CHANNEL_1);

HAL_TIMEx_PWMN_Start(&htim1, TIM_CHANNEL_1); // start complementary if needed
```

Note: desired_deadtime_ticks must be computed using the device's BDTR/DTG mapping (see the reference manual).

2.5 Synchronizing PWM with ADC for current sampling

- You often need ADC sampling in the middle of PWM on-time (sample current while MOSFETs are stable).

- Use the timer **TRGO** or compare event as the external trigger for ADC conversions. Configure TRGO to occur on CC1/Update/Compare events and connect ADC external trigger (EXTSEL) to that timer TRGO.

- Use center-aligned mode if you want symmetric sampling relative to edges.

Example concept:

85

- Set TIM1 to generate CC1 event at the edge where you want the ADC to sample.

- Configure ADC external trigger (e.g., ADC_ExternalTrigConv_T1_CC1) and set sample time accordingly.

2.6 Motor control use cases

- **Brushed DC servo / hobby motor**: single PWM channel for H-bridge gate drivers.

- **Brushed DC with direction**: two PWMs or PWM + direction GPIO.

- **Brushless DC (BLDC)**: use 3-phase complementary PWM with dead-time, hall-sensor or back-EMF sensing for commutation.

- **Field-Oriented Control (FOC)**: requires three-phase PWM, high-frequency ADC sampling for current measurement, timers generating synchronized PWM and TRGO for ADC triggers. Consider using advanced timers on H7/F7/G4 for performance.

3. Input Capture and Output Compare Modes

3.1 Input Capture: measuring time intervals, frequency, duty

Input capture latches CNT into a CCR on an external event (rising/falling edge). Typical uses:

- Measure pulse width, period, duty cycle, and frequency (e.g., measuring RPM sensor or pulse sensor).

- Implement software frequency counters and timers.

Algorithm to measure pulse width (single channel, rising→falling):

1. Configure channel for capture on rising edge. On first capture, store t_rise.

2. Configure channel for capture on falling (or use second channel configured for falling) to store t_fall.

3. ticks = (t_fall − t_rise) & CNT_MASK (handle wrap-around).

4. time_seconds = ticks / TIM_clk_effective, **where** TIM_clk_effective = TIM_clk / (PSC + 1).

5. Duty = pulse_ticks / period_ticks if both period and pulse width measured.

Example (numbers):

- If TIM_clk_effective = 1 MHz and ticks = 2500, then pulse width = 2500 / 1,000,000 = 0.0025 s = 2.5 ms.

HAL input capture snippet:

// Start input capture with interrupt

HAL_TIM_IC_Start_IT(&htim2, TIM_CHANNEL_1);

// Callback:

void HAL_TIM_IC_CaptureCallback(TIM_HandleTypeDef *htim) {

  if (htim->Instance == TIM2 && htim->Channel == HAL_TIM_ACTIVE_CHANNEL_1) {

    uint32_t capture = HAL_TIM_ReadCapturedValue(htim, TIM_CHANNEL_1);

    // store and compute differences

  }

}

IC prescaler & filter

- Input capture often supports an **input prescaler** to count 1 in N events (useful for very high-frequency inputs).

- **Digital filter** (in CCMR register) helps filter out bounce/noise on the captured input; set an appropriate filter length.

3.2 Output Compare (OC) modes

Output-compare toggles or forces an output when CNT matches CCR. Modes:

- **Toggle**: flip pin on match — good for generating square waves.

- **Active/Inactive on match**: set/clear output on match.

- **PWM1 / PWM2**: output high while CNT < CCR (or inverted) — used for PWM generation.

- **Force idle / pulse**: generate single pulses by forcing a compare event.

OC is often used with interrupts (CCx interrupt) to execute code at specific time points with hardware timing accuracy.

OC example (toggle):

- Set OC mode to toggle with CCRx = N. The timer toggles the pin each time counter == CCRx → produces $f = TIM\_clk / (2*(CCR+1)*(PSC+1))$ roughly.

3.3 PWM input mode

Some timers support **PWM input mode** where the timer internally measures pulse width and period using two capture channels and generates direct readouts for period/duty — handy for decoding servo pulses (50 Hz with varying duty) and remote-control inputs.

---

4. Timer Interrupts and Event Triggering

4.1 Common interrupt events

- **Update interrupt (UIF)**: occurs at overflow (or underflow in center-aligned mode).

- **Capture/Compare interrupts (CC1/CC2/...)**: occur when CNT == CCRx.

- **Trigger interrupts**: some timers can generate TRGI and TRGO events triggering other peripherals.

4.2 Starting interrupts using HAL

HAL_TIM_Base_Start_IT(&htim6);   // start basic timer with update interrupt

HAL_TIM_IC_Start_IT(&htim2, TIM_CHANNEL_1); // input capture

HAL_TIM_PWM_Start_IT(&htim3, TIM_CHANNEL_1); // PWM start with interrupts if needed

Handle callbacks:

void HAL_TIM_PeriodElapsedCallback(TIM_HandleTypeDef *htim) {

 if (htim->Instance == TIM6) {

  // timer tick work

 }

}

For capture/compare callbacks:

void HAL_TIM_OC_DelayElapsedCallback(TIM_HandleTypeDef *htim) {

 if (htim->Instance == TIM3) {

  // CC event

 }

}

4.3 NVIC and priorities

- Configure NVIC priority with HAL_NVIC_SetPriority(TIMx_IRQn, preemptPriority, subPriority).

- Keep ISRs short; minimal work — set flags or enqueue messages for background tasks.

- If using FreeRTOS, consider using deferred interrupt processing via xTaskNotifyFromISR() or xQueueSendFromISR().

4.4 Timer as master/slave, TRGO, and synchronization

- Timers can be **masters** (emit a TRGO on update/compare event) and **slaves** (start/stop in response to triggers).

- **Common uses**:

  - Synchronize multiple PWM generators (multi-phase motors, multi-channel PWM).

  - Use a timer as a timebase for ADC conversions (via TRGO) to sample at precise points.

  - Chain timers for high-resolution long-period timers when a single timer can't reach desired period.

HAL Master config example:

TIM_MasterConfigTypeDef sMasterConfig = {0};

sMasterConfig.MasterOutputTrigger = TIM_TRGO_UPDATE; // or TIM_TRGO_OC1 etc.

sMasterConfig.MasterSlaveMode = TIM_MASTERSLAVEMODE_ENABLE;

HAL_TIMEx_MasterConfigSynchronization(&htim1, &sMasterConfig);

HAL Slave config example:

TIM_SlaveConfigTypeDef sSlaveConfig = {0};

sSlaveConfig.SlaveMode = TIM_SLAVEMODE_TRIGGER;

sSlaveConfig.InputTrigger = TIM_TS_ITR0; // internal trigger line

HAL_TIM_SlaveConfigSynchro(&htim3, &sSlaveConfig);

4.5 Using DMA with timers

- Timers generate DMA requests on update, CCx, or TRGO events.

- Common patterns:

  - **Waveform output by DMA**: DMA supplies CCRx values from a buffer for arbitrary waveforms (e.g., audio PWM, sine lookup table).

- Capture via DMA: DMA moves captured CCRx results to memory without CPU involvement (useful for high-speed capture bursts).

- Use circular mode for continuous streaming and double-buffering for safe handover of buffers.

Example: use DMA to write a table of CCR values to TIMx->CCR1 in circular mode to synthesize a waveform.

5. Practical Examples

5.1 Edge-aligned PWM with HAL (TIM3 CH1)

```
// Configure htim3 elsewhere (clock, GPIO AF, etc.)

htim3.Init.Prescaler = 0;

htim3.Init.CounterMode = TIM_COUNTERMODE_UP;

htim3.Init.Period = 3599;  // ARR = 3599 -> 20 kHz (72 MHz timer)

HAL_TIM_PWM_Init(&htim3);


TIM_OC_InitTypeDef sConfigOC = {0};

sConfigOC.OCMode = TIM_OCMODE_PWM1;

sConfigOC.Pulse = 1800; // 50% duty

sConfigOC.OCPolarity = TIM_OCPOLARITY_HIGH;

sConfigOC.OCFastMode = TIM_OCFAST_DISABLE;

HAL_TIM_PWM_ConfigChannel(&htim3, &sConfigOC, TIM_CHANNEL_1);


HAL_TIM_PWM_Start(&htim3, TIM_CHANNEL_1);
```

5.2 Input capture to measure pulse width (TIM2 CH1)

```
// TIM2 configured with PSC so TIM_clk_effective comfortable

HAL_TIM_IC_Start_IT(&htim2, TIM_CHANNEL_1);


/* callback */

volatile uint32_t last_rise = 0, last_fall = 0;

volatile uint8_t have_rise = 0, have_fall = 0;


void HAL_TIM_IC_CaptureCallback(TIM_HandleTypeDef *htim) {

 if (htim->Instance == TIM2) {

  uint32_t val = HAL_TIM_ReadCapturedValue(htim, TIM_CHANNEL_1);

  // determine edge using CCER and capture flags or configure separate channels for rising/falling

  // store val as needed

 }

}
```

5.3 Dead-time and complementary outputs (conceptual)

- Use advanced timer (TIM1/TIM8).

- Configure BDTR dead-time field to required nanoseconds per device formula.

- Start both main and complementary channels (HAL_TIMEx_PWMN_Start).

6. Best Practices, Pitfalls, and Debugging

6.1 Best practices

- **Always enable timer peripheral clock** before configuring.

- Use **CubeMX** to validate pin AFs and timer channel mappings.

- Prefer **DMA + interrupts** for heavy data flows — avoid busy polling.

- **Shadow registers**: if ARR and CCR are buffered, write new values and wait for update event to take effect, or force an update (__HAL_TIM_GenerateEvent(&htim, TIM_EVENTSOURCE_UPDATE)).

- For motor drivers, always configure **dead-time and break**; test with a resistive dummy load first.

- Use **center-aligned** for symmetric switching when torque ripple or common-mode EMI is a concern.

6.2 Common pitfalls

- **Forgetting APB/timer clock doubling**: leads to 2× or 0.5× frequency mistakes.

- **ARR overflow**: ARR must fit the timer's counter width — use PSC when needed.

- **Not handling wrap-around** in capture subtraction — always mask or handle CNT wrap properly.

- **Incorrect GPIO AF**: PWM won't appear if the pin AF is wrong.

- **Dead-time units**: different families have different BDTR scaling; compute carefully.

- **Cache & DMA**: on M7/H7, data buffers used by DMA must be in non-cached memory or you must manage cache coherency.

6.3 Debugging tips

- Use an **oscilloscope** or logic analyzer to verify frequency, duty, dead-time, and waveform edges.

- Toggle a debug GPIO briefly in an ISR to measure ISR latency.

- Use timer registers readback (CNT, CCRx, SR flags) to inspect behavior in real time via debugger (or instrumented code sending values over UART/ITM).

- For motor control, test with PWM disabled initially; use scope on gate-driver outputs.

7. Low-Power and Timer Behavior

- Some timers stop in deep low-power modes; **LPTIM** is designed to run in Stop/Standby with very low power.

- If you need PWM or wake timing while sleeping, use LPTIM or RTC alarms. For high-frequency PWM during low power, there's usually a trade-off — high-speed timers consume power.

---

8. Suggested Labs and Exercises

1. **Simple PWM** — generate a 1 kHz PWM, vary duty with a potentiometer (ADC).

2. **High-frequency PWM** — generate 20 kHz PWM and measure jitter.

3. **Input capture** — measure frequency of an external tachometer or signal generator.

4. **Encoder** — configure timer encoder interface and read position at different speeds.

5. **Dead-time & break** — configure complementary outputs with dead-time and test break input handling under simulated fault.

6. **DMA-driven waveform** — use a sine lookup table and DMA to update CCR for arbitrary waveform PWM.

---

9. Quick Reference Cheat-Sheet

- Frequency formula: $f = TIM\_clk / ((PSC+1)*(ARR+1))$

- Center-aligned frequency: $f\_center = TIM\_clk / (2*(PSC+1)*(ARR+1))$

- Duty: $duty\% = 100 * CCR / (ARR+1)$

- For timer clock: if $APB\_prescaler > 1$ then $TIM\_clk = PCLKx * 2$ (verify for your MCU)

- Use HAL_TIM_PWM_Start() / HAL_TIM_PWM_Stop() for HAL, or LL equivalents for tighter control

- For ADC sync: set timer TRGO to a compare/update event and configure ADC external trigger accordingly

- For motor safety: always test break behavior and dead time with a safe load

Chapter 7: Analog Interfaces — Comprehensive Guide

Analog interfaces bridge the continuous real world and the digital domain inside STM32 microcontrollers. This chapter covers everything you need to design, measure, and process analog signals reliably: ADC configuration and usage, DAC applications, sampling and filtering theory applied to real designs, and sensor interfacing plus calibration strategies. Wherever relevant I show practical HAL examples, math you can apply directly, layout and hardware tips, and debugging/test methods.

---

1. Analog-to-Digital Converter (ADC) — Configuration and Use

1.1 ADC capabilities and common modes

STM32 ADCs (family-dependent) support a combination of these modes:

- **Single conversion** — one sample on demand.

- **Continuous conversion** — repeated sampling of one channel.

- **Scan / multi-channel** — sequence through several channels.

- **Triggered conversion** — start by timer TRGO, external input, or software.

- **DMA transfer** — push samples to RAM with minimal CPU load (circular or normal).

- **Differential or single-ended** (only on families that support differential).

- **Injected channels** — high-priority conversions (motor control / synchronized sampling).

- **Hardware oversampling** (on some families) — built-in oversample/decimate engine.

Always consult your MCU's reference manual for exact features (number of bits, sample-times, calibration routines, oversampling, internal channels such as VREFINT, temperature sensor, battery sense, and how many ADCs exist and can be synchronized).

1.2 ADC fundamentals and units

- **Resolution**: N bits (common values: 12, 10, 8, 16 on some families). ADC output range is $0 ..$ $2^N - 1$.

- **Reference voltage (VREF)**: ADC converts analog voltage relative to VREF (usually VDD/VDDA). Absolute accuracy depends heavily on VREF stability/accuracy.

- **LSB size**: $LSB = VREF / (2^N)$. Example: For 12-bit ADC and VREF=3.3 V, $LSB = 3.3 / 4096 \approx 0.000805664$ V ≈ 0.8057 mV.

- **Quantization error** (ideal RMS): $\sigma\_q = LSB / \text{sqrt}(12)$.

- **Ideal SNR for full-scale sine**: $SNR\_q(dB) \approx 6.02 \cdot N + 1.76$ dB.

- **Effective Number Of Bits (ENOB)** from measured SNR:
  $ENOB = (SNR\_measured - 1.76) / 6.02$.

1.3 Acquisition and source impedance (sample-and-hold)

The ADC samples by charging a small internal capacitor (sample-and-hold). The source driving the ADC must be able to charge that capacitor within the **sampling time**.

- Model: input source with source impedance R_s feeding sampling capacitor C_s.

- Time constant: $\tau = R\_s \cdot C\_s$.

- Settling requirement: to reach final voltage within error ε (fractional), require
  $$t\_acq \geq -\tau \cdot \ln(\varepsilon).$$

- If you want, e.g., 0.1% error ($\varepsilon = 0.001$), then $t\_acq \approx 6.9 \cdot \tau$.

Practical rule-of-thumb

- Aim for $R\_s \leq 1\ k\Omega$ when using short ADC sample times. If R_s is higher (e.g., tens of kΩ), increase sample time in ADC config or use a unity-gain buffer (op amp) to lower source impedance.

- Use a small RC or T-network and an op amp buffer for high-impedance sensors (thermistors, high-value dividers).

1.4 ADC clock, sample time and throughput

- ADC conversion time = acquisition time + conversion cycles (clock-dependent). Higher ADC clock gives higher throughput but can increase noise and degrade accuracy.

- Many STM32 ADCs expose selectable **sample times** (in ADC clock cycles). Increase sample time for:

  - Higher input source impedance,

  - Higher accuracy (lower distortion),

  - Higher resolution by allowing accurate charge of sample cap.

- For multi-channel scans, remember each channel has its own acquisition delay; total time per sequence = sum of (acquisition + conversion) for each channel.

1.5 DMA and continuous streaming

Use DMA for continuous sampling or for bursts (e.g., audio, waveform capture). Typical pattern with HAL:

```
// buffer: uint16_t adc_buf[NUM_SAMPLES * NUM_CHANNELS];
```

```
HAL_ADC_Start_DMA(&hadc1, (uint32_t*)adc_buf, BUF_LEN);


// callbacks:

void HAL_ADC_ConvHalfCpltCallback(ADC_HandleTypeDef* hadc) {

 // process first half of buffer

}

void HAL_ADC_ConvCpltCallback(ADC_HandleTypeDef* hadc) {

 // process second half of buffer (circular DMA)

}
```

Double-buffering (ping-pong) and circular mode enable continuous acquisition while software processes the other half of the buffer.

1.6 ADC calibration and accuracy

Two aspects: **factory/MCU calibration** and **application calibration**.

- **On-chip calibration**: many STM32 ADCs include calibration routines (single button invocation via API or register). Use at startup or after wide temperature shifts; consult your RM for the exact sequence.

- **Application-level calibration**:

  1. **Offset (zero)**: measure ADC reading when input is forced to known 0 V (short to ground through same front-end). offset_raw = ADC_raw_at_0V.

Span (gain): apply a known reference voltage (e.g., VREF or an external precision source) and measure raw_ref. Compute scale:

scale = (V_ref - V_zero) / (raw_ref - raw_zero)

Converted_voltage = (raw_sample - raw_zero) * scale + V_zero

  2. Often V_zero is 0 and V_ref = measured VREF (or an external source).

- **Two-point linearization** corrects offset and gain; multi-point calibration can correct non-linearity across range.

- Use **VREFINT** (internal reference) channel and its factory calibration constant where provided to compute actual VREF (improves absolute voltage measurement).

1.7 Noise, SNR, and techniques to improve effective resolution

- **Quantization sets a floor**; noise above quantization increases ENOB.

- **Averaging**: simple moving average reduces random noise by $sqrt(N)$ of samples (N = number averaged). Averaging increases SNR by 3 dB per doubling of samples (0.5 bits per doubling).

- **Oversampling + decimation**: collect M samples at a much higher rate, then decimate. To improve resolution by k bits you need oversampling factor $M = 4^\wedge k$.

  o   Example: to gain 1 bit, M = 4; to gain 2 bits, M = 16.

- **Hardware oversampling** (if supported on your MCU) can be configured to reduce CPU load.

- **Shielding, layout and filtering**: proper layout, star ground patterns, and short analog traces reduce noise.

- **Averaging vs low-pass filtering**: moving average is an FIR filter with latency; IIR (exponential) filters are computationally cheap but introduce phase lag.

1.8 Digital filtering examples

Moving average (window of length N):

```
float moving_average(float *buf, int len) {

  float sum = 0;

  for (int i=0; i < len; ++i) sum += buf[i];

  return sum / len;

}
```

First-order IIR low-pass (exponential):

$$y[n] = \alpha \cdot x[n] + (1-\alpha) \cdot y[n-1] \quad \text{where } 0 < \alpha \le 1$$

Choose $\alpha = dt / (RC + dt)$ where RC is time constant and dt is sampling interval.

1.9 Practical ADC checklist

- Measure or stabilize VREF. If absolute accuracy matters, use an external precision reference or calibrate against VREFINT.

- Match ADC sample time to source impedance.

- Buffer high-impedance sensors with rail-to-rail op amp if needed.

- Place analog decoupling caps close to VDDA/VREF pins; use a ground plane.

- Use DMA in circular double-buffer mode for streaming; process half-buffer in callbacks.

- If using multiple ADCs or injected channels for synchronized sampling, use timers and TRGO to synchronize conversions.

2. Digital-to-Analog Converter (DAC) — Applications and Design

2.1 DAC basics

- **Resolution**: N bits (often 12-bit on STM32 families that include DAC).

- **Output range**: 0 .. VREF (or VREF/2 in differential configurations if supported).

- **Update rate**: set by software writes or by hardware triggers (timers) and can be automated with DMA.

- **Buffering**: DAC outputs often pass through an on-chip output buffer (check the voltage range, drive capability, and settle time) or you may need an external op amp for low impedance or gain.

2.2 Typical DAC use cases

- **Analog waveform generation** (audio, test signals): use DMA + timer to update DAC at the desired sample rate.

- **Analog control signals**: generate reference voltages to external circuits (bias voltages, sensor excitation).

- **Sine/triangle generation**: table-driven waveform output (DMA feeding DAC).

- **Audio**: simple low-rate audio; for high-quality audio, external codecs are usually chosen.

2.3 DAC with timer trigger + DMA example (HAL)

// Assume dac_buf[] contains a 12-bit waveform table, LENGTH samples

// 1) Configure TIMx to generate TRGO at sampling rate

// 2) Configure DAC channel with TIMx TRGO as trigger

HAL_DAC_Start(&hdac, DAC_CHANNEL_1);

HAL_DAC_Start_DMA(&hdac, DAC_CHANNEL_1, (uint32_t*)dac_buf, LENGTH, DAC_ALIGN_12B_R);

- Use HAL_DAC_Start_DMA and a timer that triggers at the sample frequency for precise timing.

- For continuous playback, use circular DMA mode.

- Add a reconstruction filter after DAC (low-pass) to remove stepwise quantization / image frequencies.

2.4 DAC smoothing and output filtering

- The DAC output is a staircase. Use a **reconstruction filter** (low-pass, active or passive) to smooth to an analog waveform.

- Choose filter cutoff f_c well below Nyquist ($f_s / 2$) to attenuate images; a simple RC low-pass has cutoff $f_c = 1/(2\pi RC)$.

- For audio-quality or precise signals use 2nd-order active filters (Sallen-Key) or higher-order filters for steeper roll-off.

2.5 DAC settling time and drive requirements

- DAC output changes need time to settle to a new value. If your system requires fast updates with low glitch, check the DAC datasheet for **settling time** and **glitch impulse** specs.

- If driving low impedance loads, buffer with op amp; the DAC's on-chip buffer usually provides only limited drive (mA-level).

- For rail-to-rail outputs choose appropriate op amp and supply rails to avoid saturating or clipping.

2.6 Using DAC for calibration and reference

- DAC can be used to generate calibration voltages for sensor excitation (trim voltage), or to inject test signals into ADC inputs for system-level tests.

- Be careful: if you use DAC output to generate reference-like voltages, verify drift and temperature coefficients—external precision references are better for metrology.

---

3. Signal Sampling and Filtering

3.1 Nyquist, aliasing, and anti-aliasing

- **Nyquist theorem**: sample frequency f_s must be strictly greater than twice the highest frequency component f_max to avoid aliasing: $f\_s > 2 \cdot f\_max$.

- **Anti-aliasing filter (AAF)**: analog low-pass filter applied before ADC to attenuate frequencies above $f\_s/2$. Design must consider:

  - Desired passband ripple and stopband attenuation.

  - The slope of the filter (first order gives only −20 dB/decade; often insufficient).

  - For hobby or low-performance applications, a single-pole RC at $f\_c \approx 0.4 \cdot (f\_s/2)$ is sometimes used, but use multi-order for critical systems.

Design steps for AAF

1. Choose f_s based on signal bandwidth and required oversampling (often sample at several times Nyquist to make filter easier).

2. Choose desired stopband attenuation at f_alias ≈ f_s/2 (e.g., −60 dB).

3. Pick filter order (Butterworth/Chebyshev) to meet attenuation. Active filters (multiple op amp stages) let you get steeper slopes with unity gain.

3.2 Anti-imaging (post-DAC)

- Symmetric problem when using DAC: images at harmonics of the sample rate. Use a reconstruction filter to remove them.

3.3 Windowing and spectral leakage (if performing FFT)

- When you process sampled data with FFT, apply a window (Hann, Hamming, Blackman) to reduce spectral leakage and interpret amplitudes correctly.

- Window choice trades frequency resolution vs sidelobe attenuation.

3.4 Digital filters: FIR vs IIR

- **FIR** (finite impulse response): always stable, linear phase possible, good for precise filtering but can require many taps for steep roll-off.

- **IIR** (infinite impulse response): fewer coefficients for given response, but nonlinear phase and possible stability issues if not designed carefully.

Use CMSIS-DSP for optimized filter implementations on Cortex-M (FIR/IIR, decimation, FFT).

3.5 Practical sampling patterns

- **Synchronous sampling with timers**: use timer triggers to start ADC conversions for deterministic timing—essential for control loops and coherent sampling.

- **Burst sampling**: use DMA to gather bursts at high sample rate, then process offline or decimate.

- **Triggered sampling for event capture**: start conversion on external events to measure transient signals.

4. Sensor Interfacing and Calibration

4.1 Front-end analog design patterns

- **Voltage divider**: simple for thermistors and potentiometers, but watch source impedance and buffering.

- **Wheatstone bridge + instrumentation amplifier**: standard for strain gauges, load cells, and RTDs in bridge form.

- **Transimpedance amplifier (TIA)**: for current-output sensors (photodiodes); TIA converts current to voltage with gain = Rf.

- **Charge amplifier**: for piezo sensors.

- **Thermocouples**: require low-noise amplifier and cold-junction compensation; consider dedicated ICs for precision.

- **RTD (PT100)**: use current source and measure voltage drop; often boosted with differential amplifier and bridge for improved linearity.

4.2 Examples and practical tips

Thermistor (NTC)

- Use resistor divider and measure voltage across NTC.

- Non-linear: linearize in software using Steinhart–Hart equation or look–up table.

- Protect against self-heating by using low excitation current or duty cycled measurement.

Load cell / strain gauge

- Use Wheatstone bridge and a precision instrumentation amplifier (INA) or ADC with built-in PGA.

- Low-level signals (mV) require low-noise layout, shielding, and careful grounding.

- Use differential ADC input if available, or sample both bridge outputs and subtract.

Photodiode

- Use TIA with low input bias op amp and appropriate feedback resistor for desired sensitivity.

- Provide optical filtering and ensure fast enough bandwidth.

Gas sensors / chemical sensors

- Often require specific conditioning circuits (heater control, current measurement), long warm-up and calibration.

4.3 Calibration strategies

1. Factory calibration

- Performed with precise reference voltages and conditions; store coefficients in nonvolatile memory (option bytes, EEPROM, flash sector).

- Include metadata: temperature at calibration, date, and revision.

2. Two-point linear calibration

- Measure raw ADC at V_low and V_high (e.g., 0 V and Vref or known precision sources).

- Compute gain and offset to map raw to volts.

3. Multi-point calibration

- Fit polynomial or piecewise linear function for non-linear sensors—store LUT or coefficients.

4. Runtime/field calibration

- Self-calibration using known system loads or references (e.g., short-to-ground for zero offset, measure internal VREFINT for scale).

- Temperature compensation using onboard temperature sensor or additional RTD/thermistor.

5. Drift correction

- Periodic re-calibration or background measurements can correct for drift (e.g., measure VREF periodically).

6. Uncertainty and error budget

- Build an error budget: list major error sources (ADC quantization, VREF error, amplifier offset, resistor tolerance, noise).

- If absolute accuracy is required, select precision references, low-drift resistors (0.1% or better), and temperature compensation.

4.4 Software linearization and compensation examples

Steinhart–Hart for thermistors:

$$1/T = A + B \cdot \ln(R) + C \cdot (\ln(R))^3$$

where R is thermistor resistance and A/B/C are coefficients from datasheet or calibration.

Two-point linear scale:

```
float convert_adc_to_voltage(uint32_t raw, uint32_t raw0, float v0, uint32_t raw1, float v1) {

  float slope = (v1 - v0) / (float)(raw1 - raw0);

  return v0 + slope * (raw - raw0);

}
```

Digital compensation for sensor temperature sensitivity

- Measure sensor temperature and apply polynomial correction value_corrected = value_measured + f(T).

5. Measurement, Debug and Validation Techniques

5.1 Bench equipment & methods

- **Precision source**: calibrated voltage source for span calibration.

- **Oscilloscope/logic analyzer**: examine ADC trigger timing, sample-hold behavior, and DAC waveforms.

- **Multimeter** (4-wire if needed): verify reference rails and bias currents.

- **Function generator**: for SNR and linearity testing with sine waves.

- **Spectrum analyzer / FFT**: evaluate noise and harmonic content.

5.2 Quantify noise and ENOB

1. Capture N samples of ADC at fixed input (e.g., mid-scale).

2. Compute mean and standard deviation σ.

3. **RMS noise** $\approx \sigma * \text{LSB\_voltage}$.

4. Compute SNR for a full-scale sine input:
   $\text{SNR\_meas\_dB} = 20 \cdot \log10(\text{signal\_rms} / \text{noise\_rms})$.

5. $\text{ENOB} = (\text{SNR\_meas\_dB} - 1.76) / 6.02$.

5.3 Linearity testing (INL/DNL)

- Sweep a precision ramp across ADC input and compare digital output to ideal code; compute DNL (difference between successive codes minus 1 LSB) and INL (accumulated error).

- For production, run ramp test and histogram to detect stuck codes or large DNL.

5.4 PCB layout rules for analog accuracy

- Keep analog traces short and away from digital switching traces.

- Use ground plane; for mixed-signal use split planes only with careful star-point tie and attention to return currents.

- Place decoupling caps close to VDDA and VREF pins.

- Route sensitive analog inputs away from clocks and MOSFET driver signals.

- Add guard rings for high-impedance nodes if needed.

6. Common Pitfalls & How to Avoid Them

- **Ignoring VREF**: absolute voltage measurements are as good as VREF. Use precision reference or measure VREF via VREFINT and calibrate.

- **Source impedance too high**: leads to droop on sample capacitor and distortion. Use buffers or increase sample time.

- **Insufficient anti-aliasing**: high-frequency signals alias into passband; always filter accordingly.

- **Wrong ADC sample time**: too short → inaccurate readings; too long → lower throughput than needed.

- **DMA buffer overruns**: size buffers correctly and handle half/full DMA callbacks; use cache maintenance on cache-enabled MCUs (invalidate/clean).

- **Assuming ideal DAC**: DAC output is stepped and needs reconstruction filtering for smooth analog signals.

- **Mixing grounds** poorly: returns create noise; maintain coherent ground strategy.

7. Example Workflows and Code Patterns

7.1 ADC multi-channel circular DMA (HAL) — conceptual

1. Configure ADC in scan mode for the channels you need (set sample times per-channel).

2. Configure DMA in circular mode to transfer NUM_CHANNELS * SAMPLES_PER_CHANNEL.

3. Start: HAL_ADC_Start_DMA(&hadc, (uint32_t*)buf, buf_len);

4. Handle half/full complete callbacks to process chunks while DMA continues.

7.2 DAC waveform generation (HAL + Timer + DMA) — conceptual

1. Create a waveform table dac_table[L] (normalized to 0..4095 for 12-bit).

2. Configure TIMx to TRGO at sample rate f_s.

3. Configure DAC to trigger on TIMx TRGO.

4. Start with HAL_DAC_Start_DMA(&hdac, DAC_CHANNEL_1, (uint32_t*)dac_table, L, DAC_ALIGN_12B_R);

5. Add analog reconstruction filter after DAC.

8. Labs and Exercises

1. **ADC basics**: sample a potentiometer single-channel, print voltage over UART, compare with multimeter.

2. **Sampling time experiment**: drive ADC input via resistor divider with different R and change sample time; measure accuracy vs sample time.

3. **DMA streaming**: collect 10k samples at maximum ADC rate into RAM, compute mean/stddev and estimate ENOB.

4. **Anti-aliasing filter**: design and implement a 2nd-order Butterworth AAF for fs = 10 kHz and test aliasing with a 30 kHz sine.

5. **DAC waveform + LPF**: output a 1 kHz sine from DAC with 8-bit table at fs = 48 kHz, then compare raw staircase vs filtered waveform on scope.

6. **Sensor calibration**: interface an NTC thermistor, calibrate with ice water (0°C) and boiling water (~100°C), build Steinhart-Hart coefficients and compare with datasheet values.

9. Quick Reference — Useful Formulas

- $LSB = VREF / 2^N$

- Quantization RMS $\approx LSB / sqrt(12)$

ADVANCED STM32 MICROCONTROLLERS

- Ideal SNR (dB) $\approx 6.02 \cdot N + 1.76$

- ENOB = (SNR_dB - 1.76) / 6.02

- $t\_acq \geq -R\_s \cdot C\_s \cdot \ln(\varepsilon)$ (settling for specified fractional error ε)

- RC low-pass cutoff: $f\_c = 1 / (2\pi RC)$

- Oversampling factor for k extra bits: $M = 4^\wedge k$ (e.g., 1 bit $\to$ 4×, 2 bits $\to$ 16×)

Chapter 8: Serial Communication Protocols — Complete Guide for STM32

Reliable serial communication is central to embedded systems: debug consoles, sensor buses, memory cards, motor controllers, vehicle networks, and USB devices all use serial protocols tuned to different trade-offs (speed, determinism, topology, physical layer). This chapter explains the main serial protocols you'll use on STM32: UART/USART, I²C, SPI, CAN & LIN, and USB (device & host). For each I cover electrical/physical layer notes, STM32-specific configuration patterns, code examples (HAL/LL patterns), DMA/interrupt best practices, protocol quirks, debugging tips, and production considerations.

1 UART / USART — Debugging and Data Transfer

What UART/USART is

- UART = universal asynchronous receiver/transmitter. Asynchronous byte framing: start bit, data bits (5–9), optional parity, stop bits (1/1.5/2).

- USART in STM32 can do synchronous and asynchronous modes (but most use it as UART). Supports modem-like control (RTS/CTS), LIN, Smartcard, IrDA (in some devices).

Electrical layers and transceivers

- MCU pins are TTL/CMOS (0–VDD). For PC-style serial use a level shifter like **MAX232** (RS-232 ±12V).

- For multi-drop half-duplex networks, use **RS-485/RS-422** transceivers (DE/RE pins). Hardware DE (driver enable) support exists on many STM32 USARTs — prefer it because toggling DE in software can break timing if DMA is used.

- For direct MCU-to-MCU, use TTL-level (3.3V) direct connections. Never connect 5V TTL directly unless the MCU pins are 5V-tolerant.

Configuration essentials (what to pick)

- **Baud rate**: e.g., 115200, 921600. Accuracy important; choose MCU clock and USART DIV so actual baud error is small (prefer <2% for many devices, <0.5% for sensitive protocols).

- **Frame**: data bits (8 most common), parity (none, even, odd), stop bits (1 typical).

- **Flow control**: none or hardware RTS/CTS (use if receiving device may be slow).

- **Mode**: polling, interrupt-driven, DMA-driven — choose by throughput and CPU budget.

Baud-rate and oversampling

STM32 USART supports oversampling by 16 (default) or by 8 (higher speed but slightly higher receiver sensitivity). Oversampling choice affects BRR calculation and effective tolerance; CubeMX and HAL handle BRR computation automatically when you set baud in the IDE.

STM32 patterns — HAL examples

Simple polling transmit

```
// assumes huart2 created by CubeMX

uint8_t msg[] = "Hello UART\r\n";

HAL_UART_Transmit(&huart2, msg, sizeof(msg)-1, HAL_MAX_DELAY);
```

Interrupt-driven receive (byte-by-byte)

```
uint8_t rx;

HAL_UART_Receive_IT(&huart2, &rx, 1);

// in callback:

void HAL_UART_RxCpltCallback(UART_HandleTypeDef *huart) {

 if (huart == &huart2) {

  process_byte(rx);

  HAL_UART_Receive_IT(&huart2, &rx, 1); // re-arm

 }

}
```

DMA circular receive into ring buffer (recommended for continuous streams)

- Use HAL_UART_Receive_DMA() with a buffer sized for your application (e.g., 512–4096 bytes). Maintain a read pointer and check __HAL_DMA_GET_COUNTER() or use DMA half/full interrupts.

```
#define RX_BUF_LEN 512

uint8_t rx_buf[RX_BUF_LEN];


HAL_UART_Receive_DMA(&huart2, rx_buf, RX_BUF_LEN);


// in DMA half/full callbacks (or use IDLE line detection)

void HAL_UART_RxCpltCallback(UART_HandleTypeDef *huart) { /* handle second half */ }

void HAL_UART_RxHalfCpltCallback(UART_HandleTypeDef *huart) { /* handle first half */ }
```

Tip: Use UART **IDLE-line detection** (interrupt on IDLE) to know when a packet ends when protocol is packet-based but lengths vary.

Flow control & RS-485

- For RTS/CTS set HardwareFlowControl = UART_HWCONTROL_RTS_CTS in HAL init.

- For RS-485 half-duplex use hardware DE support (HAL_RS485Ex_Transmit_IT/DMA) or drive DE pin with the USART DE feature; otherwise assert DE manually but carefully time the DE deassert after last character transmitted (use TC flag or DMA transfer complete + small delay).

Common issues & debugging

- **Baud mismatch** → framing errors. Check actual baud error (use MCU clock measurement or scope).

- **Framing/Parity errors** → bad configuration on either side.

- **Missed data** → use DMA ring buffer; increase priority; tune FIFO thresholds if supported.

- **Noise** on long lines → use shielded twisted pair, differential transceivers (RS-485).

- Debug tools: logic analyzer, oscilloscope, USB->serial adapters, and stm32cubemon or serial terminal.

2 I²C — Master/Slave and Multi-Device Networking

Protocol basics

- Two-wire bus: **SDA** (data) and **SCL** (clock). Open-drain lines, require pull-up resistors.

- Master generates clock; multi-master arbitration supported (SDA low dominates); clock stretching enables slaves to hold SCL low to delay the master.

- Addressing: **7-bit** (most common) and **10-bit** addressing. SMBus is a variant with stricter electrical/timing rules.

Electrical & pull-ups

- Pull-up resistor choice depends on bus capacitance and speed: roughly $R = V_{pull} / I\_pull$. Typical values range 1k–10k. For 100 kHz with small bus capacitance use larger resistors (4.7k–10k); for 400 kHz and large bus capacitance use smaller (1k–3.3k).

- Bus capacitance limit ~400 pF (I²C spec); keep short traces or use buffers (PCA9600/IBIS solutions) for long runs.

Modes and speeds

- Standard (100 kHz), Fast (400 kHz), Fast-Plus (1 MHz), High-Speed (3.4 MHz). Not all STM32 I²C peripherals support all modes; check datasheet.

STM32 usage patterns

Master write (HAL)

uint8_t data[] = {0x01, 0x02};

HAL_I2C_Master_Transmit(&hi2c1, (uint16_t)(dev_addr<<1), data, sizeof(data), HAL_MAX_DELAY);

Master read with repeated start (no STOP between write and read)

HAL_I2C_Master_Transmit(&hi2c1, dev_wr_addr, &reg, 1, HAL_MAX_DELAY);

HAL_I2C_Master_Receive(&hi2c1, dev_rd_addr, buf, len, HAL_MAX_DELAY);

CubeMX/HAL handle repeated start automatically if you call Master_Transmit then Master_Receive (but watch flags in LL if you implement manually).

Slave mode

- Configure I²C as slave and use callbacks HAL_I2C_SlaveRxCpltCallback / HAL_I2C_AddrCallback for address match. Slave mode is trickier: ensure you meet timing and buffer availability. Interrupt-driven or DMA-driven slave implementations require careful handling.

DMA for high-throughput

- Use DMA for large bursts (e.g., sensors streaming data). Combine with interrupts for error handling.

Multi-master & clock stretching

- Multi-master: devices monitor bus while transmitting; arbitration resolves conflicts. Avoid software bit-banging multi-master unless you understand arbitration rules.

- Clock stretching: some slow devices (I²C EEPROMs, sensors) hold SCL low; master must handle it. STM32 hardware supports clock stretching but on very fast master clocks watch for stretch timeouts and enable appropriate features in CubeMX.

Error handling & recovery

- Bus stuck (SDA low) recovery: toggle SCL up to 9 times to clock out a stuck slave byte (often caused by slave stuck while driving SDA). Then generate STOP.

- If peripheral gets stuck, reinitialize I²C peripheral and toggling SCL may be required.

Addressing pitfalls

- Be careful with 7-bit vs 8-bit representations: many libraries expect 7-bit addresses left-shifted or not — check HAL expects 7-bit shifted left in hi2c calls (HAL uses 7-bit left-shift or internally shifts? In HAL you pass the 7-bit address shifted left by 1 when calling? **Check CubeMX docs** — when in doubt use (dev_addr<<1) per many HAL examples).

SMBus/PMBus specifics

- SMBus adds timeouts, host alerts, and stricter electrical specs. If designing power management or battery systems, consider SMBus-compliant chips and implement required timeouts.

3 SPI — High-Speed Full-Duplex Bus

SPI fundamentals

- Full-duplex, master-driven synchronous serial. Signals: **SCLK, MOSI, MISO, NSS/CS**.

- Modes defined by CPOL (clock polarity) and CPHA (clock phase) with 4 mode variants (0..3). Choose mode to match the slave device's expectation.

- Data order: MSB-first or LSB-first.

Electrical and topology

- SPI is point-to-point or multi-slave with separate chip-select lines (no bus arbitration).

- For long runs or multiple devices, consider tri-state and buffering (74HC125) or dedicated SPI bus extenders.

STM32 configuration essentials

- Select SPI mode (CPOL/CPHA), data size (8/16 bits), baud rate prescaler (powers of two), MSB/LSB, and NSS management (hardware NSS vs software-managed CS).

- Some STM32 families have SPI with FIFO, DMA request support, and hardware CRC generation.

HAL master transmit-receive (blocking)

uint8_t tx[] = {0x9A, 0xBC};

uint8_t rx[2];

HAL_SPI_TransmitReceive(&hspi1, tx, rx, 2, HAL_MAX_DELAY);

DMA-based for high throughput

- Configure TX and RX DMA streams to run simultaneously (double-buffer if continuous). For full duplex streaming (e.g., sensors, audio), DMA minimizes CPU load.

Half-duplex & simplex

- Some devices use half-duplex where MOSI shares MISO pin. STM32 supports half-duplex mode (MOSI as bidirectional pin), but beware the slave timing for direction switching.

NSS/CS handling

- **Hardware NSS**: the SPI peripheral can manage NSS pin automatically in master/slave modes; convenient for multi-master or multi-byte frames where edge-aligned activation is needed. However hardware NSS is inflexible for multi-slave single-master with multiple CS lines; you will often manage CS in GPIO manually.

- **Software CS**: manually assert/deassert CS GPIO around SPI transfer and call HAL SPI transmit/receive. Ensure CS is asserted low before the clock begins and deasserted only after last bit and any required delay.

Clocking: prescalers and max speed

- SPI CLK = APB clock / Prescaler. The available prescalers are discrete (2,4,8,...). For very high rates, ensure your slave can handle the clock and signal integrity is acceptable.

Protocol-level concerns

- **Mode mismatch** leads to data shifts/garbled bytes. Test with scope.

- **Byte vs word sizes**: if using 16-bit data frames, configure the SPI to 16-bit to transfer 2 bytes atomically — useful for DACs expecting 16-bit words.

- **Chip-select timing**: some devices expect CS low for entire frame including dummy clocks — follow datasheet.

Debugging SPI

- Use a logic analyzer to capture SCLK, MOSI, MISO, CS. Check sampling edge and bit order.

- Confirm MOSI data by viewing with CS asserted; if bytes shift, verify CPOL/CPHA combination.

4 CAN & LIN — Automotive and Industrial Networks

CAN (Controller Area Network)

Protocol overview

- Multi-master, message-based bus (not address-based). Messages have **identifiers** (11-bit standard or 29-bit extended) which determine priority (lower numerical ID = higher priority).

- Uses non-destructive bitwise arbitration: if two nodes send at once, the lower ID wins without corruption.

- Error-detection and frame retransmission are built-in; nodes maintain error counters and can go **Bus Off** when thresholds reached.

Physical layer

- High-speed CAN (ISO 11898-2) uses differential pair **CAN_H / CAN_L** with 120Ω termination at both ends. Use CAN transceivers (e.g., MCP2551, ISO1050, or TI/Infineon transceivers).

- CAN-FD extends payload up to 64 bytes and allows higher data-phase bitrate — requires FD-capable transceiver.

STM32 details

- STM32 has integrated CAN controllers (Classic CAN and on some parts CAN-FD). The MCU CAN peripheral needs a transceiver on the board. CubeMX generates HAL code and filter configuration templates.

Bit timing & configuration

Bit-timing parameters: **prescaler, TS1 (tseg1), TS2 (tseg2), SJW (synchronization jump width)**. They control sample point and bit rate. Tools or calculators (often built into CubeMX) help compute settings from peripheral clock.

Filters and acceptance

- Hardware acceptance filters let the controller receive only messages matching configured IDs or masks — essential for reducing CPU load.

Transmit/receive flow (HAL)

CAN_TxHeaderTypeDef txHeader;

uint8_t txData[8];

uint32_t txMailbox;

txHeader.StdId = 0x123;

txHeader.IDE = CAN_ID_STD;

txHeader.RTR = CAN_RTR_DATA;

txHeader.DLC = 8;

HAL_CAN_AddTxMessage(&hcan, &txHeader, txData, &txMailbox);

Receive via interrupt or polling; use HAL_CAN_ActivateNotification() to enable
CAN_IT_RX_FIFO0_MSG_PENDING.

Error handling & states

- Monitor CAN->ESR and peripheral error counters. If you go Bus Off, follow datasheet steps to recover (some hardware can auto-recover after bus idle, others require software reset).

Debugging tools

- CAN bus analyzers (PC tools), Vector/CANoe or Peak PCAN, and inexpensive USB-CAN adapters. Use a scope to check differential waveforms and 120Ω termination.

LIN (Local Interconnect Network)

Overview

- Single-wire, low-cost serial bus used in automotive for simple devices (comfort modules). Master/slave architecture with scheduled frames.

- Uses baud rates up to 20 kbps (typical 19200) and simple checksum methods (classic vs enhanced). Break field initiates frame from master.

STM32 usage

- Many STM32 USARTs have **LIN mode** to generate break fields and manage parity; you implement LIN by using USART LIN mode or by bit-banging in a pinch. CubeMX can enable LIN/Smartcard modes.

LIN specifics

- Master sends break (dominant low) followed by sync and identifier; slaves respond in specified time slot. Strict timing rules must be met.

5 USB — Device and Host Implementation

USB is a complex stack. STM32 provides middleware for device & host roles; CubeMX and STM32Cube middleware ease setup.

USB basics

- USB roles: **Device** (peripheral), **Host** (controller), **OTG/Dual-role** (can switch).

- Transfer types: **Control** (endpoint 0), **Bulk**, **Interrupt**, **Isochronous** — each for specific use cases (control/configuration, bulk data e.g., mass storage, interrupt for HID, isochronous for audio/video).

- USB speeds: Low (1.5 Mbps), Full (12 Mbps), High (480 Mbps) — many STM32 parts support FS, some with HS via ULPI external PHY.

Device implementation (common use-cases)

- **CDC-ACM**: virtual COM port — common for debug/console.

- **MSC (Mass Storage)**: expose an SD card or flash as USB drive (combine with FATFS).

- **HID**: keyboards, mice, simple custom data.

- **Composite devices**: combine CDC + MSC or CDC + HID.

STM32 device stack

- CubeMX can enable USB Device class (CDC, MSC, HID) and generate code: descriptors, endpoint configuration, callbacks. Use USBD_* APIs or HAL wrapper.

Device example (CDC): CubeMX generates usbd_cdc_if.c with CDC_Receive_FS() callback invoked on bulk OUT packets — you implement CDC_Transmit_FS() to send back.

Host implementation

- Host mode allows STM32 to control attached USB devices (e.g., read a FAT-formatted USB stick via MSC host class). CubeMX can generate USB Host middleware (USBH_* APIs).

Host class examples

- **USBH_MSC**: mass storage host, combines with FATFS to read/write files.

- **USBH_HID**: reads HID reports (keyboards/mice).

- Host requires more RAM and stack; make sure MCU has enough resources.

OTG & Dual-role

- OTG-capable STM32 parts can negotiate roles with a USB OTG cable/ID pin. OTG added complexity (ID detection, VBUS control), but is handy for devices that must act as both host and device.

Hardware details

- USB FS device needs D+ or D- pull-up resistor (1.5 kΩ typically) to signal speed to host; ST boards have these integrated. For OTG, VBUS detection pin and power switch with current limiting are required for host mode to supply 5V.

Endpoint & buffer considerations

- Endpoints require dedicated buffer memory (PMAs on some families or dedicated USB SRAM). Endpoint allocation and size is critical — CubeMX helps but for advanced uses tune buffer sizes to avoid stalls.

Power & certification

- As a USB device, you must honor current limits (100 mA default, then request up to 500 mA for USB2.0 unless self-powered). For USB Host, provide a current-limited 5V supply (OTG power switch with current limiting and status).

Debugging USB

- Use USB analyzers (software like Wireshark with USBPcap on PC) and USB protocol analyzers. On-device use USBD_Connect/USBD_Disconnect to simulate plug/unplug for testing.

Cross-Protocol Topics & Best Practices

DMA vs Interrupts

- For high-throughput links (UART at high baud, SPI streaming, ADC-driven I²C sensors, USB bulk transfers), prefer DMA to keep CPU free. Use interrupts for event-driven or low-rate traffic.

- Combine DMA with circular buffering and half/full interrupts for streaming patterns.

Clocking & peripheral availability

- Confirm peripheral clocks enabled (RCC). Peripheral behavior depends on APB/AHB bus states and prescalers — check CubeMX generated clock configuration. Some peripherals (USB, I²S-derived via SPI) require particular clock sources (48 MHz domain) and PLL settings.

Synchronization and real-time constraints

- For deterministic systems (motor control, fieldbus), carefully plan priorities: ISRs for time-critical handling, DMA for throughput, tasks for heavy processing. Use RTOS primitives (xSemaphoreGiveFromISR, xTaskNotifyFromISR) for safe deferred processing.

Electrical & signal integrity

- For differential buses (CAN, RS-485), always use matched twisted pair and proper 120Ω termination for CAN. For RS-485 multipoint, use biasing resistors to define idle state. For I²C use appropriate pull-ups and keep line lengths short.

Protocol testing tools

- Logic analyzer (Saleae), oscilloscope, USB analyzer, CAN bus adapter (PCAN or ValueCAN), bus pirates for ad-hoc testing. Use those early to validate physical layer and timing.

Error handling & robustness

- Implement retries on recoverable errors (NACK on I²C writes, retransmit on UART frame error), backoff strategies for repeated failures, watchdog to recover stuck states, and logging for field diagnostics.

Practical Example Patterns

UART: using IDLE detection with DMA ring buffer

- Start DMA circular into large RX buffer. In USARTx_IRQHandler, detect IDLE flag (indicates end-of-frame) and compute len = BUF_SIZE - DMA_CNDTR. Process trailing data and clear IDLE flag; this avoids needing delimiters.

I²C: combined write-then-read to read registers

- Master sends device address + register address (no stop), then repeated start and master read. Use HAL blocking or combined HAL_I2C_Mem_Read() which performs this atomically.

SPI: DMA TransmitReceive for large bursts

- Configure TX & RX DMA channels and start HAL_SPI_TransmitReceive_DMA() with huge buffers. Use DMA transfer-complete callbacks to process data.

CAN: filter & FIFO

- Configure hardware filters to accept only desired IDs and route them to FIFO0. Use interrupts on RX FIFO 0 pending and HAL_CAN_GetRxMessage() to decode.

USB: CDC loopback

- Use CubeMX to enable USB Device CDC. Implement CDC_Receive_FS() to pass received data to application and CDC_Transmit_FS() to respond — good for serial-over-USB debug.

Troubleshooting Quick Reference

- No data received: check peripheral clocks, pin AF settings, and physical wiring (TX/RX swapped?).

- Garbage at high speeds: check baud/clock rate accuracy and signal integrity (overshoot, ringing).

- DMA not working: confirm DMA channel/stream mapping and peripheral request mapping; check cache coherency on Cortex-M7/H7 (clean/invalidate D-cache for DMA buffers).

- I²C bus stuck: check SDA low → toggle SCL 9 times then STOP. Evaluate stuck slave.

- SPI mismatch: verify CPOL/CPHA and bit order. Check CS timing and ensure CS asserted for whole frame.

- CAN not passing: ensure proper termination, transceiver power, and correct bit timing.

Chapter 9: Memory Management in STM32 — Comprehensive Guide

Memory management is central to reliable embedded firmware. On STM32 devices this spans internal flash and SRAM topologies, emulating non-volatile EEPROM, attaching external memories (QSPI/NOR, SDRAM, NAND, SD), and designing robust bootloaders and firmware update (FOTA/DFU) schemes. This chapter explains the practical architecture details, APIs, pitfalls, and robust strategies you can apply in production systems.

---

1. Flash and SRAM Architecture

1.1 Memory map and roles (high-level)

STM32 devices expose a unified memory map with regions for:

- **Flash (internal non-volatile)** — code, constants, persistent configuration.

- **SRAM** — stack, heap, runtime data, DMA buffers.

- **Peripheral registers**.

- **Option bytes / backup area** (device-dependent).

- **Backup SRAM / VBAT domain** — retains data during power-off when VBAT present (if available).
  Different families add specialized RAM:

- **ITCM / DTCM / TCM** (instruction/data tightly-coupled memory) for M7 — zero-latency access for critical code/data.

- **AXI SRAM / OCRAM / CCM** — used for DMA or deterministic access.

- **Cache** (I-cache / D-cache) — present on M7/H7; affects DMA coherency.

1.2 Flash organization & operation

Physical layout

- Flash is organized in **sectors/pages/rows** (naming varies by family). Sectors are the minimum erasable unit; programming is typically word/doubleword sized.

- Some devices support **dual-bank** flash where banks can be independently erased and used for banking/failover.

Key characteristics

- **Erase-before-write**: you must erase a sector (sets bits to 1) before programming bits to 0.

- **Granularity**: erase unit (sector), program unit (half-word, word, double-word) — check the device RM and use HAL constants (FLASH_TYPEPROGRAM_WORD, FLASH_TYPEPROGRAM_DOUBLEWORD, etc.).

- **Limited cycles**: typical flash endurance ~10^4–10^5 cycles — avoid frequent full-sector rewrites.

- **Erase/program latency**: sector erase can take milliseconds; programming is faster but still non-zero — design update flows accordingly.

- **Option bytes**: small non-volatile configuration area (boot configuration, RDP) — programming option bytes requires special handling.

Flash controller API (typical HAL flow)

1. HAL_FLASH_Unlock()

2. (Optionally) __HAL_FLASH_CLEAR_FLAG(...)

3. If needed, erase sector: FLASH_EraseInitTypeDef + HAL_FLASHEx_Erase()

4. Program: HAL_FLASH_Program(type, address, data)

5. HAL_FLASH_Lock()

Example: simple safe 32-bit program

HAL_FLASH_Unlock();

uint32_t address = 0x08020000;

uint32_t data = 0x12345678;

if (HAL_FLASH_Program(FLASH_TYPEPROGRAM_WORD, address, data) != HAL_OK) {

 // handle error (check HAL_FLASH_GetError())

}

HAL_FLASH_Lock();

Best practices

- Always check status (HAL_FLASH_GetError()), and verify by reading back.

- When erasing, use PAGE/SECTOR identifiers (CubeMX or RM tells units).

- Minimize flash writes (use buffered logging, wear-leveling, external storage for frequent writes).

- For multi-threaded systems, protect flash operations with mutexes; they are blocking and may impact timing.

1.3 SRAM types, use-cases and placement

- **Main SRAM**: general-purpose RAM used for stack/heap.

- **CCM (Core-Coupled Memory)**: tightly-coupled to CPU, fast but not DMA-coherent on many devices; ideal for deterministic code/data.

- **DTCM/ITCM**: very low-latency memory for time-critical code and data.

- **Backup SRAM**: powered from VBAT, retains across main power off.

- **External SRAM (via FMC/QSPI)**: larger storage but may be slower.

Placement & linker considerations

- Use the linker script to place performance-critical code/data in TCM or CCM sections (.itcm, .dtcm, .ccmram) and mark buffers used by DMA in non-cacheable regions.

- Example linker snippet (GCC style) to place data in .ccmram:

```
.ccmram (NOLOAD) : {

 . = ALIGN(4);

 _sccm = .;

 *(.ccmram .ccmram.*)

 . = ALIGN(4);

 _eccm = .;

} >RAM_DTCM
```

Then in C:

```
__attribute__((section(".ccmram"))) volatile uint32_t time_critical_buffer[256];
```

DMA & caches

- On cache-enabled cores (M7/H7) you must **clean/invalidate D-cache** before/after DMA transfers:

    - Before DMA (CPU → peripheral): SCB_CleanDCache_by_Addr(...).

    - After DMA (peripheral → CPU): SCB_InvalidateDCache_by_Addr(...).

- Alternatively, place DMA buffers in non-cacheable RAM (some MCUs provide non-cacheable SRAM regions).

2. EEPROM Emulation Techniques

Many STM32 MCUs lack true EEPROM. Emulation uses flash sectors to store small key/value pairs with wear-leveling and atomic update semantics.

2.1 Common patterns

- **Two-page scheme (circular page)** — maintain two flash pages: one active, one receive. Appends new records sequentially; when page full, copy valid key/value pairs to the other page and erase the old one.

- **Log-structured (append-only)** — store updates as new entries; lookup is the latest entry for a key.

- **Wear-leveling** — rotate physical pages used to store logical data to spread erase cycles.

- **Garbage collection** — when space runs low, compact and copy latest values to fresh page.

2.2 State machine (typical two-page example)

Page status flags: ERASED, RECEIVE_DATA, VALID_PAGE.

- On write:

    1. Find VALID_PAGE.

2. Append new (virtual address, data, CRC) record.

3. If page full, set other page to RECEIVE_DATA, copy latest values for each variable, set VALID_PAGE, erase old page.

2.3 Implementation tips

- **Atomicity**: write full words with CRC; use power-loss safe sequence (write new page then mark it VALID).

- **Minimize erases**: store multiple variables per sector; batch updates.

- **Metadata**: store version counter or sequence number for each record to detect the latest.

- **Use hardware CRC** (HAL_CRC_Calc) to verify record integrity.

- **Use FRAM or external EEPROM** if available — FRAM has high endurance and simplifies design.

2.4 Example pseudocode: write a variable

```
bool eeprom_write(uint16_t virtual_address, uint32_t data) {

 page = find_valid_page();

 if (page full) {

  if (!page_transfer()) return false;

  page = find_valid_page();

 }

 uint32_t record = pack(virtual_address, data);

 uint32_t addr = find_next_free_word(page);

 HAL_FLASH_Program(FLASH_TYPEPROGRAM_WORD, addr, record);

 return verify(addr, record);

}
```

2.5 Using ST-provided libraries

ST has sample EEPROM emulation libraries for many series — they implement the above patterns and are a good starting point. Study them to adapt for your endurance/space needs.

---

3. External Memory Interfacing (SDRAM, NOR, NAND, QSPI, SD/MMC)

External memory provides capacity and flexibility but introduces complexity: timing, ECC, bad-block handling, and initialization order.

3.1 NOR & QSPI/OSPI (execute-in-place)

- **QSPI / OctoSPI**: serial NOR flash that can be memory-mapped (XIP) allowing code execution directly from external flash.

- **Advantages**: large code/asset storage without internal flash; fast read bandwidth in quad/octo modes.

- **Caveats**:

  - Booting directly from external flash often requires a bootloader to configure QSPI and enable memory-mapped mode.

  - Writes/erases still require command sequences (sector erase, page program) and respect erase granularity and limited cycles.

  - Some QSPI NOR parts support XIP and single-instruction reads; ensure driver and MPU/caches are configured correctly.

Typical HAL flow to enable memory-mapped QSPI

1. Initialize QSPI_HandleTypeDef.

2. Configure read mode and enabling memory-mapped mode HAL_QSPI_MemoryMapped(&hqspi, &cmd, &cfg).

3. Then read like memory: (uint8_t*)0x90000000 (device-dependent remap address).

Best practices

- Use DMA for bulk transfers (write/erase sequences).

- For critical code, place minimal bootloader in internal flash that sets up QSPI and jumps to application in XIP region.

3.2 SDRAM via FMC — large volatile off-chip RAM

- **Use case**: frame buffers (TFT), large data buffers, complex UI.

- **Initialization**: SDRAM requires a specific power-up sequence (clock config, precharge, auto-refresh cycles, mode register set).

- **Controller**: FMC provides timing parameters (CAS latency, refresh rate, row/column bits).

- **Caveats**:

  - SDRAM is volatile — must initialize before use each power-on or resume from reset.

  - For boot-time code requiring large memory, execute from internal flash and then initialize external SDRAM.

Tips

- Use CubeMX-generated init sequence and verify timings against SDRAM datasheet.

- Connect data/address lines carefully: length matching, proper termination.

3.3 NAND flash

- NAND is block-based and requires:

  - Bad block management (BBM),

  - ECC (hardware or software),

  - Wear-leveling and garbage collection.

- For simplicity, prefer **managed flash** (eMMC/SD) or NOR if code XIP is required. If you must use raw NAND, use an existing flash file system (e.g., UBIFS, YAFFS) and leverage hardware ECC where available.

3.4 SD / eMMC (SDMMC)

- SD cards & eMMC provide removable or embedded block storage. Use SDMMC peripheral or SPI mode for SD.

- Combine with **FATFS** for file access. Use DMA for best throughput and implement safe file-system sync procedures to avoid corruption.

3.5 ECC and data integrity

- Use hardware ECC for NAND or external memories if controller provides it; otherwise use CRC or stronger hashes.

- Always store metadata (CRC, version, timestamp) with images and key data structures.

4. Bootloaders and Firmware Upgrade Methods

A robust bootloader strategy is essential for secure, safe firmware upgrades. There are many approaches — risk/reliability tradeoffs center on where the new image is stored and how atomic the swap is.

4.1 Boot sources and device boot ROM

- Most STM32 MCUs have a **system bootloader (ROM)** that can boot from UART/USB/SPI/I2C/CAN depending on device. This is useful for flashing devices in the field or manufacturing.

- **Custom bootloader** in internal flash gives you complete control: authentication, A/B updates, encrypted images.

4.2 Firmware layout strategies

1. **Single bank (in-place)**: simplest — write new image over old one. Risky: power loss mid-write can brick device.

2. **Dual-bank (A/B)**: keep two application banks; write new firmware to inactive bank, verify it, then switch. If boot to A fails, fall back to B.

3. **Shadow/Swap**: store image in external flash or internal spare region then atomically swap via vector relocation.

4. **Golden image**: keep a small, verified "golden" factory image to recover if both banks fail.

Recommended: dual-bank or shadow approach for reliability in production.

4.3 Update sequence (dual-bank pattern)

1. Bootloader checks a metadata area for update request (flags + metadata: size, CRC, signature).

2. If update requested:

   ○ Write image to inactive bank (use DMA/erase-program with progress/verify).

   ○ Verify via CRC32 or cryptographic signature (ED25519/ECDSA) using public key stored securely.

   ○ Set pending flag indicating new image validated.

3. Reboot bootloader pointer or set option byte to point VTOR to new bank.

4. Boot new image; on first run, app performs sanity checks and sets valid flag. If checks fail, bootloader rolls back to previous image.

Atomic commit: use two-phase commit pattern — only flip "active" flag after full verification.

4.4 Secure update best practices

- **Authenticate images**: use digital signature verification (ECC/RSA) before activation.

- **Encrypt images** if confidentiality is required — use AES-GCM or similar and store keys in secure hardware (TPM or secure element).

- **Use monotonic counters** for anti-rollback: store secure monotonic counters (hardware or protected storage) to prevent installing older signed images.

- **Protect bootloader & keys**: set readout protection, and use TrustZone features where available to isolate key material.

- **Atomic metadata updates**: mark states via flash words that are written in a safe order so power loss leaves bootloader in a recoverable state.

4.5 OTA and transport layers

- **Transport**: HTTP(S), MQTT, CoAP, LwM2M, BLE DFU, LoRa, serial YMODEM/XMODEM, USB DFU.

- **Chunking & resume**: large images need chunked downloads with checksums per chunk and resume support.

- **Power loss considerations**:

    - Write to inactive bank + verify before commit.

    - Maintain progress pointers and publish them in persistent area.

- **Delta updates**: transmit binary diff (bsdiff, bspatch) to reduce bandwidth, then reconstruct and verify — more complex but efficient.

4.6 Example bootloader pseudocode (simplified)

```
int main(void) {

SystemInit();

if (new_image_pending()) {

  if (verify_image(inactive_bank_addr)) {

    set_active_bank(inactive_bank_addr);

    reboot();

  } else {

    clear_new_image_flag();

  }

}

jump_to_active_application();

}


void jump_to_active_application(void) {

uint32_t app_stack = *((uint32_t*)APP_ADDR);
```

```
uint32_t app_reset = *((uint32_t*)(APP_ADDR + 4));

SCB->VTOR = APP_ADDR;

__set_MSP(app_stack);

((void(*)(void))app_reset)();

}
```

4.7 DFU and built-in bootloaders

- **USB DFU** and **ST's system bootloader** let you upgrade firmware without custom bootloaders. They are handy for manufacturing and field service. If they meet security/robustness requirements, you can rely on them.

- For production devices that require signed or encrypted firmware, implement a custom bootloader that verifies signatures and optionally decrypts images.

4.8 Rollback and recovery strategies

- On first boot after update, application should:

    o Validate integrity and self-test critical peripherals.

    o Signal bootloader (via flag) that boot succeeded.

- If the bootloader doesn't receive success signal after timeout, it should revert to previous bank or golden image.

- Provide manual recovery options (boot into system memory bootloader via BOOT pins or a hardware jumper).

5. Practical Considerations, Tools & Code Snippets

5.1 CRC and image verification

Use hardware CRC peripheral where available:

```
uint32_t calc_crc(uint8_t *buf, size_t len) {
```

```
CRC->CR = 0; // reset CRC hardware (device dependent)

for (size_t i = 0; i < len; i += 4) {

  CRC->DR = *(uint32_t*)(buf + i);

}

return CRC->DR;

}
```

For signatures use established crypto libs (mbedTLS, wolfSSL) and prefer ECDSA/EdDSA over RSA for smaller keys.

5.2 Example: safe flash update loop (erase + program + verify)

```
bool flash_write_chunk(uint32_t dst, uint8_t *src, size_t len) {

 for (size_t i = 0; i < len; i += 8) {

  uint64_t word;

  memcpy(&word, src + i, 8);

  if (HAL_FLASH_Program(FLASH_TYPEPROGRAM_DOUBLEWORD, dst + i, word) != HAL_OK)

    return false;

 }
 // verify

 return memcmp((void*)dst, src, len) == 0;

}
```

Note: adjust program granularity per device (word/doubleword).

5.3 Cache and DMA care (M7/H7)

- Before reading/writing flash or external memory with DMA, perform:

- SCB_CleanDCache_by_Addr((uint32_t*)addr, size); before DMA (if CPU wrote to buffer).

- SCB_InvalidateDCache_by_Addr((uint32_t*)addr, size); after DMA (if DMA wrote to buffer).

5.4 Bootloader & option bytes

- Option bytes manage readout protection (RDP), BOR levels, and sometimes boot configuration.

- Changing option bytes usually triggers a device reset and must be done carefully (e.g., using HAL_FLASHEx_OBProgram()).

5.5 Production programming & unique IDs

- Use STM32_Programmer_CLI or vendor tools to mass-program and set device-specific metadata (serial number, calibration constants) into flash/option bytes.

- Use device unique ID (UID) for cryptographic key derivation or serial numbers.

6. Common Pitfalls & How to Avoid Them

- **Power loss during update**: always write new image to separate bank and validate before switching.

- **Ignoring cache maintenance**: leads to corrupted data after DMA.

- **Erasing too often**: leads to premature flash wear—use wear-leveling and external EEPROM/FRAM for frequent writes.

- **Wrong program granularity**: use correct program width or you will get HAL errors.

- **Not reserving bootloader area**: ensure bootloader region is protected and does not get accidentally erased.

- **Unsigned images in the field**: opens the device to malicious firmware; use signing and secure boot.

7. Quick Reference & Recommendations

- **Use dual-bank updates** for field devices where uptime matters.

- **Prefer external FRAM or EEPROM** for frequent small updates; use flash only when necessary.

- **Sign & verify firmware.** Use hardware security features (TrustZone, secure elements) when available.

- **Place DMA buffers in non-cacheable RAM or maintain cache coherency**.

- **Always verify** each programmed image by CRC and integrity checks.

- **Document memory map** (bootloader, app A/B, config, logs) in project design docs and maintain consistent linker scripts.

Chapter 10: Interrupts and Real-Time Operation in STM32 Microcontrollers

Real-time operation is at the core of many embedded systems, and the STM32 family is designed with powerful interrupt and task-handling capabilities that allow developers to achieve deterministic, low-latency performance. Understanding interrupts, the Nested Vector Interrupt Controller (NVIC), Direct Memory Access (DMA), and real-time operating systems (RTOS) integration is crucial for building robust STM32 applications.

Nested Vector Interrupt Controller (NVIC)

ADVANCED STM32 MICROCONTROLLERS

The **NVIC** is the hardware block inside STM32 microcontrollers (and other ARM Cortex-M cores) that manages all interrupt and exception requests. It is tightly coupled with the ARM Cortex-M processor and provides fast and deterministic interrupt handling.

Key Features of NVIC:

- **Vectorized Interrupt Handling**: Each interrupt source has its own vector address pointing directly to its Interrupt Service Routine (ISR).

- **Nested Interrupts**: Higher-priority interrupts can preempt lower-priority ones.

- **Configurable Priorities**: Supports multiple priority levels (usually 16 or more depending on the STM32 series).

- **Low Latency**: Hardware automatically saves core registers upon entering an ISR and restores them upon exit.

How NVIC Works in STM32:

1. **Interrupt Request**: A peripheral or external pin asserts an interrupt request.

2. **Priority Check**: NVIC compares the priority with the currently running process.

3. **Context Save**: If the new interrupt has higher priority, current execution is suspended, and the processor state is saved.

4. **ISR Execution**: The appropriate ISR is executed from the vector table.

5. **Return from Interrupt**: Context is restored, and normal execution resumes.

Programming NVIC in STM32:

```
// Enable EXTI line 0 interrupt

HAL_NVIC_SetPriority(EXTI0_IRQn, 2, 0);

HAL_NVIC_EnableIRQ(EXTI0_IRQn);
```

Here:

- EXTI0_IRQn is the interrupt number.

- Priority 2 (lower number = higher priority).

- Sub-priority 0 is for ordering interrupts with the same main priority.

External Interrupt Configuration

External interrupts allow STM32 to respond to events like button presses, sensor triggers, or other digital signals without constantly polling input pins.

Sources of External Interrupts:

- **GPIO Pins**: Configurable through the EXTI (External Interrupt/Event Controller).

- **Peripheral Interrupts**: Such as UART RX complete, ADC conversion complete, etc.

Configuring External Interrupts:

1. **Pin Mode**: Set the GPIO pin to interrupt mode (GPIO_MODE_IT_RISING, GPIO_MODE_IT_FALLING, or both).

2. **EXTI Mapping**: Map the pin to an EXTI line.

3. **NVIC Setup**: Enable the corresponding EXTI interrupt in NVIC.

4. **ISR Implementation**: Define the ISR to handle the event.

Example (Button Interrupt on PA0):

```
// Configure PA0 as interrupt on rising edge

GPIO_InitTypeDef GPIO_InitStruct = {0};

GPIO_InitStruct.Pin = GPIO_PIN_0;

GPIO_InitStruct.Mode = GPIO_MODE_IT_RISING;

GPIO_InitStruct.Pull = GPIO_NOPULL;

HAL_GPIO_Init(GPIOA, &GPIO_InitStruct);


// Enable NVIC
```

```
HAL_NVIC_SetPriority(EXTI0_IRQn, 2, 0);

HAL_NVIC_EnableIRQ(EXTI0_IRQn);


void EXTI0_IRQHandler(void)

{

  HAL_GPIO_TogglePin(GPIOB, GPIO_PIN_0); // Toggle LED

  HAL_GPIO_EXTI_IRQHandler(GPIO_PIN_0);  // Clear interrupt flag

}
```

DMA (Direct Memory Access) for High-Efficiency Transfers

DMA in STM32 enables peripherals to transfer data to/from memory without CPU intervention. This drastically reduces CPU load and improves real-time performance.

Key Benefits:

- **CPU Offloading**: Allows the CPU to perform other tasks while data transfers occur.

- **High Throughput**: Suitable for high-speed peripherals like ADC, SPI, UART, or memory-to-memory copying.

- **Low Power**: Reduces active CPU cycles.

DMA Workflow:

1. Configure DMA channel/stream for the source and destination addresses.

2. Define data length and transfer direction.

3. Enable the DMA request in the peripheral.

4. DMA automatically moves data and triggers an interrupt when complete.

Example: Using DMA for ADC Sampling

```
HAL_ADC_Start_DMA(&hadc1, (uint32_t*)adcBuffer, 128);
```

Here:

- adcBuffer will be filled with 128 samples directly by DMA without CPU loops.

RTOS Integration with FreeRTOS and ThreadX

When applications grow complex, a **Real-Time Operating System (RTOS)** helps manage multiple concurrent tasks effectively. STM32 supports integration with **FreeRTOS**, **ThreadX**, and other RTOS kernels.

Benefits of RTOS in STM32 Projects:

- **Task Scheduling**: Preemptive multitasking with priority control.

- **Inter-task Communication**: Queues, semaphores, and mutexes.

- **Timing Services**: Delays, periodic execution, and timeouts.

- **Scalability**: Suitable for small and large applications.

FreeRTOS on STM32:

- Comes pre-integrated in **STM32CubeMX**, allowing easy configuration.

- Supports **tickless mode** for low-power operation.

- Can work alongside interrupts and DMA for hybrid real-time systems.

ThreadX on STM32:

- Known for low latency and high performance.

- Integrated into **Azure RTOS** with networking, USB, and file system components.

Example: FreeRTOS Task Creation

void BlinkTask(void *pvParameters)

{

```
for(;;)

{

    HAL_GPIO_TogglePin(GPIOB, GPIO_PIN_0);

    vTaskDelay(pdMS_TO_TICKS(500));

}

}


xTaskCreate(BlinkTask, "LED Blink", 128, NULL, 1, NULL);

vTaskStartScheduler();
```

Here:

- A task toggles an LED every 500 ms while the RTOS scheduler handles other tasks.

Best Practices for Interrupts and Real-Time Operation in STM32

- Keep ISR code **short and efficient**.

- Use **volatile** keyword for variables shared between ISRs and main code.

- Prioritize interrupts carefully—too many high-priority interrupts can cause starvation.

- Combine **DMA** and **interrupts** for optimal performance.

- When using RTOS, **avoid blocking calls** in ISRs.

- Use **critical sections** to protect shared resources in multitasking environments.

Chapter 11: Low Power and Energy Optimization — Comprehensive Guide

Reducing power consumption is essential for battery-powered and energy-constrained embedded systems. This chapter explains the hardware and software techniques you'll use on STM32 microcontrollers to minimize energy use while meeting performance and latency requirements. We cover the power modes (Sleep, Stop, Standby), dynamic clock scaling and clock gating, how to measure and profile current precisely, and practical design patterns for battery-powered applications.

1. Power Modes: Sleep, Stop, and Standby

ADVANCED STM32 MICROCONTROLLERS

STM32 devices implement multiple low-power modes with different trade-offs between current draw, state retention, and wake-up latency. Exact names and characteristics vary across families — always check the device datasheet and reference manual for numbers — but the concepts below apply broadly.

1.1 Sleep mode

- **What it does:** CPU core halted (WFI/WFE), peripheral clocks normally continue (depending on configuration). SRAM and peripherals retain state.

- **Use case:** short, very frequent idle gaps where peripheral activity continues (e.g., hardware timers, UART, DMA).

- **Wake latency:** very short (instructions resume quickly after wake).

- **API (HAL example):**

```
// Enter CPU sleep until next interrupt

__WFI(); // or via HAL:

HAL_PWR_EnterSLEEPMode(PWR_MAINREGULATOR_ON, PWR_SLEEPENTRY_WFI);
```

- **Tips:** keep ISRs short; use peripheral-driven events to avoid unnecessary wakeups.

1.2 Stop mode (deep-sleep)

- **What it does:** Stops main clocks and PLL; core and many peripherals halted. Most SRAM can be retained (family-dependent). RTC and some low-power peripherals (LPTIM, RTC, certain GPIO/EXTI lines) can remain active to wake the system. On many STM32 families you can choose regulator mode (MAIN/LOW-POWER).

- **Use case:** long sleeps where CPU inactivity dominates and you need very low current with periodic wakes (e.g., sensor report every minute).

- **Wake latency:** higher than Sleep because clock sources (PLL/HSE) must be re-enabled and configured (could be a few hundred microseconds to many milliseconds depending on PLL lock and core type).

- **HAL example (enter STOP, wake on EXTI/RTC):**

// Ensure PWR clock enabled

__HAL_RCC_PWR_CLK_ENABLE();

// Enter Stop mode, wakeup via WFI

HAL_PWR_EnterSTOPMode(PWR_MAINREGULATOR_ON, PWR_STOPENTRY_WFI);

// Upon return: reconfigure system clocks (HAL example)

SystemClock_ReConfigAfterStop(); // re-set PLL, flash latency, SystemCoreClock

- **Note:** after STOP wake, the system typically resumes from same code path (no reset), but you must restore system clock config because STOP often switches system clock to HSI or MSI.

1.3 Standby mode (deepest)

- **What it does:** Core powered down, most SRAM and state lost except backup domain if VBAT present and backup SRAM retained. Only limited wake sources (RTC alarm, tamper/wakeup pin, reset) remain. On wake, device behaves as reset and boots from the vector table — treat as power-on.

- **Use case:** months/years of idle time (device effectively "off" except for a periodic RTC).

- **Wake latency:** long; full boot sequence.

- **HAL example (enter Standby):**

// Enable wakeup pin (example)

HAL_PWR_EnableWakeUpPin(PWR_WAKEUP_PIN1);

// Clear wakeup flags

__HAL_PWR_CLEAR_FLAG(PWR_FLAG_WU);

// Enter Standby

HAL_PWR_EnterSTANDBYMode();

- **Tips:** store critical state in backup registers/backup SRAM (VBAT) or persist to nonvolatile memory before entering standby.

1.4 Choosing among modes

- Use **Sleep** when peripherals must stay active and wake latency must be minimal.

- Use **Stop** for deep savings while keeping fast resume possible (but plan clock reinit).

- Use **Standby** for maximum savings when you can accept a full reboot.

2. Dynamic Clock Scaling and Peripheral Clock Gating

Reducing clock frequency and disabling peripheral clocks are among the most effective ways to lower dynamic power consumption.

2.1 Dynamic Frequency Scaling (DFS)

- **Principle:** reduce CPU and peripheral clock speeds when full performance is unnecessary. CPU dynamic power scales roughly with frequency and supply voltage ($P \propto C \cdot V^2 \cdot f$). Lower f (and optionally V) reduces dynamic power.

- **Typical approach:** run at high frequency for compute bursts, then scale down to a lower frequency for idle/background tasks.

- **Steps (safe pattern):**

    1. Stop time-critical interrupts or enter a controlled critical section.

    2. Switch system clock to a safe source (HSI or MSI) temporarily if you need to reconfigure PLL.

    3. Reconfigure PLL/clock multipliers/dividers to desired frequency.

    4. Switch SYSCLK to the new clock and update SystemCoreClock.

    5. Update flash latency if necessary.

6. Re-enable interrupts.

Example pattern (HAL pseudo-code):

// Reduce system clock from high-speed to low-speed

__disable_irq();

__HAL_RCC_PWR_CLK_ENABLE(); // if needed

// Optionally switch to HSI first

RCC_ClkInitTypeDef clkinit;

HAL_RCC_GetClockConfig(&clkinit, &flashLatency);

// configure PLL with lower multipliers (use HAL_RCC_OscConfig, HAL_RCC_ClockConfig)

HAL_RCC_OscConfig(...); // new PLL params

HAL_RCC_ClockConfig(...); // switch SYSCLK to new PLL

SystemCoreClockUpdate();

__enable_irq();

Important cautions:

- **Flash latency:** higher clock requires higher flash wait states. When increasing clock, set flash latency before switching; when decreasing, you may lower latency after switch.

- **Peripherals needing fixed clocks:** USB, SDIO, CAN, some timers require specific derived clocks (48 MHz for USB, SDMMC). If you alter PLL settings, ensure those peripherals still have proper clock sources or stop them before reconfig.

- **Caches (M7/H7):** if changing clocks or memory mapping, manage caches carefully; e.g., disable cache or clean/invalidate before changes to avoid coherency issues.

2.2 Voltage scaling

- Some STM32 series support voltage scaling (PWR ranges) where lower operating voltages permit fewer flash wait states and can save dynamic power. Reduce voltage range when frequency reduced, subject to datasheet limits.

2.3 Peripheral clock gating

- Turn off clocks for unused peripherals using RCC gating macros:

```
__HAL_RCC_USART1_CLK_DISABLE();

__HAL_RCC_SPI1_CLK_DISABLE();
```

- Use HAL/LL to enable clocks only when needed and disable them promptly after use.

- For complex drivers, add explicit power_on() / power_off() functions that manage clock gating, pin states, and peripheral resets.

3. Current Measurement and Power Profiling

Accurate measurement is essential to quantify savings, find wakeup spikes, and validate battery life.

3.1 Measurement techniques overview

- **Multimeter (DMM):** simple spot-check for average current (accurate but slow, misses short spikes).

- **Oscilloscope + current probe / shunt + differential amplifier:** captures transient currents and compute energy per event.

- **Monsoon Power Monitor / Otii Arc / STLINK-V3PWR / Keysight SMU:** specialized tools that measure current with high resolution and can log and profile energy; some provide programmable loads and scripts.

- **Shunt resistor + ADC:** measure V_shunt across a known resistor with a differential amplifier and the MCU ADC — requires attention to ground/reference and amplifier offset.

3.2 Basic shunt measurement (practical)

- **Low-side vs high-side measurement:**

- *Low-side* (between ground and GND pin) easiest but disturbs common ground — often OK for bench tests, avoid for sensitive circuits.

- *High-side* (between Vbat/regulator and Vsys) preferred; use differential amplifier or dedicated current-sense amplifier (INA219/INA226/INA233) to avoid ground disturbance.

- **Choosing R_shunt:** tradeoff between measurable voltage and voltage drop:

  - If expected current is up to 100 mA, and you want a measurable 100 mV at max current, choose R = 100 mV / 100 mA = 1 Ω. That introduces 100 mV drop; acceptable in many cases.

  - For low-power sleep currents (μA), use larger sensing gain (amplifier) or specialized monitors. For 10 μA detection, a 1 Ω shunt gives 10 nV — not measurable; need amplifier or SMU.

Formula: $I = V\_shunt / R\_shunt$

3.3 Measuring transient wakes and energy per event

- Use oscilloscope with sampling rate ≥ 1 MS/s (preferably 10+ MS/s) across shunt or current probe. Integrate area to compute charge/energy:

  - **Instantaneous power:** $P(t) = V(t) * I(t)$ (where V(t) is supply voltage, often ~3.3 V).

  - **Energy for event:** $E = \int P(t)\, dt$ over event time.

- For simpler battery-life estimates, compute average current:

  - $I\_avg = (I\_active * t\_active + I\_sleep * t\_sleep) / T\_period$

  - **Battery life (hours)** = $Battery\_capacity\_mAh / I\_avg\_mA$

Example (step-by-step arithmetic):
Scenario: device active 2 s per hour at 20 mA, sleeps otherwise at 10 μA. Battery 500 mAh.

1. Convert sleep current to mA: $10\,\mu A = 0.01$ mA.

2. Active contribution (mA·s): $I\_active * t\_active = 20$ mA $* 2$ s $= 40$ mA·s.

3. Sleep duration: t_sleep = 3600 s − 2 s = 3598 s.

4. Sleep contribution (mA·s): I_sleep * t_sleep = 0.01 mA * 3598 s = 35.98 mA·s.

5. Total per hour (mA·s): 40 + 35.98 = 75.98 mA·s.

6. Average current (mA): I_avg = 75.98 mA·s / 3600 s = 0.021105555... mA ≈ 0.021106 mA which is 21.1056 μA.

7. Battery life (hours): 500 mAh / 0.021105555 mA ≈ 23,689.66 hours.

8. Battery life (days): 23,689.66 / 24 ≈ 987.07 days ≈ 2.70 years.

(You should re-run with your exact numbers and datasheet sleep/active currents for precise planning.)

3.4 Practical profiling checklist

- Use high-bandwidth measurement for short wakes (<1 ms) to capture spikes.

- Log with waveform tools and compute area under curve to get energy per event.

- Use both average and worst-case measurements (peak currents) — battery and regulator must support transient peaks.

- Validate wake latency by toggling a debug GPIO at the start and end of ISR and measuring with oscilloscope.

4. Designing for Battery-Powered Applications

Hardware and software choices both shape battery life. Plan from day one: battery chemistry, regulator, measurement, and power management.

4.1 Battery selection and basics

- **Cell chemistry:** Li-ion / LiPo (high energy density, needs proper charger & protection), alkaline, NiMH, primary Li-SOCl2 for ultra-long shelf life. Choose by energy density, temperature range, cost, self-discharge, and safety/regulation.

- **Capacity rating:** given in mAh at specified discharge rate; usable capacity depends on load profile (higher drain reduces usable capacity).

- **Internal resistance:** affects voltage under load and heating during peaks.

4.2 Power conversion: LDO vs Switching regulator

- **LDO (linear regulator):**

  - Pros: low noise, simple, small, low quiescent current variants exist.

  - Cons: efficiency = Vout/Vin; for large Vin−Vout and high current, wasted energy in heat.

- **Switching regulator (buck, buck-boost):**

  - Pros: higher efficiency at higher currents and with large Vin−Vout; good for high average currents.

  - Cons: switching noise (EMI), more complex layout, quiescent current of some regulators can be higher (choose low quiescent options for ULP).

- **Design rule:** if average load > ~50–100 mA, switching converter usually wins body efficiency; for ultra-low duty-cycle high peaks or very low average currents, a low-Iq LDO or hybrid approach (buck for peaks + LDO for low noise) might be better.

4.3 Power-path, charging, and protection

- Choose an appropriate charger IC for rechargeable batteries (e.g., Li-ion charge controllers with fuel-gauge support if needed).

- Add battery protection (over-voltage, under-voltage, over-current, thermal cutoffs) for Li-ion cells.

- Consider hot-swap / power-path ICs for enabling system while charging.

4.4 Handling peak currents

- Use bulk capacitance (low-ESR electrolytic/capacitors and ceramic decoupling) near regulator to handle short peaks without regulator dropout.

- For wireless bursts (Wi-Fi/Bluetooth), peak currents can be several hundred mA; ensure regulator can handle surge or add local reservoir capacitor (e.g., 100 µF low ESR).

4.5 Firmware patterns for low-power devices

- **Event/batch processing:** accumulate sensor data and transmit in bursts to amortize the cost of radio start-up.

- **Duty cycling:** keep radios off as much as possible; plan network/report intervals with energy budget in mind.

- **Sensor offloading:** use low-power sensor hubs or comparator interrupts to wake MCU only for relevant events.

- **Peripheral autonomous modes:** use DMA, timers, and peripheral gating so work occurs without waking CPU.

- **Minimize wake duration:** maximize work done per wake (but don't over-run memory/stack constraints).

- **Use tickless RTOS:** reduce periodic wakes due to OS tick; only wake on real events.

4.6 Firmware robustness for battery failures

- Implement graceful shutdown when battery voltage is below safe thresholds (measure VBAT and save state).

- Add periodic checkpointing of critical state to nonvolatile memory if a full shutdown is possible.

4.7 System-level power budgeting

- Build a power budget spreadsheet with:

  - Active-mode currents for each subsystem (radio TX/RX, sensor sampling, CPU heavy tasks).

  - Sleep-mode currents.

  - Duty cycle per activity.

- ○ Estimate average current and battery life.

- Iterate design choices (regulator, radio duty cycle, sensor selection) to meet target life.

---

5. Low-Power Hardware & Layout Tips

- Place decoupling capacitors close to MCU VDD/VSSA/VDDA pins.

- Use separate analog ground plane for sensitive ADC front-ends (or careful split plane with single star point).

- Keep high-current traces (antenna feeds, motor drivers) away from sensitive analog traces.

- For low leakage, select MOSFETs and components with low gate leakage and low Iq.

- Add solder jumpers or pads to disconnect/regulate power domain for peripheral isolation during testing.

- Use low-leakage pull-ups or provide option to remove pull-ups that draw current in sleep.

---

6. Software Recipes and Code Examples

6.1 Enter Stop mode and restore clocks (HAL example)

```
// Prepare for stop

HAL_RTCEx_DeactivateWakeUpTimer(&hrtc); // example

// Clear wake up flag and enable wake source

__HAL_PWR_CLEAR_FLAG(PWR_FLAG_WU);

HAL_PWR_EnableWakeUpPin(PWR_WAKEUP_PIN1);


// Enter stop mode (WFI)

HAL_PWR_EnterSTOPMode(PWR_MAINREGULATOR_ON, PWR_STOPENTRY_WFI);
```

```
// After wake: reconfigure system clock

SystemClock_Config(); // user function generated by CubeMX

SystemCoreClockUpdate();
```

6.2 Example: dynamic scaling — quick frequency change pattern

```
// Example: temporarily reduce clock for background tasks

__disable_irq();


// Switch to HSI as SYSCLK to free PLL for reconfig:

RCC_ClkInitTypeDef clkInit;

uint32_t flashLatency;

HAL_RCC_GetClockConfig(&clkInit, &flashLatency);

__HAL_RCC_HSI_ENABLE();

while(__HAL_RCC_GET_FLAG(RCC_FLAG_HSIRDY) == RESET);


// Switch system clock to HSI

HAL_RCC_ClockConfig(&clkInit, FLASH_LATENCY_0); // adapt params


// Reconfigure PLL for lower frequency, re-enable and switch back.

// After reconfiguration:

SystemCoreClockUpdate();

__enable_irq();
```

Implementations differ per device. Use CubeMX to generate safe examples and then customize.

6.3 Using LPTIM/RTC for ultra-low-power timing

- Configure **LPTIM** or **RTC** alarm as wake source. Both can run in low-power modes and have low drift options.

- Use LSE (32.768 kHz crystal) for accurate RTC wakeups.

---

7. Validation, Testing and Checklist

7.1 Measurement checklist

- Verify quiescent currents for each mode (Sleep/Stop/Standby) with battery attached.

- Capture wake-up current spike waveforms (scope) and compute energy per wake.

- Validate regulators transient response for peak currents.

- Test wake sources: EXTI, RTC, LPTIM, USART, USB, and confirm expected behavior in STOP/Standby.

- Test brown-out and reset behavior under low battery conditions.

7.2 Software checklist

- Replace polling loops with event-driven or DMA patterns.

- Ensure caches are cleaned/invalidated when using DMA on cache-enabled MCUs.

- Check that peripheral clocks are disabled when idle.

- Protect flash and NV memory wear (e.g., log batching, EEPROM emulation).

- Test fail/recovery scenarios (power loss during flash writes, partial boot).

7.3 Hardware checklist

- Proper decoupling and bulk capacitance for peak currents.

- Battery protection circuit in place for Li-ion.

- Low quiescent regulator selected that matches average load needs.

- Wake pins accessible and documented.

8. Example Calculations & Quick Reference

- **Average current (general)**: I_avg = (Σ (I_i * t_i)) / T_period.

- **Battery life**: Life_hours = Battery_capacity_mAh / I_avg_mA.

- **Energy per event (Joules)**: E = V_supply * I_avg_A * duration_seconds.

- **Shunt measurement**: I = V_shunt / R_shunt.

Example (recap) (active 2 s/hr @ 20 mA, sleep rest @ 10 µA, battery 500 mAh):

- Active mA·s = 20 * 2 = 40 mA·s

- Sleep mA·s = 0.01 * 3598 = 35.98 mA·s

- Total = 75.98 mA·s

- Average mA = 75.98 / 3600 ≈ 0.0211056 mA = 21.1056 µA

- **Battery life** ≈ 500 / 0.0211056 ≈ 23,689.7 **hours** ≈ 987.07 **days** ≈ 2.70 years.

9. Common Pitfalls and How to Avoid Them

- **Not measuring—guessing:** always measure real hardware; datasheet numbers are guides.

- **Ignoring wake spikes:** short radio or flash writes can consume a lot of energy; capture with scope.

- **Forgetting clock reconfiguration after STOP:** system may run at HSI/MSI after wake; you must restore PLL and SystemCoreClock.

- **Cache & DMA mismatches on M7/H7:** leads to corrupted buffers — always manage caches around DMA transfers.

- **Using high-Iq regulators:** high quiescent current may dominate average consumption in low-duty devices.

- **Leaving peripherals enabled:** e.g., ADC or SPI clocks left on can waste µA–mA.

10. Roadmap: How to Approach Low-Power Optimization in a Project

1. **Define target:** required battery life, operational profiles (tx/sec), and acceptable wake latencies.

2. **Instrument early:** add sense resistor pads, test points, and measurement hooks on prototype.

3. **Baseline measurement:** measure current in active and sleep states before optimization.

4. **Eliminate obvious drains:** disable LEDs, unused peripherals, and debug UART in production builds.

5. **Software architecture:** move to event-driven, batch operations, and peripheral offload (DMA/LPTIM).

6. **Tune clocks and voltages:** reduce clock frequency and voltages where possible.

7. **Iterate with measurement:** profile changes, quantify savings, and re-optimize.

8. **Stress-test across temp and battery conditions:** behavior and battery life vary with temperature and battery internal resistance.

Chapter 12: Working with Sensors and Actuators in STM32

STM32 microcontrollers are widely used for real-world interfacing due to their rich peripheral set, flexible I/O configuration, and support for various communication protocols. Sensors allow STM32 devices to acquire environmental data, while actuators enable them to control mechanical or electronic systems. Understanding how to efficiently interface with these devices is crucial for building responsive, reliable embedded systems.

Temperature, Humidity, and Pressure Sensors

Environmental sensors are common in IoT, industrial automation, and scientific monitoring. STM32 MCUs can interface with both **analog** and **digital** sensor types.

1. Temperature Sensors

- **Analog Sensors**: Examples include LM35 and TMP36, which output a voltage proportional to temperature. The STM32's **ADC** is used to read and scale the value.

- **Digital Sensors**: Examples include DS18B20 (1-Wire protocol) and TMP102 (I2C protocol). These often have built-in calibration and require less signal processing.

Implementation Considerations:

- Use averaging or low-pass filtering to reduce noise in analog readings.

- Apply compensation formulas for sensors with non-linear characteristics.

- Consider internal STM32 temperature sensors for basic system thermal monitoring.

2. Humidity Sensors

- **Capacitive Humidity Sensors** like DHT22 or AM2301 measure changes in capacitance.

- **Digital MEMS Sensors** such as SHT3x (I2C) offer high precision and integrated temperature compensation.

Best Practices:

- Use timing-accurate protocols for sensors like DHT22.

- Calibrate periodically in high-humidity environments to maintain accuracy.

3. Pressure Sensors

- **Analog Sensors**: BMP180's predecessor modules output voltages proportional to pressure.

- **Digital Barometric Sensors**: BMP280, BME680 use I2C/SPI for accurate readings and additional environmental data.

Integration Tips:

- Implement oversampling in sensor configuration for improved stability.

- Correct altitude calculations using temperature compensation.

IMU (Accelerometer, Gyroscope, Magnetometer) Integration

In robotics, drones, and motion-tracking applications, Inertial Measurement Units (IMUs) combine multiple motion sensors in one package.

1. Accelerometers

- Measure linear acceleration in one or more axes (e.g., ADXL345 via I2C/SPI).

- Require digital filtering to remove vibration noise.

2. Gyroscopes

- Measure angular velocity; useful for stabilization and navigation (e.g., L3G4200D).

- Integrate readings over time for orientation estimation, but beware of drift.

3. Magnetometers

- Detect magnetic fields for compass heading (e.g., HMC5883L).

- Require hard and soft iron calibration for accuracy.

4. Combined IMU Modules

- MPU6050 (Accelerometer + Gyroscope) or MPU9250 (Accelerometer + Gyroscope + Magnetometer) integrate all functions.

- Use sensor fusion algorithms (Kalman filter, Madgwick filter) for accurate 3D orientation.

STM32-Specific Tips:

- Leverage **I2C Fast Mode (400 kHz)** or **SPI** for high-frequency IMU data acquisition.

- Use **DMA transfers** to offload CPU during continuous sensor streaming.

Servo and Stepper Motor Control

Actuators like motors allow STM32 systems to physically interact with the environment.

1. Servo Motors

- Controlled using **PWM signals** (typically 50 Hz with 1–2 ms pulse width).

- Example: SG90 micro servo.

- Use STM32's **general-purpose timers** for precise control without CPU overhead.

Implementation Notes:

- For multiple servos, use hardware PWM channels to avoid timing jitter.

- Use stable power sources as servos can generate electrical noise.

2. Stepper Motors

- Used in CNC, 3D printers, and positioning systems.

- Controlled using **step and direction signals** via driver modules (A4988, DRV8825).

- STM32 timers can generate the required pulse frequency and acceleration profiles.

Best Practices:

- Use acceleration ramp algorithms to avoid mechanical stress.

- Implement **microstepping** for smoother motion and higher resolution.

Display Modules (LCD, OLED, TFT)

Visual output devices allow STM32-based systems to present data, status, and interactive user interfaces.

1. Character LCDs (HD44780)

- Simple text displays (16x2, 20x4).

- Use 4-bit or 8-bit parallel interface, or I2C via backpack modules.

2. OLED Displays

ADVANCED STM32 MICROCONTROLLERS

- High contrast, low power (SSD1306 is common).

- Use I2C or SPI communication.

- STM32 can use graphics libraries like **u8g2** or **LittlevGL** for easy rendering.

3. TFT LCDs

- Support full-color graphics (ILI9341, ST7789).

- Require higher data throughput via SPI or FSMC (Flexible Static Memory Controller) for parallel connections.

Optimization Tips:

- Use **DMA SPI transfers** for smooth animations.

- Implement double-buffering in graphics applications to prevent flicker.

Key Takeaways for STM32 Sensor & Actuator Integration

- Always select the right communication protocol based on speed, wiring complexity, and reliability.

- Apply hardware debouncing, filtering, or shielding where necessary.

- Use STM32 hardware features like **DMA, timer-based PWM**, and **low-power modes** for efficient operation.

- Modularize code to make sensor and actuator drivers reusable across projects.

Chapter 13: Advanced Features of STM32

The STM32 microcontroller family is not just a collection of general-purpose embedded processors — it's a platform designed to meet the needs of advanced, high-performance, and security-critical applications. In addition to the typical MCU peripherals, STM32 devices integrate a range of advanced hardware features that enable signal processing, real-time computation, secure communications, and connectivity for the modern IoT landscape. Mastering these features can significantly expand what you can achieve with STM32.

Floating Point Unit (FPU) Usage

Many STM32 models, especially those based on **ARM Cortex-M4, M7, M33, and M55 cores**, integrate a hardware **Floating Point Unit (FPU)** for accelerating mathematical operations.

Key Benefits:

- **Performance Boost:** FPUs allow direct hardware execution of floating-point arithmetic, bypassing the need for slow software emulation.

- **Reduced Code Size:** With hardware floating-point instructions, compilers can generate more compact code.

- **Lower Power Consumption:** Faster execution means the MCU can complete tasks quicker and return to low-power modes sooner.

Enabling and Using FPU:

1. **Compiler Settings:** In STM32CubeIDE, set -mfpu=fpv4-sp-d16 (for Cortex-M4/M7 single precision) and -mfloat-abi=hard for hardware floating point.

2. **CMSIS and HAL Support:** Most math functions in CMSIS-DSP and STM32 HAL libraries automatically use the FPU when available.

3. **Application Examples:**

   - Complex trigonometric calculations in robotics control loops.

   - Real-time physics simulations in gaming controllers.

   - Audio signal filtering and spectral analysis.

Digital Signal Processing (DSP) Capabilities

Cortex-M4, M7, and higher cores feature **DSP extensions** that allow the execution of single-cycle multiply-accumulate (MAC) operations, SIMD (Single Instruction, Multiple Data) operations, and optimized arithmetic.

Core DSP Functions:

- **FIR and IIR Filtering:** Implementing low-pass, high-pass, and band-pass filters efficiently.

- **FFT (Fast Fourier Transform):** Frequency-domain analysis for audio, vibration, or communication systems.

- **Matrix Operations:** Useful in computer vision, robotics kinematics, and control algorithms.

CMSIS-DSP Library:

- ARM provides a **highly optimized DSP library** for STM32, containing functions like convolution, correlation, FFT, vector operations, and statistical analysis.

- Functions are pre-optimized to take advantage of the MCU's DSP instructions.

Use Cases:

- Vibration analysis in predictive maintenance systems.

- Audio equalization and noise suppression.

- Real-time sensor fusion for drones and autonomous vehicles.

Hardware Cryptography and Secure Boot

Modern STM32 devices such as **STM32L4+, STM32H7, STM32WB, and STM32U5** incorporate **security-oriented peripherals** for protecting firmware, data, and communications.

Hardware Crypto Engines:

- **AES, DES, 3DES**: Symmetric encryption for fast, secure data transfer.

- **RSA, ECC:** Asymmetric cryptography for authentication and key exchange.

- **SHA-1, SHA-256:** Secure hash algorithms for data integrity verification.

- **True Random Number Generator (TRNG):** Generates hardware-quality random numbers for encryption keys.

Secure Boot & Firmware Protection:

- **Root of Trust (RoT):** Ensures only signed firmware can run on the device.

- **Read/Write Protection:** Locks specific Flash sectors against unauthorized access.

- **Secure Firmware Update:** Uses encrypted and signed updates to prevent malicious code injection.

Applications:

- Secure payment terminals.

- IoT devices requiring encrypted communication.

- Industrial controllers with IP protection needs.

Ethernet, Wi-Fi, and Bluetooth Integration

Many STM32 devices integrate or support external modules for **network and wireless connectivity**, enabling them to act as smart connected nodes.

Ethernet:

- Available in high-performance families like **STM32F7, STM32H7**.

- Supports **10/100 Mbps MAC** with hardware checksum offloading for efficient TCP/IP stacks.

- Commonly used with **LwIP** (Lightweight IP) stack for embedded networking.

Wi-Fi:

- STM32 can integrate with modules like **ESP8266, ESP32**, or ST's own Wi-Fi solutions (e.g., **SPWF series**).

- Useful for IoT devices requiring cloud connectivity.

Bluetooth:

- **STM32WB series** comes with an integrated dual-core MCU, running both application code and Bluetooth Low Energy (BLE) stack.

- Suitable for wearable tech, sensor beacons, and wireless control systems.

Example Use Cases:

- Ethernet-based industrial controllers with real-time monitoring dashboards.

- Wi-Fi-enabled smart home devices reporting data to cloud servers.

- BLE-based wireless medical devices streaming patient data to mobile apps.

Key Takeaways

- **FPUs** are essential for math-heavy applications, dramatically reducing computation time.

- **DSP instructions** unlock real-time signal processing capabilities for audio, sensors, and control systems.

- **Hardware cryptography and secure boot** protect devices from tampering and secure sensitive data.

- **Networking capabilities** extend STM32 into IoT and Industry 4.0 environments.

By leveraging these advanced features, developers can push STM32 far beyond simple embedded control, enabling it to power high-performance, secure, and connected systems in demanding industries.

Chapter 14: Debugging and Testing — Comprehensive Guide for STM32

Reliable debugging and a structured testing strategy turn intermittent prototypes into robust products. This chapter covers the full practical toolbox you'll use day-to-day and in CI: on-chip debugging with ST-LINK, SWD vs JTAG, instruction/data trace, how to use oscilloscopes and logic analyzers effectively, and how to build automated, reproducible test pipelines for embedded firmware.

1. Debugging Methodology — a repeatable process

Before individual tools, adopt a debugging discipline:

1. **Reproduce** — make a minimal, repeatable test case. Record exact steps and inputs.

2. **Isolate** — simplify software and hardware to narrow the fault domain (e.g., disable peripherals).

3. **Observe** — capture runtime evidence (logs, traces, register snapshots, waveforms).

4. **Instrument** — add measurements (GPIO toggles, timing counters, logging) rather than blind printf.

5. **Hypothesize & Test** — propose an explanation, make a small, reversible change, and retest.

6. **Fix & Regression** — add a regression test that reproduces the bug and stays green after fix.

2. On-Chip Debugging with ST-LINK

ST-LINK is ST's debugger/programmer family. It supports SWD, SWO/ITM, flash programming, and a VCP (virtual COM port) for simple logging.

2.1 Typical workflows

- **CubeIDE**: integrated ST-LINK support — build, flash, set breakpoints, live inspect memory/regs.

- **OpenOCD + GDB** (CLI): for headless CI or advanced scripting. Start OpenOCD, then attach arm-none-eabi-gdb to target.

- **STM32CubeProgrammer**: flashing and option-byte management in GUI/CLI for production programming.

2.2 Common ST-LINK tasks & commands (conceptual)

- Connect under reset if target refuses to halt.

- Use ST-LINK's virtual COM for printf()-like logs, or use SWO/ITM for low-overhead logging.

- ST-LINK V3 variants support extra features (GPIO, power measurement on some models).

2.3 Practical tips

- Always connect **VTref** so the probe auto-detects IO voltage.

- Keep SWD cable short to avoid signal integrity issues.

- If ST-LINK cannot connect: try "Connect under reset", lower SWD clock speed, or hold MCU in bootloader (BOOT0) to prevent code from disabling debug pins.

3. SWD and JTAG Protocols

3.1 SWD (Serial Wire Debug)

- Modern, two-wire debug protocol (SWDIO, SWCLK). It's compact and supported by all Cortex-M devices.

- SWO is a single additional pin (one-wire) for trace/ITM.

Pinout (common minimal):

- SWDIO, SWCLK, GND, NRST, VTref. Add SWO if required.

3.2 JTAG

- Four or five pins (TDI, TDO, TCK, TMS, optional TRST). Useful if you need boundary-scan, but most Cortex-M workflows prefer SWD.

3.3 When to choose what

- Prefer **SWD** for normal development — fewer pins and full debug support.

- Use **JTAG** only if you need advanced boundary-scan features.

4. Breakpoints, Watchpoints, and Trace

4.1 Breakpoints

- **Hardware breakpoints**: supported in ROM; limited number (per debug unit). They halt the CPU on an address match.

- **Software breakpoints**: replace an instruction with BKPT — requires flash write if setting in flash and may not be permitted in production.

4.2 Watchpoints (Data Breakpoints)

- Trigger when a watched memory address is read/written. Useful for catching unexpected memory corruption.

4.3 SWO / ITM / DWT trace

- **ITM**/SWO: low-overhead printf-style channel for streaming messages and events (very useful in real time).

- **DWT (Data Watchpoint and Trace)**: cycle counter (DWT->CYCCNT) and event counters for timing and profiling.

- **ETM (Instruction Trace)**: high-fidelity instruction-level trace (requires trace probe like J-Link Pro or ULINKpro and dedicated trace pins).

Example: enable DWT cycle counter

// Enable DWT cycle counter (for timing)

if (!(DWT->CTRL & DWT_CTRL_CYCCNTENA_Msk)) {

  CoreDebug->DEMCR |= CoreDebug_DEMCR_TRCENA_Msk;

  DWT->CYCCNT = 0;

  DWT->CTRL |= DWT_CTRL_CYCCNTENA_Msk;

}

// Later: read DWT->CYCCNT for cycles elapsed

5. Capturing and Decoding Hard Faults and Fault Status Registers

When firmware crashes with a HardFault, it's vital to capture the stacked registers and fault status registers:

- **Stacked registers**: r0–r3, r12, lr, pc, xPSR (pushed by hardware).

- **Fault registers**: SCB->CFSR (Configurable Fault Status), SCB->HFSR, SCB->BFAR, SCB->MMFAR.

Example improved HardFault handler (stores registers for post-mortem)

```
void HardFault_Handler(void) {

  __asm volatile (

  "tst lr, #4           \n"

  "ite eq               \n"

  "mrseq r0, msp        \n"

  "mrsne r0, psp        \n"

  "b HardFault_HandlerC \n"

  );

}



void HardFault_HandlerC(uint32_t *stack) {

  uint32_t r0  = stack[0];

  uint32_t r1  = stack[1];

  uint32_t r2  = stack[2];

  uint32_t r3  = stack[3];

  uint32_t r12 = stack[4];

  uint32_t lr  = stack[5];

  uint32_t pc  = stack[6];

  uint32_t psr = stack[7];
```

```
// Save to reserved RAM or send over UART/ITM

CrashInfo.r0 = r0; // example struct in retained RAM

CrashInfo.pc = pc;

CrashInfo.lr = lr;

// Optionally capture CFSR/HFSR

CrashInfo.cfsr = SCB->CFSR;

CrashInfo.hfsr = SCB->HFSR;

// spin or reset safely

while (1);

}
```

Symbolicate PC

Use ELF to map PC to source line:

```
arm-none-eabi-addr2line -e build/app.elf 0x08001234
```

This gives file and line number for the PC captured.

---

6. Using GDB / OpenOCD for Headless Debugging

6.1 Typical sequence

1. Start OpenOCD:

```
openocd -f interface/stlink.cfg -f target/stm32f4x.cfg
```

2. Start GDB:

arm-none-eabi-gdb build/app.elf

(gdb) target remote localhost:3333

(gdb) monitor reset halt

(gdb) load

(gdb) continue

6.2 Useful GDB commands

- info registers — view CPU registers.

- x/32x $sp — dump stack memory.

- bt — backtrace.

- monitor — heterogenous OpenOCD monitor commands (e.g., monitor reset halt).

---

7. Low-Overhead Logging Techniques

printf() is easy but has latency and size costs. Use these alternatives:

7.1 ITM/STM32 SWO (best for low overhead)

- Configure SWO in debugger, send data via ITM stimulus ports. ITM has minimal impact and works while CPU is running.

- Example with printf via ITM:

```
int _write(int fd, char *ptr, int len) {

 for (int i = 0; i < len; ++i) {

  while (!(ITM->PORT[0].u32 & 1));

  ITM->PORT[0].u8 = ptr[i];
```

```
}

    return len;

}
```

7.2 UART with DMA and ring buffer

- Use DMA circular buffer and an idle-line detection interrupt to know when a packet ends; this offloads CPU.

7.3 Event recording

- Use a binary event recorder or a compact logging format that logs events with IDs and timestamps (saves flash space and speeds post-mortem analysis).

---

8. Logic Analyzers and Oscilloscopes in Firmware Debugging

Hardware observation is often the fastest way to find timing and signal problems.

8.1 Logic analyzer (e.g., Saleae, Sigrok)

Useful for digital buses: UART, I^2C, SPI, CAN, PWM, GPIO toggles.

Use cases

- Decode protocols (UART frames, I^2C transactions).

- Measure timing (ISR latency, event-to-event delay).

- Capture long traces and search for abnormal patterns.

Example: measure ISR latency

- Toggle a GPIO at ISR entry and exit; capture with logic analyzer and compute time difference.

8.2 Oscilloscope

- Use for analog signals, analog front-end debugging, power rails, and high-speed timing.

- For power spikes and transient current measure with a current probe or via shunt resistor on scope (differential amplifier if measuring high-side).

Best practices

- Use proper probing (ground spring for small loops to reduce noise).

- For differential signals (CAN), use a differential probe or measure across resistor and use math functions.

- Use long captures for intermittent events (many modern scopes record long periods and let you zoom in).

8.3 Capture examples and checks

- **UART issues**: check signal level, frame timing, parity, noise.

- **I²C stuck bus**: capture SCL/SDA to see stuck low or clock stretching. Use analyzer to see ACK/NACK patterns.

- **SPI timing**: verify CPOL/CPHA matches device expectation and CS timing.

- **PWM & motor drivers**: check dead-time and complementary outputs; verify no shoot-through.

9. Performance Profiling and Timing Measurement

9.1 Cycle-accurate timing

- Use DWT->CYCCNT for microsecond/nanosecond-level measurement scaled by SystemCoreClock.

9.2 Instruction-level trace (ETM)

- Use ETM with a trace probe if you need instruction-level performance profiling and branch trace.

9.3 Software profiling techniques

- Instrument functions with entry/exit timestamps. Store aggregated counters and durations for hotspots.

---

10. Unit Testing, Integration Testing, and Test Doubles

A layered test strategy:

10.1 Unit tests (host-run)

- Isolate business logic from hardware by abstracting HAL behind interfaces.

- Compile and run logic code on host (Linux/Windows) with unit test frameworks (Unity, GoogleTest).

- Use mocking frameworks (CMock, Fake functions) to simulate peripherals.

- Benefits: fast, part-of-pipeline CI, easy code coverage measurement.

10.2 Integration tests (on device or QEMU)

- Exercise drivers with hardware abstractions or emulated peripherals (QEMU for Cortex-M can run code with some peripheral models).

- Use hardware-in-loop (HIL) where device under test interacts with test harness (sensors, power supplies, controlled loads).

10.3 System tests / Acceptance tests

- End-to-end tests on product hardware. Use fixtures that can power-cycle, inject signals, and read outputs (GPIOs, ADCs, UARTs).

10.4 Test doubles and fakes

- Replace HAL with a fake layer that records calls; assert interactions (useful for communication stacks and state machines).

---

11. Automated Testing and Continuous Integration (CI)

Automation brings repeatability, speed and confidence — essential for teams shipping firmware.

11.1 Core CI steps for embedded firmware

1. **Build**: compile for target (arm-none-eabi-gcc) with deterministic flags.

2. **Static analysis**: run clang-tidy, cppcheck, MISRA checks, clang-format for style.

3. **Unit tests**: run host-compiled tests (fast).

4. **Integration tests**: optional QEMU or hardware tests (on test rigs).

5. **Artifact generation**: .elf, .hex, .bin, size reports, map files.

6. **On-target tests**: flash device and run self-test suite; collect logs and test results.

11.2 Example GitHub Actions (conceptual)

- Job: build (arm toolchain), run unit tests (host), run static analysis, upload artifacts.

- For hardware tests, set up a self-hosted runner connected to test benches that can run OpenOCD and serial log capture to run on-target tests.

11.3 On-target automated test patterns

- **Self test harness**: firmware exposes test commands over UART that return PASS/FAIL for specific tests.

- **Rig controller**: Raspberry Pi or PC controlling power, relays, and communications to program the device, run tests, and collect results.

- **Test guard**: if a test fails, log details, archive core dump, mark build as failed.

11.4 Example on-target test flow (scripted)

1. Reboot tester to clean state.

2. Use STM32_Programmer_CLI or openocd to flash test image.

3. Power-cycle target to ensure bootloader/flash behavior.

4. Connect to UART, run test commands, parse pass/fail.

5. If fail, save serial log and core dump (if available) and power-cycle to recover.

11.5 CI metrics to track

- Build success rate.

- Test pass percentage and flaky test count.

- Code coverage (unit test coverage).

- Static analysis warnings over time.

- Code size and memory regression (map file diff alerts).

12. Hardware Regression Testbeds / Burn-in

- Build fixture with a fixture harness that connects IOs to test controller.

- Implement endurance tests (stress loops, power cycles, environmental chambers).

- Use automated logging and alerting; snapshot failing unit and isolate.

13. Static Analysis, Fuzzing, and Security Testing

- **Static analysis**: clang-tidy, cppcheck, and commercial tools (Coverity, Klocwork) find memory & concurrency issues early.

- **Fuzz testing**: fuzz protocol parsers (UART, CAN, USB) with random inputs to find crashes. Run fuzzers on host versions of parsers.

- **Binary hardening**: address vulnerabilities by using stack canaries, pointer sanitization in host tests, and code reviews.

14. Practical Debugging Examples & Recipes

14.1 Intermittent UART corruption

- Capture serial with logic analyzer. If idle noise or line level changes, try adding pull-ups, shielding, or differential transceivers.

- Use DMA with ring buffer to avoid CPU overrun.

14.2 Latency spike in control loop

- Toggle debug GPIO at ISR entry/exit and capture on scope to compute worst-case latency across events.

- Use trace to find which higher-priority ISR preempts your handler.

14.3 DMA data corrupted on M7/H7

- Ensure DMA buffers are in non-cacheable memory or perform SCB_CleanDCache_by_Addr() before DMA reads and SCB_InvalidateDCache_by_Addr() after DMA writes.

14.4 Bricked board after enabling RDP

- Beware: raising Read-Out Protection (RDP) may require a full chip erase to recover using ST tools. Keep a development flag and test carefully.

---

15. Logging, Post-Mortem and Telemetry

- Persist crash info to a reserved flash page or backup SRAM so you can read it after reboot. Include stack pointer, PC, LR, CFSR, and timestamp.

- Send lightweight telemetry (event IDs, counters) off-device before system-critical ops; this helps remote diagnosis.

---

16. Checklist — Quick Reference

When starting to debug

- Reproduce failure reliably.

- Capture serial logs & core dumps.

- Attach debugger (either ST-LINK or J-Link).

- If not connecting, try "connect under reset" and check BOOT pins.

When measuring timing

- Use DWT->CYCCNT for cycle accurate timing.

- Use oscilloscope / logic analyzer for hardware timing measurements.

For DMA + cache

- Use non-cacheable memory sections or manage cache manually.

For CI

- Automate builds, static analysis and unit tests.

- Add on-target test harness and run nightly/system-level tests.

---

17. Tools & Recommended Setup

- **Debugger/Programmer**: ST-LINK V2/V3, SEGGER J-Link.

- **Debug server**: OpenOCD, pyOCD, ST-LINK server.

- **IDE**: STM32CubeIDE, VS Code + PlatformIO, Keil, IAR.

- **Logic analyzer**: Saleae or Sigrok-compatible capture device.

- **Oscilloscope**: 50+ MHz for logic, more for high-speed signals; differential probe for power.

- **CI**: GitHub Actions, GitLab CI, self-hosted runners for hardware rigs.

- **Static analysis**: clang-tidy, cppcheck, MISRA/C checker.

- **Unit test frameworks**: Unity (ThrowTheSwitch), CMock for C; GoogleTest for host-side C++ tests.

---

18. Final Advice — make debugging cheap and fast

- Design boards with **test points and convenient SWD header** and make BOOT pins accessible.

- Reserve **non-volatile slots** for crash logs and manufacture info.

- Integrate **self-test** commands into firmware early; use them in automated test rigs.

- Keep your debug environment scripted: flashing, logging, and tests should be one command away.

Chapter 15: Project Development Workflow — From Idea to Production (Comprehensive Guide)

A predictable, repeatable project workflow turns ideas into reliable products. Below is a practical, end-to-end playbook—technical, hands-on, and ready to use—for embedded projects centered on STM32: idea & requirements → prototype → PCB → firmware lifecycle under git → documentation and maintainability. Use the checklists and templates as working artifacts you can drop into your project.

From Idea to Prototype

1. Requirements, scope & validation

- **Write clear goals**: primary function, constraints (size, weight, power, cost), target lifetime, and regulatory targets.

- **Prioritize**: make an MVP list vs stretch features. Keep the first prototype focused on proving the riskiest assumptions.

- **Acceptance criteria**: numeric specs (sample rates, latency, battery life, throughput) so tests are clear.

2. System architecture & partitioning

- Block diagram: MCU, sensors, radios, power, storage, human interface.

- Partition responsibilities: what runs on MCU, what on co-processors or modules, which features can be deferred.

- Define interfaces (I²C/SPI/UART/CAN/USB/Ethernet), timing budgets and performance budgets.

3. Component & risk analysis

- For each critical part (MCU, radio, power IC), list risks: availability, temperature range, lifetime, cost.

- Pick a primary and at least one alternative for key parts (footprint-compatible when possible).

- Do an early feasibility spike for the riskiest item(s).

4. Prototype strategies (choose based on risk)

- **Software-first**: simulate peripherals or use inexpensive dev boards (Nucleo/Discovery). Good when computing/software is main risk.

- **Hardware-first**: breadboard or mezzanine for mechanical constraints and analog circuitry.

- **Hybrid**: use an off-the-shelf module (Wi-Fi, BLE, PMIC) and design a simple carrier board with SWD headers.

5. Rapid prototyping toolbox

- Use ST Nucleo / Discovery or Black/Blue Pill boards for fast MCU bring-up.

- For sensors & radios, use pre-certified modules to avoid RF/regulatory delays.

- Use KiCad or Eagle for schematics & board layout; generate simple prototypes (2-layer) for iteration.

- For advanced peripherals (QSPI, SDRAM) use ST eval boards to validate sequences before custom PCB.

6. Bring-up plan / smoke tests (must do before anything else)

1. Power rails: verify voltages and currents.

2. Connect SWD and confirm probe detects MCU (VTref connected).

3. Hold MCU in system boot if needed (BOOT0) to avoid boot code interfering.

4. Flash a *smoke-test* firmware:

   - Toggle an LED.

   - Blink and print MCU unique ID via UART/ITM.

   - Read and print supply voltage and temperature sensor.

5. Test critical analog: measure ADC reading of a known divider.

6. Check communications: UART loopback, I²C scan, SPI echo.

7. Iteration cycles

- Keep iterations small (hardware changes should aim for 1–2 defects fixed per revision).

- Maintain a hardware-change-log and firmware-change-log in repo.

- Prototype → validate → update schematic/layout → produce next prototype.

PCB Design Considerations for STM32

Good PCB design accelerates bring-up, reduces mysterious failures, and speeds certification.

1. Schematic best practices

- **Power rails**: clearly label VDD, VDDA, VREF, VBAT, VDD_IO. Use net ties or explicit power-enable switches if powering different domains separately.

- **Reset & boot**:

  - NRST pin to push button and supervisor reset IC (recommended).

  - BOOT0 pulled to required state with pad to override for programming.

- **Clocks**: add footprints for HSE/ LSE crystals and an option for oscillator modules (0 ohm link).

- **SWD header**: expose SWCLK, SWDIO, NRST, GND, VTref, and optionally SWO/TRACE pins. Put header near MCU.

- **Programming pads** and test points: include pogo pad groups for production flashing.

- **Connector pinouts**: label orientation and critical nets (USB D+/D−, CAN H/L).

- **Protection**: TVS diodes on external connectors (USB, CAN, power), series resistors on IOs if needed.

2. Power design

- **Regulator selection**: choose LDO vs switching (buck) by average power and noise sensitivity.

  - Use low quiescent regulators for battery standby.

  - Add a small LDO for ADC/analog reference if the main regulator is noisy.

- **Decoupling**: one 0.1 µF ceramic cap as close as possible to each VDD pin + one 10 µF (or larger) bulk cap near regulator output. For VDDA add separate decoupling.

- **Ferrite beads & pi filters** to isolate noisy domains (photlets with power analyzers).

- **Power sequencing** if required by MCU family (check datasheet). Add supervision if clarifying reset.

3. Layout: signals & planes

- **Ground plane**: solid plane under MCU and analog circuits. Avoid splits under crystals and ADC traces.

- **Power plane**: use a plane for VDD; avoid narrow long traces for VDD to reduce IR drop.

- **Via stitching** around ground plane edges and under high-speed components.

- **Short traces** for crystals and oscillator loading caps; no vias under crystal.

- **Length matching & impedance** for high-speed signals (USB D+/D−, RNG, SDRAM, Ethernet).

- **Differential pairs**: maintain pair spacing and length match for USB/USB-HS, Ethernet.

- **Thermal relief** on ground via for hand soldering of large pads but keep copper area for heat dissipation on power parts.

4. High-speed & memory interfaces

- **USB**: D+/D− pair routing, controlled impedance ~90Ω differential, place series resistors if recommended, add ESD protection and place pull-up resistor footprints.

- **Ethernet**: magnetics, MDI pair routing, 50Ω single-ended/100Ω differential as required; place transformer/magnetics near connector.

- **SDRAM/OSPI/QUADSPI**: follow venders' reference designs; match length per byte lane and address bus; use proper termination and decoupling.

- **DDR/SDRAM**: leave complex layout to experienced designers—use vendor reference and impedance control.

5. Analog & sensor layout

- Place ADC front-end (buffers, filters) close to ADC pins and keep traces away from switching supplies.

- Use guard traces around high-impedance nodes and connect to ground at a single point.

- Place VREF decoupling close to ADC VREF pin.

6. RF & antennas

- Keep antenna clear area per module datasheet; respect keepout; add test pads for antenna port.

- If using chip antenna, keep recommended ground and matching network; provide option for external antenna (U.FL).

7. Testability & production

- **Test points**: for supply rails, I/O, SWD, UART, crystal signals, low-level power measurement.

- **Programming connector**: position accessible for fixture pogo-pin programming.

- **DFT**: add boundary-scan if applicable; include jumper configurations for test modes.

- **Panelization**: plan for mechanical panelization and fiducials for assembly.

8. BOM & sourcing

- Lock package and footprint to common distributor parts. Keep alternative part numbers in BOM for each critical part.

- Include manufacturer part numbers, footprint library references, and 3D models for assembly.

9. EMC/EMI mitigation

- Keep digital switching currents near decoupling caps.

- Add common-mode chokes and pi filters on external interfaces (USB, power).

- Use ground stitching and split analog/digital grounds carefully.

- Place large switching components away from sensitive analog traces.

10. Prototype checklist (before sending for fab)

- Schematic: clear nets, passive values filled, reference designators unique.

- Footprints verified with datasheet (3D/I/O orientation).

- Critical nets checked: SWD header, power rails, boot pins, crystal footprints.

- DRC clean, rule checks, gerber preview, assembly drawings, pick-and-place.

- BOM complete with manufacturer/alt/manufacturer PN and suggested suppliers.

Firmware Version Control with Git

A disciplined git workflow makes teams productive and reduces regressions.

1. Repository layout (recommended)

/project-root

  /hardware   # schematics, PCB files, BOM, gerbers

  /firmware

    /app   # application sources

    /bsp   # board support (pin mappings)

    /drivers   # peripheral drivers

    /middleware   # RTOS, stacks

    /tests   # host/unit tests

    /tools   # scripts: build, flash, test

/cmake or Make # build system files

/docs   # README, QUICKSTART, ARCHITECTURE

/.github   # CI workflows, issue templates

/ci-scripts

/releases   # release notes and artifacts (or use Releases)

2. Branching model

- **Trunk-based** (recommended for embedded teams):

    - main/master is always releasable.

    - Feature branches: short-lived feature/xxx merged by PR.

    - Use feature flags for incomplete features if needed.

- **Gitflow** is useful for teams that need long-lived release branches, but it can complicate firmware CI and release automation.

3. Commit message conventions

- Use **imperative** style: Add, Fix, Refactor.

- Optionally use **Conventional Commits** for automated changelogs:

    - feat(bluetooth): add DFU trigger command

    - fix(i2c): handle NACK on sensor read

    - chore(build): update toolchain to gcc 10.2

- Keep messages descriptive and link to issue/ticket IDs.

4. Pull requests and code review

- Require at least one reviewer for non-trivial PRs.

- PR template should include: summary, testing done, impact, checklist (builds, unit tests, docs updated).

- Use CI to run builds and tests before allowing merge.

5. Tagging and releases

- Use **Semantic Versioning** (MAJOR.MINOR.PATCH). Tag releases and attach artifacts (hex/elf/map).

- Keep CHANGELOG.md updated (use Keep a Changelog style). Automate generation from Conventional Commit messages if desired.

6. Dependency management & monorepo vs submodules

- Avoid storing large binary blobs. Use release artifacts or package registries.

- Use git submodules sparingly — they add complexity. Prefer monorepo or package management (git+versioned tarballs).

- Pin third-party library versions in third_party or package manifest.

7. CI/CD for firmware

Key pipeline stages:

1. **Build** for configured toolchains (GCC, IAR, Keil). Use matrix builds for different targets.

2. **Unit tests** (host-compiled or cross-compiled using emulator/QEMU).

3. **Static analysis**: clang-tidy, cppcheck, MISRA checks where applicable.

4. **Size & map checks**: prevent regressions in flash/RAM usage.

5. **Artifact creation**: .elf, .bin, .hex, map.

6. **On-target tests** (optional self-hosted runner): flash device and run smoke tests via serial/USB; collect logs.

7. **Release**: produce signed firmware, create release notes, upload to artifact store.

8. Security & repository hygiene

- Protect main with branch protection rules (require PR, CI success).

- Store secrets (keys, tokens) in CI secrets, never in repo.

- Sign tags (gpg --sign) for critical releases.

9. Example PR Checklist (short)

- Build passes for target configurations.

- Unit tests added/updated and passing.

- Documentation updated (README, API).

- No sensitive data committed.

- CI pipeline green.

Documentation and Code Maintainability

Good documentation + maintainable code = lower onboarding cost, faster bug fixes, fewer regressions.

1. Documentation taxonomy

- **README**: project overview, quickstart (build & flash), prerequisites.

- **QUICKSTART**: one-page guide for getting started (dev environment, flashing, running tests).

- **ARCHITECTURE.md**: block diagrams, module responsibilities, data flows, timing constraints.

- **HARDWARE/**: schematics, BOM, assembly notes, mechanical constraints.

- **API docs**: Doxygen generated for drivers & public APIs; published as HTML artifact.

- **OPERATIONS.md**: manufacturing & test instructions, programming procedure, calibration steps.

- **CHANGELOG.md**: human-readable release history.

- **ADR/** (Architecture Decision Records): record important choices and rationale (e.g., HAL vs LL; RTOS choice).

2. Code structure & good patterns

- **Layering**:

    o hal/ (thin wrapper around vendor HAL),

    o drivers/ (driver implementations calling hal),

    o services/ (application logic),

    o app/ (high-level behavior).

- **Board Support Package (BSP)**: centralize pin mappings, peripheral instances, and permits portability between boards.

- **Driver API**: small, testable, narrowly focused interfaces; avoid leaking HAL types to high-level code.

- **Configuration**: central config.h or device tree-like approach; avoid scattered #define magic numbers.

3. Coding standards & toolchain

- Adopt and enforce a style guide (e.g., Threads or MISRA where applicable).

- Use formatters & linters and enforce them with pre-commit hooks:

    o clang-format for C/C++,

- ○ clang-tidy/cppcheck for static analysis.

- Include compile_commands.json for tools that need it (clang tools).

4. Automated documentation

- Use **Doxygen** for API docs; generate in CI and publish to GitHub Pages or artifact storage.

- Keep example usages near the API doc (usage snippets).

- Auto-generate CHANGELOG from commits using Conventional Commits.

5. Testing strategy

- **Unit tests**: isolate business logic from hardware; use mocking (CMock, FakeHAL).

- **Integration tests**: test drivers with hardware or hardware simulators (QEMU when possible).

- **On-target tests**:

  - ○ Boot tests: flash and ensure application boots and reports expected hardware IDs.

  - ○ Functional tests: sensor read → known value check, actuator response verification.

  - ○ End-to-cnd tests: full system scenario (power up, sensor acquisition, publish).

- **Hardware-in-the-loop (HIL)**: simulate external events and measure responses.

6. Maintainability practices

- Small functions, single responsibility, and clear naming.

- Prefer composition over complicated inheritance or deep macros.

- Avoid global mutable state; where necessary, document lifecycle and ownership.

- Add code comments for *why*, not *what* (the code already says what).

7. Reproducible builds & dev environment

- Pin toolchain versions in CI; provide a devcontainer or Docker image for local reproducibility.

- Provide scripts to set up toolchain and flash device: ./tools/setup.sh, ./tools/flash.sh.

- If using different toolchains (GCC/IAR/Keil) keep canonical build flags documented and a machine-readable build matrix.

8. Onboarding & knowledge transfer

- Write a concise ONBOARDING.md that lists:

    - How to get a dev board, build the project, flash and run smoke tests.

    - Where to find schematics/BOM.

    - How to run CI locally.

- Record architecture walkthroughs: short video or docs explaining the main components.

9. Release & long-term maintenance

- Define a release process: create release branch, run full test suite, sign firmware, create release notes.

- Deprecation policy: document when and how APIs will be removed; keep compatibility for at least one major release cycle.

- Archive references: keep a snapshot of the BOM and supplier at time of release for later reproduction.

Useful Templates & Examples (copy-paste friendly)

Recommended repository tree (example)

project-name/
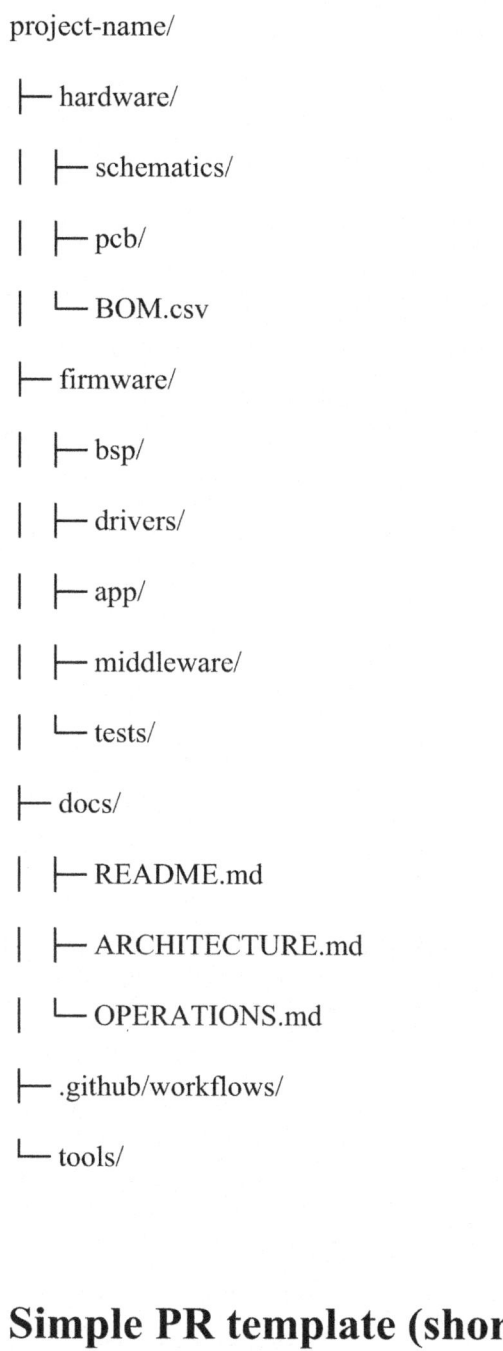
```
project-name/
├─ hardware/
│  ├─ schematics/
│  ├─ pcb/
│  └─ BOM.csv
├─ firmware/
│  ├─ bsp/
│  ├─ drivers/
│  ├─ app/
│  ├─ middleware/
│  └─ tests/
├─ docs/
│  ├─ README.md
│  ├─ ARCHITECTURE.md
│  └─ OPERATIONS.md
├─ .github/workflows/
└─ tools/
```

Simple PR template (short)

Summary

(What changed and why)

Test plan

- [ ] Build (target)

- [ ] Unit tests

- [ ] On-target smoke test (describe)

Notes

(Backwards compatibility, migration steps)

Example commit messages

- feat(sensor): add BME280 pressure/humidity driver

- fix(power): prevent regulator undervoltage on cold start

- chore(build): upgrade toolchain to gcc-11

Minimal CI build steps (conceptual)

1. checkout

2. install toolchain (cache)

3. make all for targets

4. run cppcheck, clang-tidy

5. run host unit tests

6. generate artifacts and upload

From Prototype to Production — Practical Transition Checklist

- **DFM Review**: check footprints, silk, fiducials, assembly notes.

- **DFT**: include test pads for in-circuit test; enable boundary scan if helpful.

- **EMC pre-compliance test**: fix glaring radiated/conducted emissions.

- **Production programming**: script factory programmer, set serial numbers and option bytes.

- **Test jigs & fixtures**: design pogo-pin fixtures and automated test scripts.

- **Regulatory & safety**: verify applicable standards (CE/FCC/UL), RF certification for wireless.

- **Sourcing & lifecycles**: ensure second-source parts, check lead times and MOQ.

- **Support plan**: field firmware update strategy (A/B), rollback mechanism, and secure update.

Chapter 16: Practical Projects with STM32 — Extensive, Hands-to-end Guide

This chapter walks you through five realistic, production-lean STM32 projects. For each project you'll get: goals, hardware choices, schematic/PCB notes, firmware architecture (CubeMX/HAL and LL patterns), critical code patterns, testing & debug tips, power and safety considerations, and sensible extension paths. Treat these as blueprints you can adapt to your MCU family (F0/L0/F1/F3/F4/L4/H7/etc.) — where specifics differ I call out the key device-dependent decisions.

1. LED Matrix Controller

Project goal

Drive an LED matrix (e.g., 16×16 RGB or 32×8 monochrome) with high refresh rate, smooth animations, brightness control, and optionally hardware gamma correction. Support animations from flash or streamed over serial/USB.

Hardware choices

- MCU: STM32 with enough GPIOs or SPI DMA (F4/L4/H7 are great). If using large RGB matrices, prefer a 32-bit STM32 with DMA.

- LED type:

    - **Direct LED matrix** (multiplexed rows/columns) — many GPIOs, external transistors/drivers recommended.

    - **Addressable LEDs** (WS2812/WS2811/APA102) — use single-wire timing (bit-banged or SPI/USART with DMA) or SPI-like (APA102 easier).

    - **LED drivers** (TLC5940, IS31FL3731) for constant-current control per channel (better brightness control).

- Power: 5V or 12V depending on LEDs; regulators sized for maximum LED current (reserve headroom). Large matrices need significant current and decoupling.

- Level shifting: if MCU is 3.3V and LEDs are 5V logic, use proper level shifters (74HCT, specialized buffers).

- Connectors: for modular panels add robust screw terminals or keyed headers.

Schematic & PCB notes

- Use MOSFET or transistor-per-row drivers for direct-drive matrices (N-channel low-side MOSFETs, P-channel high-side or high-side drivers for rows if needed).

- Include gate-driver resistors, flyback diodes only for inductive loads (not LEDs).

- Place decoupling caps per LED power domain; large electrolytic caps to supply transient current.

- Provide test pads for SPI/UART/Power and expose SWD for debugging.

- If using addressable LEDs, route data traces short and avoid stubs; add a small series resistor (22–100Ω) at data output and a single-bitlevel shifter if required.

Firmware architecture

Key tasks:

- Frame buffer abstraction in RAM (RGB565/8-bit-per-channel depending on memory).

- Display refresh via timer + DMA or timer + ISR:

    - For **multiplexed matrix**: use a timer ISR to strobe rows and write column data via DMA to GPIO (use a timer + DMA or SPI shift registers).

    - For **APA102 (clocked)**: use SPI + DMA to stream frames with minimal CPU.

    - For **WS2812**: encode each pixel into PWM timing (use a timer with DMA driving PWM compare buffer; on M4/M7 precisely timed).

- Gamma correction and brightness scaling on the fly or pre-computed LUT.

- Animation scheduler that updates the frame buffer in background (task/RTOS or main loop).

- Optional: double-buffering to avoid tearing (one buffer displayed via DMA while CPU writes to back buffer).

Peripherals used

- TIM for refresh interrupts and PWM generation.

- DMA to feed PWM or SPI data without CPU load.

- SPI (for APA102) or USART in SPI mode (if needed).

- GPIO port clocks and EXTI if user input required.

Code pattern: PWM-Pulse DMA for WS2812 (concept)

1. Convert each LED color to timing bit pattern (e.g., 1 → 0.8μs high/0.45μs low).

2. Fill a uint16_t DMA buffer with timer compare values representing waveform.

3. Start TIM PWM and DMA: HAL_TIM_PWM_Start_DMA(&htimX, TIM_CHANNEL_x, dma_buf, length);

4. On DMA complete interrupt, start next frame.

Example: use 24-bit color → 24 * num_pixels * bits_per_pwm entries in DMA buffer. Use circular/double-buffering to avoid gaps.

Example: APA102 via SPI + DMA (pseudocode)

// prepare frame: start-frame + LED frames + end-frame

HAL_SPI_Transmit_DMA(&hspi1, frame_buffer, frame_length);

// in callback HAL_SPI_TxCpltCallback, swap buffer or update animations

Testing & debugging

- Start with a small 8×8 matrix and verify current draw at full white before larger panels.

- Use scope to verify data timing for WS2812 or SPI for APA102.

- Measure power rail under load; watch for voltage droop and overheating.

- Use simple test patterns (single pixel, fill, checkerboard) to validate wiring.

Power & thermal considerations

- Avoid trying full-white display without calculated current capability (I_total = num_pixels × max_current_per_pixel). Include MOSFET switches or current limiting if needed.

- Provide thermal relief and measure PCB heating; use larger copper pours on power planes.

Extensions

- Add USB or SD card playback of animations.

- Add PWM-based dimming per row or CIE gamma table for color correctness.

- Support external control via MQTT/HTTP (see IoT section).

2. USB HID Keyboard / Mouse Emulation

Project goal

Make an STM32 appear to a host as a USB HID device (keyboard, mouse, or composite HID), enabling custom HID-based controllers (macros, foot pedals, gamepads).

Hardware choices

- MCU with USB FS/HS device peripheral (STM32F4, L4, H7, some F7, WB).

- USB micro-B/USB-C connector with proper D+/D− routing, ESD protection, VBUS sense, and 5V power switch if providing host power.

- Optional: mechanical switches, rotary encoders, and operator interface.

Schematic & PCB notes

- Controlled impedance routing for D+/D− if high speed required. FS usually less strict.

- Pull-up resistor on D+ or D− normally provided on MCU/eval board or STUSB for device detection — CubeMX generated USB driver assumes hardware present.

- Provide VBUS sense to detect host connection.

- Add decoupling and place ESD diodes on USB lines.

Firmware architecture

- Use **STM32CubeMX** to enable USB Device, **HID class**, generate skeleton code.

- Implement HID report descriptor corresponding to device (keyboard has standard descriptor; mouse as well).

- Implement a HID interface layer: USBD_HID_SendReport() to send reports to host.

- Samples:

      ○   Keyboard: standard 8-byte report: modifier, reserved, 6 keycodes.

      ○   Mouse: 3-4 byte report: buttons, x movement, y movement, wheel.

Example sequence: Keyboard key press

1. Build HID report with the appropriate HID keycode (e.g., 0x04 for 'a').

2. USBD_HID_SendReport(&hUsbDeviceFS, report, sizeof(report));

3. Wait for endpoint idle/IN complete (or rely on stack buffering), then send a zeroed report to signal key release.

Report descriptor (high-level)

- The HID descriptor defines usage pages, usages (keyboard, mouse), report sizes and counts. CubeMX generates a default keyboard descriptor; for composite devices you create combined descriptors.

Polling vs Interrupt

- USB Host polls endpoints; HID IN reports are typically polled at an interval defined by descriptor, usually 10–20ms for keyboard/mouse responsiveness.

HID over USB: example keyboard code (concept)

uint8_t keyreport[8] = {0};

keyreport[0] = 0; // modifiers

keyreport[2] = HID_KEY_A; // 'a' pressed

USBD_HID_SendReport(&hUsbDeviceFS, keyreport, 8);

HAL_Delay(5);

memset(keyreport, 0, 8);

USBD_HID_SendReport(&hUsbDeviceFS, keyreport, 8); // release

Testing & debugging

- Use a PC to verify device enumerates (Device Manager on Windows, lsusb on Linux).

- Use USB protocol analyzers or usbmon/Wireshark (with USB capture) to inspect HID reports if needed.

- For composite HID (keyboard + media keys), ensure correct report IDs are present.

Security & etiquette

- Ensure device only sends expected inputs (avoid accidental repeated key storms).

- For firmware upgrades, support signed firmware if device could be abused.

Extensions

- Add N-key rollover (NKRO) for advanced keyboards (requires special descriptor).

- Add Bluetooth HID (use STM32WB or external module) for wireless HID.

---

3. Sensor Data Logger with SD Card

Project goal

Collect sensor data (ADC, IMU, GPS, etc.) and reliably log to an SD card using FAT filesystem (FATFS), with time stamps from RTC, and safe power-off handling.

Hardware choices

- MCU: any STM32 with SPI or SDMMC peripheral. SDMMC hardware (SDIO) offers higher throughput than SPI mode.

- SD card socket with detect switch and write-protect pin optional.

- RTC + coin-cell backup or use LSE to preserve time across resets.

- Sensors: IMU (I2C/SPI), ADC front-end, temperature sensors, etc.

Schematic & PCB notes

- Add series resistors on SD data lines for signal integrity; place ESD protection.

- Connect card detect pin to MCU for safe insert/remove detection.

- Include power switch or soft power control to prevent card removal during writes.

- Use proper pull-ups per SD spec on CMD and DAT lines when in SPI mode.

Firmware architecture

- Initialize FATFS, mount filesystem; if absent, create a new volume with unique filename pattern (e.g., LOG0001.CSV).

- Use **circular buffer + DMA** for sensor acquisition to avoid CPU overrun.

- Batch writes (e.g., write in 512-byte blocks) and call f_sync() after critical batches to ensure data on media.

- Implement graceful shutdown on power loss: detect low battery and flush buffer / close files.

- Time stamping via RTC and calendar for human-readable CSV logs.

Peripheral usage

- ADC with DMA for continuous analog sampling.

- SPI/SDIO for SD card with DMA.

- I2C/SPI for sensors (IMU) with DMA or interrupt-driven reads.

- RTC for timestamps.

File I/O pattern & reliability

- Use append mode for log files and write in block-sized chunks to align with SD sector size.

- Use journaling pattern or dual-file strategy for atomic writes:

    - Write to a temp file or pre-allocated area, f_sync(), then rename to final file.

- Detect file system errors and remount filesystem if necessary.

Example code: write buffer to SD safely (HAL + FATFS pseudocode)

```
void flush_log_buffer(void) {

  UINT bw;

  FRESULT fr = f_write(&logFile, log_buf, log_len, &bw);

  if (fr == FR_OK && bw == log_len) {

    f_sync(&logFile); // guarantee write to card

    log_len = 0;

  } else {

    // handle write error (try remount, re-init)

  }

}
```

Power-fail handling

- Add a small capacitor that provides enough energy to flush buffers (calculate energy: $E = 0.5CV^2$) to cover worst-case flush time at card current.

- Alternatively use immediate f_sync() after each important record (slower).

Wear leveling and SD health

- SD cards manage wear internally; avoid frequent small writes — batch them to reduce write amplification.

- Log filesystem health and free space periodically. Rotate logs when nearly full.

Debugging & testing

- Use known-good SD cards from reputable manufacturers.

- Test many insert/remove cycles and forced power loss mid-write to validate recovery.

- Validate timestamps and data sanity (e.g., ranges).

Extensions

- Compress logs on-the-fly (LZ4 or RLE) to save space.

- Add web or USB mass-storage access to extract logs.

- Implement encryption/signing for confidential logs.

---

4. IoT Node with MQTT over Wi-Fi

Project goal

A battery- or mains-powered sensor node that publishes telemetry to an MQTT broker via Wi-Fi and supports remote control/OTA.

Hardware choices

- Two broad approaches:

  1. **STM32 + Wi-Fi module (AT-command)**: ESP8266/ESP32 in AT firmware or other certified module (easiest).

  2. **STM32 with integrated Wi-Fi (rare)** or use an STM32 + Wi-Fi chip with SPI/SDIO device interface managed by custom driver (higher complexity).

- Use TLS-capable module for secure MQTT (MQTTS) if required.

- Antenna and RF chain per module vendor guidelines.

Option 1: ESP8266/ESP32 as AT co-processor (recommended for speed)

- Pros: module handles TCP/TLS; MCU only speaks AT or a higher-level bridge (JSON over serial).

- Cons: need to handle module firmware quirks and AT command parsing.

Firmware architecture (with AT-module)

- Use UART or SPI to communicate with module.

- Implement an asynchronous AT-command manager that supports:

  - Connection management (connect/disconnect to AP),

  - TCP open, TLS handshake if supported,

  - MQTT client operations via module (many modules have MQTT client built-in) or implement MQTT on MCU using the module's socket interface.

- Use a state machine or RTOS tasks:

  - network_task manages Wi-Fi association and sockets,

  - sensor_task reads sensors and queues messages,

  - mqtt_task publishes/subscribes and handles reconnection/backoff.

- Use JSON or compact binary payloads; include device ID and timestamp.

MQTT details

- Topics: devices/<id>/telemetry, devices/<id>/cmd.

- QoS: choose appropriate QoS (0 for low-latency, 1 for at-least-once).

- Keepalive and LWT (Last Will and Testament) configured for device presence.

Example AT-driven publish sequence (concept)

1. AT+CWMODE=1 (station mode)

2. AT+CWJAP="ssid","pass" (connect)

215

3. AT+MQTTUSERCFG=... (configure MQTT client on module) or open TCP and send MQTT CONNECT packet by MCU.

4. AT+MQTTPUB="topic","payload",qos,retain

Security

- TLS: implement TLS on module or use module's secure client. For resource-constrained MCU, offload TLS to module.

- Certificates: store server CA or use certificate pinning; protect private keys if doing client auth.

- Use token-based auth when possible (rotate tokens).

OTA updates

- Module can often handle firmware update for itself; for MCU firmware use a secure OTA pattern:

   - Push new binary via MQTT (chunked) or request URL (HTTP(S)), store in external flash or SD, verify signature, then switch banks (dual-bank bootloader).

   - Use fallback to previous version if boot fails.

Network resilience patterns

- Exponential backoff on reconnect.

- Local cache of messages (queue) to re-send after reconnect.

- Keepalive / ping; detect and restart module on stale link.

Example: using LwIP + SPI Wi-Fi chip (advanced)

- Use STM32 + external Wi-Fi that exposes an interface LwIP can drive (rare and complex).

- LwIP + MQTT client (paho embedded MQTT or MQTT-C) on MCU gives full control and TLS, but requires more RAM/CPU.

Power considerations

- Wi-Fi is power-hungry: use sleep modes on module (deep sleep for ESP) and wake MCU on intervals or events.

- Accumulate data and send bursts to amortize connection overhead.

- Measure peak current and size power supply accordingly.

Testing & debugging

- Use local MQTT broker (Mosquitto) during development.

- Sniff traffic with Wireshark to debug TLS or MQTT handshake (TLS encrypted, see SNI/connection).

- Log connection/disconnection times and reasons.

Extensions

- Bluetooth Low Energy fallback (STM32WB).

- Edge rules in device: local threshold triggers to avoid excessive cloud traffic.

- Gateway mode: node can forward other sensor nodes via mesh.

---

5. Mini Robotics Controller with Motor Drivers

Project goal

Control small robots: DC motors (H-bridge), stepper motors, or brushless motors with closed-loop control. Provide interfaces: motor driver power management, encoder feedback, current sensing, and high-level motion commands (velocity/position).

Hardware choices

- MCU: STM32 with advanced timers (TIM1/TIM8 on advanced parts) for PWM complementary outputs and dead-time (F3, F4, H7, etc.).

- Motor drivers:

    ○ Brushed DC: H-bridge drivers (DRV8833, BTS7960) or discrete MOSFET half-bridges with gate drivers.

    ○ Brushless (BLDC): 3-phase drivers with gate drivers and current sensing (or use dedicated BLDC controllers).

    ○ Stepper: A4988/DRV8825 or more advanced drivers for microstepping.

- Sensors:

    ○ Quadrature encoders (incremental) — connect to timer encoder interface

    ○ Hall sensors for BLDC commutation

    ○ Current sense shunt + differential amplifier or integrated current-sense (INA219/INA226)

- Power: battery pack + proper regulator (buck) and protection. Include large bulk capacitors and TVS diodes.

Schematic & PCB notes

- Gate drivers near MOSFETs; keep high-current loops short and wide.

- Sense resistors on low-side or high-side with proper filtering; protect ADC inputs with op-amp front-end if needed.

- Separate power ground and signal ground carefully; consider star or split-plane technique and place sense resistor to define measurement node.

- Add current-limiting or emergency stop input with hardware cutoff (e.g., logic-level MOSFET or latching relay).

Firmware architecture

- Real-time control loop in RTOS task or bare-metal with high-priority control ISR:

    ○ **Control loop**: read encoder/IMU, run motor control algorithm (PID/FOC), output PWM via timers.

- o **Safety task**: monitor temperature, current, watchdog.

- o **Communications**: serial/USB/CAN for commands and telemetry.

- For DC motor closed-loop:

  - o Encoder → measure speed/position using timer encoder interface or input–capture.

  - o PID velocity controller outputs duty cycle to PWM.

  - o Current limit via ADC-measured shunt voltage; if above limit, clamp duty and log fault.

PWM configuration for H-bridge

- Use advanced timers with complementary channels and dead-time to avoid shoot-through when using high-side/low-side MOSFETs.

- If using half-bridges with independent low-side MOSFETs and high-side drivers, ensure correct dead-time and complementary gating.

Encoder & timers

- Use timer encoder interface mode (TIMx in encoder mode) for quadrature decoding; read CNT and compute delta per control period.

- For very high resolution, use hardware encoder interface and sample periodically.

Current sensing and ADC considerations

- Sample shunt voltage synchronized to PWM (sample in middle of PWM on-time when switching noise minimal).

- Use timer trigger to start ADC conversion (TRGO from TIM) and DMA to transfer samples into buffer.

Brushless Motor (BLDC) & FOC

- BLDC/FOC requires:

  - o 3-phase PWM with complementary outputs and dead-time (advanced timers).

- Sampling of phase currents (two shunts or single shunt) synchronized to PWM for rotor current measurement.

- Clarke/Park transforms and PID for torque/field control — needs FPU/DSP acceleration for real-time FOC (prefer M4F/M7).

- Implement sample timing such that ADC samples at the desired phase point; use injected conversions or regular conversions triggered by TIM TRGO.

Example: PID velocity loop (pseudocode)

```
float pid_update(PID_t *pid, float setpoint, float measurement, float dt) {

  float error = setpoint - measurement;

  pid->integral += error * dt;

  float derivative = (error - pid->prev_error) / dt;

  float out = pid->Kp * error + pid->Ki * pid->integral + pid->Kd * derivative;

  pid->prev_error = error;

  return clamp(out, -max_duty, max_duty);

}
```

Safety & fault handling

- Hard limits: over-current trip that cuts gate drive via MOSFET disable pin or hardware e-stop.

- Watchdogs: IWDG for recovery if control loop stalls.

- Thermal monitoring: measure MOSFET temperature (thermistor or temp sensor).

- Voltages: handle undervoltage/overvoltage with safe shutdown.

Testing & debugging

- Start with low-power tests (no motor) using LEDs or small loads.

- Use an oscilloscope to measure PWM gating, dead-time, and phase currents.

- Implement simulator mode: run control algorithm without enabling drivers, visualize commands via serial/Plotter.

- Use encoder test harness to verify quadrature decoding and speed measurement.

Extensions

- Add trajectory planner for motion profiles (trapezoidal or S-curve acceleration).

- Implement sensor fusion between encoders and IMU for better odometry.

- Add CAN bus interface for multi-motor robots.

Cross-Project Best Practices

Development & Tooling

- Start from a CubeMX project or your standard template that configures clocks, NVIC, and peripherals.

- Use FreeRTOS for complex projects with real-time, concurrency, and separation of concerns (sensor task, comms task, control task).

- Use Git for version control; tag milestones and include a reproducible build environment (Docker/devcontainer).

Use DMA & Timers to offload CPU

- DMA + timers reduce CPU overhead for all of these projects (display streaming, SD writes, ADC sampling, SPI/USART transfers).

Memory & Cache

- On cache-enabled MCUs (M7/H7), use non-cacheable memory regions for DMA buffers or use cache maintenance functions before/after DMA.

Safety and recovery

- Implement bootloader + dual-bank firmware for safe OTA/updates.

- Use hardware watchdogs and combination of software monitors to ensure recovery from stalled states.

Testing

- Simulate and unit-test algorithms on host before porting to MCU (especially PID, FOC).

- Add diagnostic modes and self-test routines accessible via serial or debug interface.

Example Bill-of-Materials (high-level sketch per project)

- LED matrix controller: MCU dev board, LED panel(s), MOSFET drivers, level shifters, power supply, connectors.

- USB HID: STM32 board with USB, pushbuttons, encoders, enclosure, USB cable.

- Data logger: STM32 dev board, SD card socket, RTC crystal + battery, sensors (IMU/pressure/temp), connectors.

- IoT node: STM32 + ESP32 module or certified Wi-Fi module, antenna, sensors, battery/regulator.

- Robotics controller: STM32, MOSFETs or driver modules, gate drivers, shunt resistors, encoders, bulk capacitors.

(For production BOMs produce per-project detailed part lists with vendors and alternates.)

Project Timelines & Milestones (suggested)

4–6 week example per project (prototype)

1. Week 1: requirements, parts procurement, initial schematic.

2. Week 2: prototype wiring with dev boards; basic bring-up (power, clock, SWD).

3. Week 3: core firmware (frame buffer/spi/USB/SD/MQTT) and peripheral DMA setup.

4. Week 4: feature integration (animations, HID reports, log rotation, MQTT topics).

5. Week 5: testing, stress tests, power measurements, debugging.

6. Week 6: iterate HW fixes, finalize firmware, prepare demo and documentation.

Longer for robotics/BLDC (may need 2–3 months for robust closed-loop and PCB revisions).

Final checklist before shipping

- Document hardware (schematics, BOM, PCB fab files), firmware (version, build artifacts), test results (power profiles, thermal).

- Implement manufacturing programming scripts (STM32_Programmer_CLI).

- Provide user and service documentation: how to update firmware, connectivity settings, safety warnings.

Chapter 17: Security and Reliability in STM32 Systems — Comprehensive Guide

Security and reliability must be designed in from the start. This chapter pulls together practical, field-proven techniques you can apply to STM32-based products to make them robust, safe, and defensible against accidental and malicious failure. It covers secure firmware update workflows (SFU), Memory Protection Unit (MPU) configuration, watchdogs and fail-safe design, and ESD/EMI protection techniques — with examples, recipes, and checklists you can act on immediately.

1. Secure Firmware Update (SFU)

A robust Secure Firmware Update scheme guarantees authenticity, integrity, and (optionally) confidentiality of firmware delivered during production or over-the-air. The overall goals are:

- **Authenticate** that firmware comes from a trusted party (signature verification).

- **Ensure integrity** (CRC/HASH) and atomic switching so power loss cannot leave device bricked.

- **Prevent rollback** to older vulnerable versions.

- **Protect keys** used for verification and provide a secure provisioning model.

1.1 SFU design patterns (practical options)

- **Single-bank in-place** — simplest but most risky (power loss can brick).

- **Dual-bank (A/B)** — write new image to inactive bank, verify signature, then switch active bank (recommended for field devices).

- **External storage + staged install** — download image to external flash or SD, verify, then flash internal bank with power-loss safe sequence.

- **Golden image + update partition** — keep a stable minimal image (recovery) and a regular application partition.

1.2 Essential SFU building blocks

1. **Signed images**: Use asymmetric signatures (ECDSA/P-256, Ed25519) signed by a secure build server. Device contains public key.

2. **Image format**: Include metadata (version, size, hash, signature, flags). Use a fixed header layout and a manifest.

3. **Atomic commit**: Only mark an update as active after full verification (two-phase commit).

4. **Rollback protection**: Maintain monotonic counter or version number stored securely (option bytes, secure element, or OTP).

5. **Recovery path**: Bootloader must be immutable and able to revert to previous working image or accept transfer via USB/serial programmer.

6. **Secure key provisioning**: Inject device-specific secrets or public keys during manufacturing using secure tools (JTAG/serial is risky — prefer trusted programming stations or secure elements).

1.3 High-level A/B update flow (recommended)

1. Bootloader checks a metadata area for an update request.

2. If update present, bootloader writes new image to inactive bank, verifying incremental checksums as it writes.

3. Bootloader verifies whole image signature (using stored public key) and optionally verifies image hash.

4. If verification passes, bootloader marks new bank PENDING and reboots to run the new image.

5. New image starts and performs a self-test (sanity, peripheral checks, watchdog interaction).

6. If new image signals OK to bootloader (flag in nonvolatile region), bootloader marks bank ACTIVE. If it fails, bootloader falls back to old bank.

1.4 Signature verification (practical notes)

- Use standard crypto (PKCS, mbedTLS, wolfSSL). Prefer elliptic-curve signatures (ECDSA/EdDSA) for smaller keys and faster verification on MCUs with crypto accelerators.

- Offload verification to hardware crypto engine if available — faster and protected key usage.

- Keep signature verification inside **bootloader/secure runtime**, not in application.

1.5 Protecting keys and anti-rollback

- Prefer **hardware-backed keys**:

  - Secure element (ATECC, SE050), or

  - MCU secure storage (TrustZone, OTP, option bytes, backed-up in secure flash) — store only public keys in read-only/locked region.

- **Monotonic counters**: store in secure hardware (secure element) or backup domain to avoid reset-based rollback. If unavailable, use signed sequence numbers with server-side tracking but accept weaker protection.

- Option bytes and RDP (Read Protection) can make extracting keys harder; use with caution and documented recovery paths.

1.6 Transport & robustness

- Use TLS (HTTPS/MQTTs) for image download if downloading over IP; modules like ESP32 can handle TLS or use an OTA gateway.

- Support chunked download with checksums, resume, and retry (e.g., store last successful block number).

- Use sufficient power/transient budget to complete final write — add a small supercapacitor or plan a battery threshold cut-off to attempt flush before shutdown.

1.7 Example pseudocode (verify & swap)

```
if (update_available()) {

  download_image_to(inactive_bank);

  if (!verify_signature(inactive_bank_header, PUBLIC_KEY)) {

    error("Bad signature");

    abort_update();

  }

  mark_bank_pending(inactive_bank);

  reboot();

}


// in bootloader on boot:

if (active_bank_is_pending()) {

  if (application_selftest_ok()) {

    mark_bank_active();
```

```
} else {

  rollback_to_previous();

}

}

jump_to_active_app();
```

1.8 Practical pitfalls and countermeasures

- **Bricking due to power loss**: avoid by two-bank schemes and atomic metadata updates (write validation flags last).

- **Key theft during provisioning**: protect with secure programming stations; avoid shipping private keys in the device.

- **Replay/rollback attacks**: use monotonic counters or sign with nonces and server checks.

- **Unsigned images in CI**: enforce signing step in build pipeline and include verification tests.

2. Memory Protection Unit (MPU) Configuration

The MPU is a first-line defense against software bugs and many classes of attacks (stack overflows, buffer overruns, accidental writes to code or peripheral regions). The MPU is available on Cortex-M3/M4/M7/M33+ (not on Cortex-M0/M0+). (For TrustZone-capable parts, use MPU in secure/non-secure configuration.)

2.1 Goals for MPU use

- Prevent execution from data regions (no-execute / XN).

- Make flash code read-only.

- Create guarded stacks (no-execute + no-access around canary).

- Protect peripheral regions and memory-mapped devices from accidental writes.

- Enforce privilege separation (if running user tasks that should not access kernel resources).

2.2 MPU concepts (practical)

- MPU regions are power-of-two sized and aligned. Typical region attributes: read/write/execute, caching/ buffering attributes (shareable/non-shareable), and subregion enables (8 subregions per region).

- On Cortex-M7, also consider cacheability: mark regions that are DMA-targets as non-cacheable or manage cache coherency manually.

2.3 Typical MPU layout (example)

Region	Base	Size	Attributes
0	Flash (code)	512KB	RO, Execute, Cacheable
1	Flash (constants)	128KB	RO, XN=0
2	SRAM (stack & heap)	128KB	RW, Execute Never (XN)
3	Peripherals	0x40000000	RW, Device, XN
4	External RAM (DMA)	0x60000000	RW, Non-Cacheable, XN
5	Guard region below stack	aligned size	No access (to capture overflow)

2.4 Example: configure MPU with CMSIS (C code)

```
#include "core_cm7.h" // or core_cm4.h
```

229

```c
void MPU_Config(void) {

  // Disable MPU

  MPU->CTRL = 0;


  // Region 0: Flash (example 512KB at 0x08000000) - RO, Exec

  MPU->RNR = 0;

  MPU->RBAR = 0x08000000;

  // Size value n encodes 2^(n+1) bytes; choose correct encoding for 512KB

  MPU->RASR = (AP_RO << 24) | (SIZE_512KB << 1) | ENABLE_REGION;


  // Region 1: SRAM - RW, XN

  MPU->RNR = 1;

  MPU->RBAR = 0x20000000;

  MPU->RASR = (AP_RW << 24) | (XN_BIT << 28) | (SIZE_128KB << 1) | ENABLE_REGION;


  // Region N: Peripherals - device type

  // ... configure subregions if needed


  // Enable MPU with background region enabled for default

  MPU->CTRL = MPU_CTRL_PRIVDEFENA_Msk | MPU_CTRL_ENABLE_Msk;

  __DSB();

  __ISB();

}
```

Use AP/SIZE macros and proper alignment. For safety-critical apps, generate region definitions and validate alignment at build-time.

2.5 Guard regions and stack protection

- Put **no-access** region immediately beyond allocated stacks to catch overflow — an access fault occurs, enabling post-mortem analysis.

- Use separate stacks for interrupts (Main Stack/Process stack) and configure MPU accordingly.

2.6 Privilege separation

- In systems that use an RTOS or implement application plugins, configure user-mode threads with restricted MPU regions and a secure kernel region for OS objects and drivers.

- Use MPU with FreeRTOS-MPU port or similar to get task-level memory protection.

2.7 Debugging MPU faults

- On fault, read SCB->MMFAR / SCB->CFSR to find offending address and reason (read/write/execute). Log/record these into retained RAM for post-mortem.

2.8 Practical pitfalls

- MPU region sizes and alignments are restrictive — plan memory layout early in design.

- On cache-capable MCUs, wrong caching attributes cause elusive DMA corruption — mark DMA buffers non-cacheable or manage caches.

3. Watchdog Timers and Fail-Safe Design

Watchdogs are essential to recover from software hangs, live-locks, or unforeseen hardware states. Use them as part of a layered fail-safe strategy.

3.1 Types of watchdogs on STM32

- **Independent Watchdog (IWDG):**

○ Runs from its own LSI oscillator (independent of main clock).

○ Cannot be stopped once started (unless option bytes permit).

○ Ideal final safety net for production devices.

- **Window Watchdog (WWDG)**:

    ○ Allows a time window to refresh; refreshing too early or too late triggers reset.

    ○ Useful to detect timing anomalies.

- **Software/Task-level watchdog**:

    ○ Implemented in firmware via supervisor task that checks liveness signals from tasks (task heartbeats) and kicks the hardware watchdog if everything is healthy.

3.2 Watchdog design patterns

- **Two-tier watchdog**:

    ○ **Tier 1**: IWDG as hardware last resort (strict, short timeout).

    ○ **Tier 2**: WWDG for detection of timing faults; or a supervisory MCU or external watchdog if safety requirements mandate redundancy.

- **Petting strategy**:

    ○ Only the supervisor module should pet (reset) the watchdog after verifying system health (all tasks have signaled).

    ○ Avoid scattering watchdog kicks across code — centralize them.

- **Windowed kicking**:

    ○ Use WWDG to ensure periodic kicks within a defined window to detect stuck-state where code is stuck in a tight loop that blindly kicks watchdog.

3.3 Watchdog example (HAL) — IWDG init & refresh

/* Initialize */

hiwdg.Instance = IWDG;

hiwdg.Init.Prescaler = IWDG_PRESCALER_64;

hiwdg.Init.Reload = 4095; // choose per required timeout

HAL_IWDG_Init(&hiwdg);

/* Refresh (in supervisor task) */

HAL_IWDG_Refresh(&hiwdg);

Compute timeout: $t = (Reload + 1) * Prescaler / LSI\_freq$. Use measured LSI freq (can vary) to compute accurate timeout.

3.4 Watchdog with RTOS

- Implement a **watchdog task** that collects heartbeat notifications from tasks (xTaskNotifyFromISR or semaphore). Only if all tasks reply within the monitoring window the watchdog is kicked.

- If a task misses heartbeat, escalate: log fault, attempt graceful restart of the task, and if unresolved, allow the watchdog to reset system.

3.5 Fail-safe hardware

- **External watchdog supervisors** (supervisory ICs) monitor power rails and can force reset if undervoltage occurs. Useful to complement internal watchdogs.

- **Power supervisors & POR/BOR** configuration: set BOR levels appropriate to your MCU to avoid operation at undervoltage.

3.6 Crash reporting & recovery

- On watchdog reset, log the reset cause (RCC_CSR, backup registers) and attempt to upload logs on next boot or store them in reserved flash for diagnostics.

- Use backup SRAM or magic tokens in flash to determine whether the system failed early or late during boot and to trigger special recovery paths.

3.7 Practical pitfalls

- Avoid infinite loops waiting for peripheral flags that are dependent on external hardware — they can prevent watchdog refresh.

- Time-critical sections should not disable watchdog for long durations; instead, feed watchdog from an interrupt that is unrelated to the long section if absolutely necessary.

4. ESD and EMI Protection Techniques

Protecting electronics from Electrostatic Discharge (ESD) and minimizing electromagnetic interference (EMI) ensures reliability and regulatory compliance. These are hardware + PCB layout techniques you must practice.

4.1 ESD protection (practical)

- **Where to protect**: all external connectors (USB, power jack, antenna, CAN/RS485, sensor connectors).

- **Typical components**:

    o **Unidirectional/bi-directional TVS diodes** (SMBJ/SMBJxxx family or smaller SMD TVS such as SMBJ/SMBJ series for power lines, little SOD523 for signal lines).

    o **Transorb** for high energy; place close to connector.

    o **Series resistors** (47–220Ω) on signal lines to limit surge current and ringing.

    o **Gas discharge tubes (GDT)** for very high-energy lines (e.g., outdoor installations).

- **Layout**:

    o Place TVS as close as possible to the connector pad.

    o Route protected trace to TVS with short wide traces; minimize loop area.

    o Ensure return path to chassis ground is short for GND surge currents.

4.2 EMI mitigation (practical)

- **Decoupling**: one 0.1µF ceramic close to every VDD pin plus 10µF bulk near regulator. Use multiple values for broad-spectrum suppression. Place capacitors between power pin and ground with shortest path possible.

- **Grounding strategy**:

  o Use continuous ground plane under digital/analog areas.

  o For mixed-signal, consider star point or split ground only when required and understand return currents.

  o Stitch ground vias around high-speed/antenna areas.

- **Cable filtering**:

  o Add common-mode chokes for differential lines (USB, Ethernet, CAN).

  o Add ferrite beads on single-ended lines to suppress high-frequency noise.

- **Signal integrity**:

  o Maintain controlled impedance for USB and Ethernet; differential pair routing and matching is critical.

  o Add series resistors (22–100Ω) at drivers to dampen reflections.

- **Clock management**:

  o Keep high-frequency clocks away from sensitive analog traces.

  o Use spread-spectrum clocking if permissible and helpful to reduce peak emissions.

- **Shielding**:

  o Metal enclosure grounded to chassis ground reduces radiated emissions significantly.

  o Keep openings (vent slots) small or use RF gasket.

4.3 Practical component examples (BOM hints)

- **TVS**: SMAJ5.0A (for power), PESD5V or similar for data lines (choose standoff voltage appropriate to signal).

- **Ferrite beads**: 0603/0805 ferrite beads with appropriate impedance at target frequencies.

- **Common-mode choke**: for USB/ETH lines (e.g., 1210 common-mode choke).

- **Transient suppressor**: Gas Discharge Tube for outdoor mains.

4.4 PCB layout rules for EMI/ESD

- Keep digital and power return currents close; avoid long loops.

- Place decoupling capacitors as close as possible to device pins and route directly to ground plane via multiple vias.

- Route high-speed signals over continuous reference plane; avoid crossing splits.

- Place ESD diodes at connectors to shield internal circuits and provide a controlled discharge path.

4.5 EMC testing & certification

- Pre-compliance testing in a lab (EMI chamber; near-field probes) helps find hotspots.

- Follow standards appropriate for markets (CE/FCC/IEC). IEC 61000 series covers immunity (including ESD, EFT). Design for immunity levels appropriate to product class (consumer, industrial, automotive).

4.6 Practical pitfalls

- Putting TVS diodes far from connector defeats their purpose.

- Large copper pours under sensitive analog circuits without careful partitioning can couple noise.

- Using very low ESR ceramics for bulk capacitance without considering inrush may stress regulators — balance capacitor choice.

---

5. System-Level Reliability Techniques

Security and ESD/EMI are part of reliability; add these system techniques:

5.1 Redundancy and graceful degradation

- **Hardware redundancy**: dual sensors or dual power paths for critical systems.

- **Software graceful degradation**: if a feature fails, fall back to reduced capability and notify operator.

5.2 Health monitoring and telemetry

- Implement self-test, periodic health reports, and remote diagnostic endpoints. Use structured event logs with severity and timestamps to support field debugging.

5.3 Flash wear-leveling and corruption handling

- Avoid frequent in-place flash writes. Use EEPROM emulation with wear-leveling or external FRAM for frequent writes.

- Always write checksums/CRC and include version metadata to enable safe rollback and detection of corruption.

5.4 Power-failure safe design

- Use dedicated power-fail interrupt or ADC to measure supply; initiate safe shutdown (flush logs, mark state) when supply drops below threshold.

- Consider using a small energy reservoir (supercapacitor) sized to complete critical writes.

5.5 Production test & provisioning

- Factory programming should provision device identity, set up keys, and mark bootloader/option bytes with RDP appropriately. Use automated, secure programming stations and keep a key-management system.

6. Testing and Validation Strategies

6.1 Security testing

- **Static code analysis**: find buffer overflows and memory issues.

- **Fuzzing**: fuzz network parsers (MQTT/HTTP/USB/CAN).

- **Penetration testing**: test firmware update path, debug port access, and default credentials.

- **Side-channel & fault injection**: if high security is required, test resistance to fault injection and physical attacks.

6.2 Reliability testing

- **Burn-in**: long-term stress under elevated temperatures and operation.

- **Fault injection**: simulate sensor faults, network failures, power transients.

- **ESD/EMC pre-compliance**: ESD gun testing and near-field scans to identify emission hot spots.

- **Power cycling & Brown-out**: test power-up/power-down behavior and verify recovery.

7. Practical Recipes & Code Snippets

7.1 Simple signed-image verification pseudo with mbedTLS

```
// high-level pseudocode

uint8_t *image = load_image_from_flash(addr);

uint8_t hash[32];

mbedtls_sha256(image, image_len, hash, 0);


// load public key (from secure storage)

mbedtls_pk_context pk;

mbedtls_pk_init(&pk);

mbedtls_pk_parse_public_key(&pk, public_key_pem, public_key_len);


if (mbedtls_pk_verify(&pk, MBEDTLS_MD_SHA256, hash, sizeof(hash),
```

```
                signature, sig_len) == 0) {
```

// signature ok

} else {

 // reject

}

Use hardware crypto accelerator if present (or mbedTLS with engine driver).

7.2 IWDG example (HAL)

IWDG_HandleTypeDef hiwdg;

hiwdg.Instance = IWDG;

hiwdg.Init.Prescaler = IWDG_PRESCALER_64;

hiwdg.Init.Reload = 4095; // adjust to desired timeout

HAL_IWDG_Init(&hiwdg);

// Then in supervisor task periodically:

HAL_IWDG_Refresh(&hiwdg);

7.3 MPU guard region example (CMSIS)

- Reserve a 4KB guard just after the stack (aligned) as a no-access MPU region. If an overflow occurs, an exception triggers and the address is recorded (MMFAR/CFSR).

---

8. Checklists (Actionable)

Security checklist (deployment-ready)

- Bootloader is immutable and stored in protected area.

- Firmware images are signed (and optionally encrypted).

- Device verifies signature in bootloader before switching active image.

- Public verification keys provisioned via secure manufacturing or secure element.

- Monotonic/anti-rollback mechanism in place.

- Recovery path (USB/ST-LINK / bootloader mode) exists and tested.

- Debug interfaces protected or documented (disable in production if required).

- Option bytes and readout protection considered and tested with recovery plan.

- OTA transport uses TLS or module-level secure transport.

- Regular key rotation and revocation plan exists.

Reliability checklist

- Hardware watchdog (IWDG) enabled.

- Supervisor/task-level watchdog checks implemented.

- Proper BOR/BOD levels configured for MCU.

- Persistent logs or backup SRAM for crash diagnostics.

- ESD protection on external interfaces.

- EMI mitigation - decoupling, common-mode chokes, controlled impedance, shielding.

- Flash wear-leveling / EEPROM emulation design in place for frequent writes.

- Power-fail protection (energy reservoir or graceful shutdown) validated.

- Production test harness and burn-in test defined.

---

9. Common Pitfalls & How to Avoid Them

- **Locking yourself out with RDP**: trial on test devices and document recovery processes. For mass production, automate safe programming.

- **Assuming SDK handles security**: validate and independently verify the chain of trust and key handling.

- **Neglecting power budget for OTA**: wireless downloads can take minutes and spike currents; measure and ensure power supply handles it.

- **Incorrect MPU sizes/alignment**: plan early; misaligned MPU regions can cause subtle faults.

- **Cache/DMA coherency errors**: always manage cache around DMA operations on M7/H7-class parts or use non-cacheable regions.

Chapter 18: Migration, Scalability, and Productization — Comprehensive Guide

Shipping a product built on STM32 is more than firmware and a PCB: it requires deliberate migration planning between MCU series, scalable production programming and test fixtures, planned regulatory compliance and EMC strategy, and long-term supply-chain and support processes. This chapter gives detailed, practical, production-ready advice you can act on today: checklists, hands-on recipes, decision criteria, and traps to avoid.

1. Migrating Between STM32 Series

ADVANCED STM32 MICROCONTROLLERS

Moving from one STM32 family to another (e.g., F0 → F3 → F4 → L4 → H7 / or to STM32WB/STM32U5) is a common need: to gain performance, power efficiency, peripherals, or cost advantages. Migration touches hardware, boot/bootloader, BSP, drivers, toolchain, timing, and verification. Do it in structured phases.

1.1 High-level migration strategy

1. **Define why**: performance, memory, analog/peripheral capability, power, cost, lifecycle. Capture acceptance criteria (e.g., "application must run at 200 Hz control loop with <2% jitter").

2. **Gap analysis**: compare features (pins, ADC resolution, DAC, timers, DMA channels, USB/ETH/CAN, crypto, FPU, caches, MPU). Produce a side-by-side table.

3. **Pin & peripheral mapping**: map every used signal to new package pins and alternate functions (AF). Flag signals that lose hardware support (e.g., dedicated CAN vs bit-banged).

4. **Software abstraction**: separate HAL/LL usage from application logic into BSP or driver layers—this minimizes rewriting.

5. **Prototype & validate**: bring up clocks, GPIO, SWD, then peripherals one-by-one (USART, I²C, SPI, ADC, timers).

6. **Performance & power profiling**: verify control loop jitter, ADC acquisition times, DMA throughput, power consumption in low-power modes.

7. **Full-system regression**: run entire test suite including time-critical tests and EMI/thermal checks.

8. **Update documentation & BOM** and finalize migration.

1.2 Things that commonly change and how to handle them

Clocks & PLL

- Different series have different clock trees and PLL behavior. Recalculate PLL parameters and flash latency.

- Checklist:

  - Recompute PLL multipliers/dividers for required SYSCLK and peripheral clocks (USB needs 48 MHz domain on many parts).

  - Update SystemClock_Config() and CubeMX settings.

- Check HAL_RCC_OscConfig and flash latency ordering (set flash latency before increasing HCLK).

Pin alternate functions

- AF numbers vary between families. Use CubeMX or ST datasheets to remap.

- Strategy: create a board.h pin mapping layer and replace hard-coded GPIO_AF values with board macros.

Peripheral differences

- ADC sample timings, resolution, calibration registers, DMA channels and request mapping differ.

- Example solution: write wrapper APIs that expose the features you use (e.g., adc_read_channel()), with family-specific backends.

Clock domain doubling (timers)

- APB prescalers and timer clock doubling rules vary; always recompute timer prescalers for correct frequencies.

Caches (M7/H7)

- If migrating to a core with caches, add cache maintenance (clean/invalidate) around DMA buffers, or allocate DMA buffers to non-cacheable memory.

- Validate DMA behavior and memory barriers.

FPU and DSP

- If migrating to MCU with FPU/DSP, enable -mfloat-abi=hard and proper -mfpu flags. Benchmark and port floating math carefully; prefer double only if needed.

MPU & TrustZone

- If adding MPU/TrustZone, add memory layout changes early and test MPU faults.

Power & low-power modes

- Low-power behavior and available modes differ. Revalidate Stop/Standby behavior, wake latency, and peripheral retention.

Bootloader & option bytes

- Option bytes and system bootloaders may differ. If relying on system bootloader for factory programming, check supported interfaces and required GPIO states (BOOT pins).

1.3 Software migration checklist (practical)

- Separate platform-independent application code from board support code (BSP).

- Create a HAL-wrapper layer: bsp_gpio.h, bsp_adc.h, bsp_timer.h, etc.

- Replace direct register accesses with macros or inline functions you can re-target.

- Update startup code and linker script (new vector table address, RAM/flash sizes, section placement).

- Reconfigure interrupts and priorities in NVIC; re-evaluate preemption priorities with RTOS.

- Run static timing checks (control loop jitter) with DWT cycle counters.

- Add cache maintenance for DMA regions (if applicable).

- Re-run unit & integration tests; add new tests for new peripherals.

1.4 Hardware migration checklist

- Create pin map and verify AF conflicts.

- Verify power rails and decoupling for the new part (VDDA, VREF, VBAT).

- Validate crystal/oscillator circuits (HSE, LSE) and their load capacitors.

- Check PCB footprint differences and thermal pad requirements.

- Update BOM with package temperature rating and body material (lead-free solderability).

1.5 Example pin-mapping pattern

Use a single header file per board with symbolic names:

// board_pins.h (example)

#define LED_STATUS_PORT   GPIOA

#define LED_STATUS_PIN   GPIO_PIN_5

#define I2C_SCL_PORT   GPIOB

#define I2C_SCL_PIN   GPIO_PIN_8

// ...

Change only this file when migrating; HAL calls remain the same.

1.6 Validation & performance profiling

- Use DWT->CYCCNT to measure ISR and control-loop latency.

- Measure ADC acquisition + conversion time under new sample times and source impedance.

- Verify DMA throughput (bytes/sec) and CPU load.

- Validate low-power current in Sleep/Stop/Standby modes using real measurement.

---

2. Production Programming and Test Fixtures

Moving from prototypes to hundreds/thousands of units requires efficient programming, reliable testing, and traceable results. This section covers programmer options, fixture types, test flows, and metrics.

2.1 Production programming options

- **In-circuit programming via SWD/JTAG**:

  - Tools: ST-LINK, SEGGER J-Link, U-Link, or production programmers that support multiple targets (e.g., SEGGER Flasher Series).

- o Pros: flexible, full control, supports option bytes and debug features.

- o Cons: slower for very large volumes unless parallelized.

- **Mass programmers / gang programmers**:

    - o Use dedicated production programmers (e.g., Adafruit or commercial gang programmers) or multiple J-link pods in parallel.

    - o Many factories use clamshell fixtures with pogo pins to program and test multiple boards simultaneously.

- **Factory bootloader / DFU over USB**:

    - o If bootloader is robust, the factory can flash via USB mass-storage or DFU at high speed; avoids SWD connection points but requires a reliable bootloader.

- **One-time programming (OTP) / secure provisioning**:

    - o For programming secrets or keys into secure elements, use dedicated secure provisioning stations with audit logs.

2.2 Test fixture types

A. Bed-of-Nails (In-Circuit Test — ICT)

- Uses a PCB testbed with pogo pins to access many nets (power, signals, Vref, clocks).

- Advantages: quick electrical checks (shorts, opens, component values).

- Disadvantages: expensive fixtures, requires test pads on PCB design.

B. Flying Probe

- Uses movable probes; good for low-volume and late changes.

- Advantage: no fixture cost; disadvantage: slower than bed-of-nails.

C. Functional Test Fixture

- Minimal test pads (power, UART, SWD, IO) and connectors to exercise functionality:

    ○ Power-up test, smoke test, LED blink, UART identity, sensor checks, radio test, CAN/ETH loopback.

- Often lower cost; run custom test firmware.

D. Boundary-Scan (JTAG)

- Use JTAG chain to test PCB interconnects without physical access to nodes. Good when you have many BGA parts and minimal test pads.

E. Burn-In Fixture

- Fixtures for long-duration power cycling / thermal stress; can exercise devices for hours/days.

2.3 Recommended production test flow

1. **Visual & AOI**: Automated Optical Inspection for component placement.

2. **In-Circuit / Flying probe**: shorts/opens, passive values, power rails.

3. **Program & ID**: program bootloader + firmware, write serial number and calibration data.

4. **Functional test**: run scripted test harness to exercise key features (UART, I2C sensors, ADC, PWM, radio TX/RX, USB enumeration).

5. **Calibration**: perform sensor calibration if needed (store calibration constants).

6. **Burn-in / stress**: optional for critical products (24–72 hrs).

7. **Final test & pack**: final functional check, label, and package.

2.4 Designing the PCB for testability

- Add **SWD header** or test pads; place them in accessible location for fixtures.

- Add **programming/test pads** near connectors. Use standard pitch to simplify fixtures (e.g., 2.54 mm or 1.27 mm pogo targets).

- Expose UART TX/RX, power rails, ADC measurement points, and key analog nodes as test pads.

- Add **test points for oscillator or clock nets**.

- Consider adding a **test-mode pin**: on boot, asserts test mode (bypass timed flows or enter production test firmware).

- For RF modules, provide access to the antenna port (U.FL) or provide RF test pads.

2.5 Programming & traceability (best practice)

- Program unique identifiers (serial numbers, manufacturing date code, hardware version) and record them in a centralized database along with:

  - Firmware version (git commit hash), calibration data, test logs and pass/fail.

- Use signed firmware images and store their digest to ensure traceability.

- Provide labels / 2D barcodes with serialized data to print on PCB or product sticker.

2.6 Test automation & software

- Use a **test controller** (PC or embedded Linux like Raspberry Pi) that:

  - Controls power switching,

  - Programs device (via ST-LINK CLI or SEGGER Flasher CLI),

  - Runs functional test scripts (expect/serial),

  - Saves logs and test results (CSV/SQL),

  - Prints labels on pass.

- Provide a **recovery path** in test software to handle intermittent failures (e.g., reflash, power cycle, rerun a test).

2.7 Production metrics to track

- **Yield (%)**: units passing final test / total units assembled.

- **First-pass yield (FPY)**: important for process control.

- **Failure modes**: categorize failures (assembly, component, design, firmware).

- **MTBF/field returns**: track returns after shipping.

---

3. Certification and Compliance (CE, FCC, EMC)

Regulatory compliance is a project-level activity—plan it early because test labs, redesigns and documentation take time and money.

3.1 What to plan for

- **Electromagnetic Compatibility (EMC)**:

  - Radiated emissions (measure in range 30 MHz–1 GHz or higher depending on product).

  - Conducted emissions (on power lines).

  - Immunity/EMS tests: ESD, EFT (fast transients), surge, conducted immunity, voltage dips.

- **Radio approvals** (if product has RF: Wi-Fi, BT, cellular, LoRa):

  - FCC (USA), IC (Canada), RED (EU), MIC (Japan), regulatory per-country.

  - Modules vs fully-integrated radios: using a pre-certified radio module reduces certification scope (modular approval), but you still must do EMC and integration testing.

- **Safety & product-specific**: UL/IEC safety standards for mains-powered or battery-powered devices.

- **Environmental & transport**: battery shipping rules (IATA), RoHS, REACH, WEEE in EU.

3.2 EMC pre-compliance (do this before full test)

- Run pre-compliance scans in-house with near-field probes and a spectrum analyzer.

- Key early tests:

  - Measure radiated emissions (near-field) to find hotspots.

- Check power-rail conducted emissions with LISN or simulated measures.

- ESD bench checks (gun) on external connectors.

- Fix items in the lab: improper grounding, noisy switching regulators, high-speed traces, and box/connector emissions.

3.3 EMC mitigation checklist

- **Layout**:

  - Solid ground plane under digital sections.

  - Short loops for high-current traces.

  - Proper decoupling — 0.1 µF + 1 µF + bulk ceramic per regulator.

- **Filtering**:

  - Ferrite beads on power inputs,

  - Common-mode choke on USB/Ethernet,

  - Pi filters on DC input.

- **Termination**:

  - Series resistors on high-speed signal drivers to damp reflections.

- **Shielding**:

  - Metal enclosure or grounded EMI gasket for sensitive circuits.

- **Clock management**:

  - Use spread-spectrum clocking where acceptable; keep crystal traces short.

3.4 Radio approvals tips

- Use **pre-certified radio modules** to reduce scope. Still:

- ○ Do **RF integration tests**: antenna placement, ground plane, cable routing, and enclosure effects.

- ○ Measure transmitter power and spurious emissions in final enclosure with intended antenna.

- Antenna change or enclosure change can invalidate modular approvals — re-test integration.

3.5 Product documentation for certification

- Test reports (pre-compliance and full compliance),

- Schematics and BOM,

- Board layout (top/bottom CAD),

- User manual and marking labels,

- RF test report if wireless,

- Declaration of Conformity and technical file (for CE/RED).

3.6 Typical certification timeline & budget

- Pre-compliance & fixes: 1–3 weeks per iteration.

- Full lab testing: 1–2 weeks (booked slot in accredited lab).

- If failures occur and board redesign is needed, add PCB respin time (~2–4 weeks).

- Budget varies enormously: a single-lab test run might be several thousand dollars; full global radio approvals can run much higher.

4. Long-Term Support and Supply Chain Considerations

A product is judged by field reliability, availability of spares, and your ability to service it over years. Plan policies and processes for long-term success.

4.1 Component selection & lifecycle management

- **Preferred vendors & second sources**: for every critical component, identify at least one alternative with compatible footprint and electrical characteristics.

- **Lifecycle status checks**: monitor vendor obsolescence notices and EoL alerts (set up alerts via distributors).

- **Design for component substitution**:

  - Use common footprints,

  - Document parametric tolerances that allow substitute parts,

  - Avoid single-source, obscure parts for critical functions where possible.

- **Last Time Buy (LTB)**: plan and budget LTB orders for components expected to be discontinued before you can redesign.

4.2 Procurement & inventory strategies

- **Safety stock**: keep buffer inventory proportionate to lead times and forecast uncertainty.

- **Consignment / vendor-managed inventory (VMI)** for large-volume production.

- **Long-term agreements** with suppliers for preferred pricing and allocation priority.

- **Multi-sourcing** and geographic diversification to hedge supply chain disruptions.

4.3 Manufacturing partners & CM selection

- Evaluate contract manufacturers (CM) for:

  - Technical capability (BGA, microassembly, RF assembly),

  - Certifications (ISO 9001, IPC standards),

  - Test & automation capability (ICT, AOI, X-ray, functional test),

  - Logistical reach, MOQ and lead times,

  - Quality metrics and warranty support.

- Start with a pilot run to verify DFM/DFA and establish yield baselines.

4.4 Quality control & incoming inspection

- **Incoming inspection**: verify Lot/Date code, perform sample testing for critical components.

- **AQL**: define acceptance quality limits for incoming boards and assembled units.

- **Serial tracking & traceability**: track batches, firmware versions, test logs and repairs.

- Use **barcoding / serialization** for traceability to support recalls and RMA.

4.5 Firmware maintenance & security updates

- Define a **software maintenance policy**:

  - Supported versions and update windows (e.g., 3 years critical patches, 5 years bug fixes).

  - Security policy for vulnerability handling and communication with customers.

- Implement secure OTA (signed updates), secure boot, and device attestation.

- Keep a public vulnerability disclosure process and SLA for patches.

4.6 Field support, RMA & repair

- Provide **field diagnostics**: logs, crash dumps, device health telemetry.

- Build repair repeatability: service manuals, calibrated test fixtures for repair shops, spare parts lists.

- Track returns and failure modes to feed back into product improvements.

4.7 Environmental & regulatory continuity

- Plan for RoHS, REACH updates, battery regulations and shipping constraints.

- Keep documentation of conformity for long-term sales and audits.

5. Scaling from Prototype to Volume — Practical Roadmap

A condensed, actionable roadmap:

1. **Prototype Stage**

   - Breadboard/dev boards, rapid PCB revs, manual programming/debugging.

   - Focus: core functionality and technical risks.

2. **Pre-Production (Pilot)**

   - Freeze schematic and mechanical variant; produce 50–200 units with professional PCB assembly.

   - Add test pads and instrumentation hooks.

   - Validate manufacturing processes and DFM issues.

   - Run full functional and EMC pre-compliance tests.

3. **Certification & Compliance**

   - Execute formal pre-compliance fixes and send for full lab certification.

   - Finalize enclosure and labeling for regulatory submissions.

4. **Pilot Production**

   - 500–2,000 units: finalize production fixtures, program tooling, automated test suites, burn-in procedures.

   - Establish supply contracts and initial inventories.

5. **Volume Production**

   - Ongoing supplier monitoring, KPIs (yield, throughput), product support and continuous improvement cycles.

6. **Sustaining & End-of-Life**

   - Plan LTB, transition plan to next-generation device, and maintain critical spare inventory.

6. Checklists and Templates

Migration Gate Criteria

- Pin mapping complete, conflicts resolved.

- BSP abstraction layer implemented and tested.

- Clock and PLL validated at target frequencies.

- DMA and cache coherency verified.

- Performance targets met (latency, throughput).

- Power modes measured and within budget.

- Full regression tests passed.

Production Release Gate Criteria

- Prototype PCBs pass DFM and thermal checks.

- Manufacturing test fixture validated (ICT/functional).

- Firmware build reproducible and signed.

- Serial/programming/labeling scripts ready and tested.

- EO/QA test plan documented with pass/fail criteria.

- Certification plan booked and pre-compliance checked.

- Supply chain and second-source plan in place.

Certification Pre-flight Checklist

- EMC pre-scan done; hotspots identified and mitigated.

- Enclosure RF behavior verified for wireless products.

- Power supply and conducted emissions measured.

- ESD basic immunity tested on external connectors.

- All user documents prepared (manuals, warnings).

Supply Chain Risk Matrix (example fields)

- Component | Criticality | Primary vendor | Secondary vendor | Lead time | MOQ | Last time buy risk

---

7. Common Pitfalls & How to Avoid Them

- **Underestimating certification time** — build time for re-spins and EMC fixes into your schedule.

- **Late DFM changes** — add test pads and SWD early; changing them later is costly.

- **No second source for critical parts** — identify alternates early and validate footprints.

- **Tight coupling of app and hardware** — keep application code portable with BSP/abstraction layers.

- **Neglecting test automation** — manual testing won't scale; invest in automated fixtures early.

- **Not tracking firmware with hardware** — always log firmware git hash and build ID into production units.

Chapter 19: Future Trends for STM32 & Embedded Systems — Extensive, Forward-Looking Survey

Below is a comprehensive, practice-oriented view of where embedded systems (and the STM32 ecosystem in particular) are headed over the next 3–10 years. I cover hardware, software, security, connectivity, power & sensors, tooling and workflows, market/industry shifts, and practical advice you can use today to future-proof designs and teams.

1. Hardware: the era of heterogeneous, specialized microcontrollers

Edge AI & tinyML accelerators on MCUs

MCUs are evolving from simple control engines into mixed-function SoCs that fuse real-time control with on-device inference. Vendors (including ST) are shipping MCUs with integrated NPUs/accelerators and toolchains that let you compile neural networks into efficient runtime kernels and run sensor-fusion or vision workloads with low latency and low power. Expect more energy-efficient purpose-built blocks (tiny NPUs, SIMD engines, dedicated convolution engines) in mid-range MCUs so applications such as always-on anomaly detection, keyword spotting, and local vision become standard. (STMicroelectronics, Edge AI and Vision Alliance)

Neuromorphic and event-driven sensing

Beyond standard neural accelerators, event-driven and neuromorphic chips (spiking neural network architectures) are moving from research into niche commercial products for ultra-low-power always-on sensing (audio, vision, vibration) where conventional sampling would be too costly. These allow processing only when events occur, enabling very long battery life for "smart-sensor" applications. Watch for ecosystem toolkits that map conventional models or rule engines to these new chips. (Tom's Guide)

Heterogeneous cores, chiplets, and on-chip accelerators

Multi-core MCUs with mixed-role cores (high-efficiency M-class core + high-performance M-class core + secure/real-time core) will proliferate for workloads that require hardened isolation (secure tasks, network stacks, inference). Chiplet packaging and modular IP will let vendors mix and match accelerators (crypto, ML, DSP) tuned for market segments (industrial, medical, consumer).

RISC-V presence alongside ARM

ARM Cortex-M will continue to dominate many embedded segments for a while, but RISC-V is accelerating its momentum — broadening the options for MCU designers and giving OEMs new supply options and license flexibility. Expect more RISC-V MCUs and hybrid platforms (ARM-based MCUs with RISC-V accelerators, or vice versa) — this affects toolchains, low-level libraries, and long-term porting plans. (MarketsandMarkets, RISC-V International)

---

2. Software and tooling: model-centric, reproducible, and multi-language stacks

TinyML, model compilers, and deployment pipelines

TinyML toolchains (TensorFlow Lite for Micro, vendor compilers like STM32Cube.AI) will be standard parts of firmware buildchains. Expect model-aware CI (automated quantization/validation), model regression testing, and standardized artifacts (quantized weights + metadata) that are versioned alongside firmware. Build pipelines will include model accuracy checks, latency/power profiling, and fallback strategies when a model fails in the field. (edgeir.com, ScienceDirect)

Higher-level languages & safer systems (Rust, safer C/C++ idioms)

Safety, concurrency, and security concerns will push more teams to evaluate Rust (or safer subsets/tools for C) for critical components (drivers, comms stacks, crypto layers). Expect mixed-language projects — low-level board bring-up in C, higher-level logic or safety-critical modules in Rust — with better FFI patterns and CI flows that compile and test across the language boundary.

Cloud-native development patterns on the edge

Edge devices will be part of "cloud-native" development cycles: container-like packaging of functionality (on capable devices), remote simulation, and full CI pipelines that include hardware-in-the-loop tests. Device SDKs will more often expose telemetry, logs and manifests that integrate with cloud toolchains for validation, OTA, and analytics.

Formal verification & model-based engineering (in high-assurance domains)

For safety-critical domains (automotive, medical), more formal methods, model-based design, and static provers will be adopted for critical subsystems. Tool support and integration into CI will broaden, making some formal verification practices a standard part of release requirements.

---

3. Connectivity & standards: interoperability and deterministic networking

Matter, Thread, and the rise of unified smart-home stacks

Matter (IP-based interoperability over Thread and Wi-Fi, provisioning over BLE) is maturing and will push module vendors and MCU ecosystems to provide turnkey stacks and sample applications for Matter endpoints and border routers. For IoT product designers, Matter reduces integration work for smart-home interoperability while increasing expectations around security and OTA support. (WIRED, CSA-IOT)

Low-power wide-area & advanced Wi-Fi / BLE

Expect continued evolution of wireless: BLE audio & LE Isochronous features, Wi-Fi 6/6E optimizations for IoT, and broader adoption of LPWAN variants where range and power matter. Coexistence (BLE + Wi-Fi) and multi-protocol SoCs will become common to cover multiple deployment scenarios.

Deterministic Ethernet / TSN in industrial IoT

Time-Sensitive Networking (TSN) and deterministic Ethernet will become more available in embedded platforms as industrial systems demand synchronized, deterministic comms for motion control and robotics. MCUs and SoCs will offer hardware offloads and driver stacks tailored for TSN.

---

4. Security: hardware roots, certified components, and secure lifecycle

Hardware Root of Trust (RoT) and certifications

Products will increasingly rely on a combined RoT approach: secure enclaves/TEE, discrete secure elements, and signed boot chains. Industry certification programs (PSA Certified, GlobalPlatform) will be used not only by high-security sectors but as market differentiators for consumer and industrial products. Expect vendors to ship certified RoT or provide easy-to-integrate secure elements for keys, counters, and attestation. (psacertified.org)

Secure update and attestation by default

Secure Firmware Update (signed + versioned + rollback protection) will be table stakes. Devices will increasingly support cryptographic attestation (prove identity & state to backend) and supply-chain-backed provisioning techniques. Bootloader design patterns (A/B banks, staged install) will be formalized across OEMs and toolchains.

Security tooling maturation

Automated firmware scanning, SBOMs (Software Bill of Materials), signed images, HSM-backed signing services, and vulnerability disclosure processes will be integrated into product life cycles. Vendors like ST are extending educational content and tooling (STM32Trust and similar) to help teams adopt hardened flows. (ST life.augmented Blog)

---

5. Power & sensing: extreme low power, always-on intelligence, and energy harvesting

Always-on sensing + event-driven processing

Combining ultra-low-power front-end sensors and low-energy wake-up processors (or neuromorphic sensors) will let devices monitor environment continuously and wake the main compute only on relevant events. This pattern substantially extends battery life for environmental sensors, security, and wearables.

Energy harvesting and power-adaptive software

Energy harvesting (solar, vibration, RF) will become viable for many sensor use-cases. Firmware will be designed to adapt to available energy levels (graceful degradation, opportunistic processing, duty-cycle tuning), supported by energy-awareness APIs and runtime policies.

---

6. Manufacturing, productization & modularization

Certified modules & reference stacks win time-to-market

Using pre-certified wireless/secure modules and validated reference designs will remain a rapid path to market — reducing certification scope for RF and security while letting OEMs focus on product differentiation.

Production automation, digital twins & lifecycle analytics

Manufacturers will further automate programming, test, and calibration (fixtures that report to the cloud), creating digital twins that map deployed device fleets to manufacturing metadata and firmware versions. This improves troubleshooting, recalls, and targeted updates.

---

7. Industry trends: RISC-V, open hardware, and geopolitics

Diverse supply & architecture choice

Geopolitical factors and desire for architectural sovereignty are accelerating RISC-V momentum in some markets. Expect a broader ecosystem of RISC-V silicon and tooling; ARM-based platforms will remain strong, so multi-architecture readiness is a sensible strategy. (MarketsandMarkets, RISC-V International)

Open-source IP & community ecosystems

Open IP, open toolchains, and larger community ecosystems will create more optionality for startups and established vendors — but commercial-grade support and long-term maintenance contracts will still be decisive in production choices.

---

8. Development workflows & DevOps for embedded

Model- and data-centric CI/CD

CI pipelines will include ML model validation, hardware-in-loop tests, and automated certification checks (static analysis, safety checks). Build artifacts will include models, SBOMs, and reproducible images. OTA pipelines will be auditable and signed end-to-end.

Hardware abstractions & portability

Teams will invest in clean BSP/driver layers and portability targets so code can be recompiled across vendor MCUs or even RISC-V cores with minimal logic changes — reducing migration cost as silicon choices evolve.

Observability and remote diagnostics

Devices will ship with structured observability: compact telemetry that supports remote debugging, crash-symbol sending (when privacy/perf allows), and rollback-safe update policies.

9. Markets, business models, and sustainability

Feature-as-a-service and subscription models

As remote management and analytics improve, expect more devices to be sold with recurring services (feature unlocks, analytics). This affects product design (OTA, license keys, secure attestation).

Environmental and lifecycle responsibilities

Design for reparability, parts reuse, recyclable packaging, and energy efficiency will be regulatory and market expectations. Devices will carry richer lifecycle metadata (materials, disposal guidelines, software status).

10. Practical takeaways — what engineers and product teams should do now

1. **Invest in edge-AI skills and toolchains.** Learn TinyML workflows, quantization, and vendor compilers (e.g., STM32Cube.AI). Integrate model tests into CI. (edgeir.com, ScienceDirect)

2. **Plan for security by design.** Add secure boot, signed updates, and consider secure elements / PSA certification early — not as an afterthought. (psacertified.org, ST life.augmented Blog)

3. **Design portable software stacks.** Abstract board support, keep application logic hardware-agnostic, and prepare for multi-architecture builds (ARM + RISC-V). (RISC-V International, MarketsandMarkets)

4. **Emphasize low-power architecture patterns.** Use event-driven sensors, duty-cycle radios, and power-adaptive firmware. Evaluate neuromorphic or always-on sensor options for extreme budgets. (Tom's Guide)

5. **Adopt modular hardware strategy.** Use pre-certified modules for radios and secure elements if you want faster time-to-market and smaller certification scope. (CSA-IOT)

6. **Upgrade your CI to include model & security checks.** Automate model-size/accuracy regression, firmware signing, SBOM generation and automated static analysis in every merge.

11. Risks and open questions

- **Fragmentation risk:** multiple connectivity standards, architectures (ARM vs RISC-V), and ML runtimes may fragment tooling and increase porting cost.

- **Supply & certification friction:** RF/enclosure changes still cause re-certification; modular strategies mitigate but don't eliminate this.

- **Security arms race:** with more capable edge devices, attackers gain incentives — secure provisioning and rapid-patch flows are mandatory.

- **Ethical & privacy constraints:** on-device AI shifts capabilities but also raises questions about data local processing, consent, and model explainability.

12. Further reading & resources (short list)

- ST's Edge AI overview and STM32Cube.AI (ST website). (STMicroelectronics, edgeir.com)

- RISC-V community and market analyses (RISC-V Foundation summaries and market reports). (RISC-V International, MarketsandMarkets)

- Matter spec and CSA resources for smart-home interoperability. (CSA-IOT, WIRED)

- PSA Certified background and secure element guidance. (psacertified.org)

- TinyML and neuromorphic surveys for low-power AI research & reviews. (ScienceDirect, Tom's Guide)

Final note

The next 3–10 years in embedded systems will be characterized by **specialized hardware**, **on-device intelligence**, **stronger security expectations**, and **tighter integration between cloud and edge**. For STM32-based teams, the pragmatic path is to adopt modular hardware, secure-by-design processes, model-aware CI, and portable BSPs so you can upgrade silicon, add tinyML features, and respond quickly to certification or supply-chain changes.

Bonus Chapter 1: STM32 Project Examples — Extensive & Actionable

Below are 15 practical project blueprints you can build with STM32 microcontrollers. Each entry includes clear goals, hardware choices, software architecture, critical implementation notes and code patterns, testing advice, BOM/PCB tips, power and safety considerations, extension ideas, and a difficulty/prerequisite tag so you can pick what suits you. Use these as templates — adapt MCU family and parts to your constraints.

1. Blinky → Robust Platform Bring-Up & Power Measurement

Goal: Minimal first project that proves board power, clock, debug, and basic I/O; measure real power in run/sleep modes.
Hardware: Any STM32 Nucleo/Discovery or custom board; LED, current sense resistor (0.1–1Ω), SWD header.
Software architecture: Tiny firmware that toggles LED, serves simple UART command set (identify, read VBUS, enter sleep), supports IWDG.
Key implementation notes:

- Configure system clock, GPIO, UART, and IWDG.

- Implement SHELL command sleep to exercise Stop/Standby modes.

- Use DWT->CYCCNT for cycle timing.
  Code pattern (LED + UART):

```
HAL_GPIO_TogglePin(LED_PORT, LED_PIN);

HAL_Delay(250);
```

Testing & validation: Verify SWD connect, UART prints, LED blink; measure current in run vs sleep; verify watchdog reset path.
BOM/PCB notes: Expose SWD, VBUS sense, and current-sense pads. Use decoupling near MCU.
Power & safety: Ensure sense resistor power rating; power-calc when measuring.
Extensions: Add ADC measurement for VDD, add tiny telemetry over UART.
Difficulty: Beginner.
Acceptance criteria: Device blinks, UART responds, current measured and documented.

---

2. Serial Bootloader & Firmware Update (UART/DFU)

Goal: Implement a robust serial bootloader supporting frame-chunked updates, CRC and resume.
Hardware: STM32 with SWD header, USB-UART adapter or direct UART header.

Software architecture: Minimal immutable bootloader (small flash sector), application bank with metadata (version, CRC, signature placeholder). Bootloader responsibilities: enter DFU mode, write image to flash with atomic commit, validate CRC, jump to app.

Key implementation notes:

- Use HAL flash APIs (HAL_FLASH_Program), erase sectors in batches, write verification after each block.

- Keep bootloader in a protected flash area and use option bytes to protect if required.

- Metadata layout: 32-bit magic, version, length, CRC32, status flags.
  Code pattern:

```
if (verify_crc(img_addr, length, crc)) { mark_valid(img_addr); jump_to(img_addr); }
```

Testing & validation: Simulate interrupted transfer and resume flows; intentional corrupted block should be rejected; test reset/rollback behavior.
BOM/PCB notes: Boot pins accessible in hardware to force system-boot if needed.
Security: For production, add signature verification (ECDSA) and signed manifests.
Difficulty: Intermediate.
Acceptance criteria: Image can be reliably uploaded, resumed across disconnects, verified, and booted.

---

3. USB HID Keyboard & Mouse Emulation

Goal: Emulate a standard USB HID keyboard/mouse using STM32 USB device peripheral.
Hardware: STM32 with USB FS (e.g., F4, L4); USB connector with ESD protection, VBUS sense.
Software architecture: STM32CubeMX generated USB Device stack with HID class; application layer maps input (buttons/encoders) to HID reports; optional composite descriptors for multi-interface.
Key implementation notes:

- Prepare proper HID report descriptor.

- Use USBD_HID_SendReport() for IN reports; ensure to send "release" report after press.
  Code snippet (keyboard):

```
uint8_t rpt[8] = {0};

rpt[2] = HID_KEY_A; // 'a'
```

USBD_HID_SendReport(&hUsbDeviceFS, rpt, 8);

Testing & validation: Enumerate on Windows/Linux/macOS; confirm lsusb and Device Manager show HID device; verify keypresses and releases.

BOM/PCB notes: Route USB D+/D− as a differential pair, add ESD and series terminations.

Extensions: NKRO, media keys, macro layers, BLE HID (STM32WB).

Difficulty: Intermediate.

4. LED Matrix Controller (multiplexed & addressable)

Goal: Drive a medium-sized RGB/mono matrix with smooth animations, brightness control, and DMA offload.

Hardware: STM32 (F3/F4/H7 recommended), MOSFET row drivers, shift registers or LED drivers (TLC5940) or addressable strips (WS2812/APA102), high-current power supply.

Software architecture: Framebuffer in RAM, DMA-driven SPI or PWM to produce bit patterns; animation task updates back buffer. Use double-buffering to prevent tearing.

Key implementation notes:

- For WS2812: encode 24-bit color into PWM timing and use TIM + DMA.

- For APA102: simple SPI+DMA streaming with start/end frames.
  Code pattern (APA102):

HAL_SPI_Transmit_DMA(&hspi, frame_buf, frame_len);

Testing & validation: Validate timing on scope; load test full-white current; thermal checks.

BOM/PCB notes: Adequate traces, current distribution copper pours, MOSFET heat dissipation.

Power & safety: Current-limited supply and proper fusing; measure inrush and provide bulk caps.

Difficulty: Intermediate → Advanced.

Acceptance criteria: Flicker-free display, animation smooth at target FPS, power/thermal within design.

5. Sensor Data Logger with SD Card & FATFS

Goal: Sample sensors and write robust timestamped logs to SD card with safe shutdown handling.

Hardware: STM32 with SDMMC or SPI; SD card socket; RTC with backup; sensors (IMU/BME280); optional supply monitor.

Software architecture: Data acquisition via DMA (ADC/I2C), circular buffer, writer thread that flushes blocks to FATFS in 512B sectors, periodic f_sync(). Use watchdog and power-fail detection to flush buffers.

Key implementation notes:

- Use SDMMC for high throughput; SPI mode for simplicity.

- Batch writes to minimize wear and ensure sector-aligned writes.

- For power failure, compute required energy to finish flush and size a capacitor accordingly or call f_sync() more frequently under low-power risk.
  Code snippet (flush):

```
UINT bw;

f_write(&file, buf, buf_len, &bw);

f_sync(&file);
```

Testing & validation: Force power removal during writes and validate filesystem resilience; check log ordering and CRC.

BOM/PCB notes: Card detect pin; ESD diodes; series resistors on SD data lines.

Difficulty: Intermediate.

Extensions: Compression, encryption, circular log rotation, USB mass storage access.

---

6. IoT Node — MQTT over Wi-Fi (with module)

Goal: Send sensor telemetry reliably to cloud using MQTT; support OTA.

Hardware: STM32 + Wi-Fi module (ESP32/ESP8266 in AT mode or certified module), sensors, battery/regulator.

Software architecture: Tasks: network_task handles module & MQTT state machine, sensor_task collects and queues samples, ota_task handles updates. Use TLS via module or offload to module if MCU lacks capacity.

Key implementation notes:

- Implement message queuing with persistence on SD or FRAM for connectivity loss.

- Use LWT for presence; implement exponential backoff reconnect.

- For OTA, implement signed A/B firmware or staged downloads.
  Testing & validation: Verify MQTT QoS 0/1/2 behavior, reconnect behavior, message duplication handling.
  Power & safety: Wi-Fi is power hungry — use sleep strategies, batch transmissions.
  Difficulty: Intermediate.
  Extensions: Edge processing (thresholding), MQTT-SN over low-power networks.
  Acceptance criteria: Device connects/reconnects, sends telemetry reliably, OTA test success.

7. BLE Peripheral — GATT Sensor & Control

Goal: Implement BLE peripheral exposing sensor data and remote control points (GATT).
Hardware: STM32WB (native BLE) or STM32 + BLE module; sensors.
Software architecture: Use vendor BLE stack (STM32WB uses M0 coprocessor). Define custom or standard services (Battery, Environmental Sensing, Device Info). Implement pairing, bonding, and secure GATT operations.

Key implementation notes:

- Advertise with proper intervals and connectable flags.

- Persist bonds in flash/backup domain; handle reconnection gracefully.
  Testing & validation: Pair with phone apps (nRF Connect), test MTU, throughput (notify/indicate). Verify connection parameters and privacy features.
  Security: Use LE Secure Connections, enforce bonding and encryption.
  Difficulty: Intermediate.
  Extensions: OTA via BLE DFU, BLE Mesh support.

8. CAN Bus Data Logger / Gateway

Goal: Interface with vehicle or industrial CAN bus, log messages, and optionally forward selected frames to USB/Ethernet.

Hardware: STM32 with CAN peripheral (F4/L4/H7), CAN transceiver, termination resistors, SD card or Ethernet connector.

Software architecture: Configure CAN filters to accept desired IDs; use FIFO and interrupt or DMA for RX; store logs on SD or forward via a higher-level protocol. Provide time stamping (RTC) and optional decoding (DLC parsing/DBC file mapping).

Key implementation notes:

- Use hardware acceptance filters to reduce CPU load.

- Provide galvanic isolation on CAN transceiver if needed.
  Testing & validation: Use CAN bus analyzer (PCAN) to inject and sniff frames; validate timing and lost-frame statistics.
  BOM/PCB notes: Transceiver selection (e.g., SN65HVD230), termination jumpers, TVS on CAN_H/L.
  Difficulty: Intermediate → Advanced.
  Extensions: Implement CANopen, J1939, or gateway to MQTT.
  Acceptance criteria: Correct frame capture, timestamping, and reliable long-term logging.

---

9. Motor Controller — DC & Stepper (Closed-loop)

Goal: Control DC or stepper motors with encoder feedback, safety limits, and smooth motion profiles.

Hardware: STM32 with advanced timers, MOSFET H-bridge or stepper driver (DRV8825), quadrature encoder, current sense amplifier.

Software architecture: High-priority control loop (timer ISR) reads encoder, computes PID, outputs PWM; lower-priority tasks handle comms and telemetry. Implement acceleration profiles and current limiting.

Key implementation notes:

- Sample current synchronized to PWM using ADC triggered by timer.

- Use encoder interface on timers for accurate position/speed.
  Testing & validation: Step response tests, step/settle time, track error under load. Safety tests: overcurrent, emergency stop.
  BOM/PCB notes: Gate drivers near MOSFETs, large copper and decoupling for motor supply, sense resistor placement.
  Difficulty: Advanced.
  Extensions: Add CAN control, trajectory planning, auto-tuning PID.
  Acceptance criteria: Motor follows commanded velocity/position within specified error and safe shutdown on fault.

10. Field-Oriented Control (FOC) for BLDC

Goal: Implement high-efficiency BLDC control using FOC with current control and position feedback (encoder/HALL).
Hardware: STM32 with FPU/DSP (M4F/M7), advanced timers with complementary outputs and dead-time, three-phase inverter and current sensing.
Software architecture: Real-time FOC pipeline: Clarke/Park transforms, PI current regulators, space vector PWM generation. Use fast loops (<=1 kHz current loop depending on motor).
Key implementation notes:

- Synchronize ADC to PWM for current sampling at safe points.

- Use floating-point math and CMSIS-DSP or hand-optimized fixed-point on constrained MCUs.
  Testing & validation: Motor characterization (phase resistance/inductance), d/q current step response, thermal checks.
  Safety: Disable outputs on fault, watchdog, hardware cutoff.
  Difficulty: Expert.
  Extensions: Sensorless FOC, torque control, regenerative braking.
  Acceptance criteria: Smooth torque control, stable under load, no dangerous oscillations.

---

11. IMU-based Attitude Estimation (AHRS)

Goal: Build a robust attitude estimator (roll/pitch/yaw) from accelerometer, gyroscope, magnetometer using sensor fusion.
Hardware: STM32 with I²C/SPI IMU (MPU6000/9250, ICM-20948), optional barometer and GPS.
Software architecture: Sensor acquisition task (DMA/interrupt), filtering and fusion algorithm (Madgwick, Mahony, or Kalman), output to control or logging tasks. Consider offloading to DSP/FPU.
Key implementation notes:

- Calibrate accelerometer bias, gyroscope bias, and magnetometer hard/soft iron.

- Use sensor timestamps to handle variable sampling intervals.
  Code snippet (Madgwick call):

```
MadgwickAHRSupdate(gx,gy,gz, ax,ay,az, mx,my,mz);
```

Testing & validation: Static test (level), spin test to check drift, compare to reference IMU/optical tracker.

Difficulty: Intermediate → Advanced.

Extensions: Integrate with motor control or drone flight controller.

Acceptance criteria: Attitude stable, drift within spec after bias compensation.

---

12. Audio Capture & Playback (I²S + Codec)

Goal: Record and play audio with STM32 using I²S and external codec or PDM mic, implement effects or compression.

Hardware: STM32 with I²S or SAI, CODEC (e.g., WM8731) or I²S microphone, SD card for storage, headphone amp.

Software architecture: Use DMA for continuous audio streaming to/from buffers, implement ring buffer, possibly use CMSIS-DSP for FFT/effects, use FATFS for file storage.

Key implementation notes:

- Use double buffers and DMA interrupts to process blocks in real time.

- Ensure audio clocks/stability and avoid jitter (use PLL and MCLK as required).
  Testing & validation: Measure latency, SNR, distortion; verify file compatibility (WAV 16-bit PCM) and playback integrity.
  BOM/PCB notes: Analog layout hygiene, decoupling, ground islands, audio jacks and ESD.
  Difficulty: Intermediate → Advanced.
  Extensions: Implement voice activity detection, compression (ADPCM), Bluetooth audio sink.
  Acceptance criteria: Clean capture/playback at target sample rate and latency.

---

13. Touch Interface + GUI (TFT + LVGL)

Goal: Build interactive UI with touchscreen, menus, and graphics using LittlevGL (LVGL).

Hardware: STM32 with enough RAM (ideally >64KB framebuffer), TFT display (SPI or parallel) and resistive/capacitive touch controller (XPT2046 or FT5406).

Software architecture: LVGL as UI layer, display driver using DMA SPI or FMC, input driver for touch sampling and debouncing. Use two layers if hardware supports.

Key implementation notes:

- Use GPU/accelerated features where available, minimize redraws for responsiveness.

- Place framebuffer in fast RAM region (DTCM/CCM) as required.
  Testing & validation: Touch accuracy, hysteresis, ghost touch tests, UI responsiveness under load.
  BOM/PCB notes: Proper connector for display, route parallel bus with impedance control if used.
  Difficulty: Intermediate.
  Extensions: Add animations, multi-language, firmware update via UI.
  Acceptance criteria: Responsive UI, accurate touch, no missed events.

14. TinyML Edge Inference (Keyword Spotting / Anomaly Detection)

Goal: Run a quantized ML model on-device (wake-word detection, anomaly detection), integrate with sensor pipeline and low-power wake strategy.
Hardware: STM32 with enough flash/RAM and optional NPU (STM32H7, U5, or Cube.AI-targeted MCU). Low-power always-on front-end recommended.
Software architecture: Preprocess signal (MFCC, feature extraction), run TFLite-Micro model or vendor runtime (Cube.AI), post-process results and trigger actions. Integrate model as artifact in firmware with version metadata.
Key implementation notes:

- Quantize model to int8 for smallest RAM; profile memory and latency on target hardware.

- Use interrupt-driven or event-based wake chain to reduce average power (run full model only when front-end flag triggers).
  Testing & validation: Validate model accuracy on edge dataset (not just training/test), run on-device inference and measure latency/power.
  BOM/PCB notes: Microphone front-end layout and analog filtering; shield analog traces.
  Difficulty: Advanced (ML + embedded).
  Extensions: On-device continuous learning, federated updates, streaming inference.
  Acceptance criteria: Model meets accuracy and latency targets on device under real-world conditions.

15. Industrial Data Acquisition & Protocol Gateway (Modbus, EtherCAT)

Goal: Aggregate sensor/actuator data and expose it over industrial protocols (Modbus RTU/TCP, EtherCAT) with deterministic timing and reliability.

Hardware: STM32 with Ethernet MAC (F7/H7 families) and optional EtherCAT slave controller, galvanic isolation, RS485 transceivers for Modbus.

Software architecture: Real-time acquisition task, protocol stack tasks (FreeRTOS + lwIP/MODBUS), ring buffers for deterministic sampling, priority-aware scheduling. Use hardware timers for deterministic sampling and timestamping.

Key implementation notes:

- Implement jitter-bounded sampling using timers and DMA.

- For industrial reliability, add watchdogs, redundancy where needed, and NVRAM for configuration.

  Testing & validation: Conformance to Modbus specs; latency/jitter tests for bus cycles; interoperability with SCADA or PLC. EMC immunity testing is important for industrial environments.

  BOM/PCB notes: Robust connectors, isolation barriers, surge protection, and industrial-grade components.

  Difficulty: Advanced → Expert.

  Extensions: Add MQTT/OPC-UA gateway, secure TLS-connectivity to cloud, redundancy cluster features.

  Acceptance criteria: Reliable deterministic acquisition and correct protocol responses under load and fault conditions.

Final Notes: Choosing & Scaling Projects

- **Pick depending on learning goals:** Start with 1–3 (Blinky, Bootloader, USB HID) for fundamentals; progress to 4–9 for real-world interfacing; 10–15 are advanced domain projects (control, ML, industrial).

- **Reuse building blocks:** HAL/LL BSP layers, DMA patterns, logging, OTA, and test harness code should be shared across projects to accelerate development.

- **Testing & CI:** For any project, create unit tests (host-run) and on-device smoke tests that can be automated in production. Log git commit hashes into firmware for traceability.

- **Safety & security by default:** Design watchdogs, fail-safes, secure boot/updates, and ESD/EMI mitigation from the start — retrofitting is expensive.

- **Documentation:** For each project maintain README, architecture diagram, BOM, and bring-up checklist.

Bonus Chapter 2:STM32 — Top 25 FAQs (Extensive & Practical Answers)

Below are 25 frequently asked questions about STM32 development, each answered in depth with practical advice, code patterns, debugging tips and production considerations. Use this as a living reference while designing, coding, debugging and shipping STM32-based products.

---

1) How do I pick the right STM32 for my project?

Short answer: match CPU performance, peripherals, memory, power, package/pins, and security features to your requirements — and always check supply/channel availability.

Longer checklist & approach

- **Define requirements**: CPU load (control loops, DSP, ML?), RAM/Flash needs (code size + buffers), peripherals (USB/ETH/CAN/SPI/I²C/SDIO/ADC/DAC/SDRAM/QSPI), power budget, real-time latency, and required HW security (crypto/secure boot).

- **Series guide (very briefly)**:

  - Ultra-low-power: **STM32L0/L1/L4/L5/U5** families.

  - Performance with good DSP/FPU: **F4 (M4), F7/H7 (M7), U5 (M33+)**.

  - Wireless integrated: **STM32WB** (BLE), STM32WL (LoRa).

  - Connectivity heavy: STM32 with Ethernet (F7/H7).

- **Peripherals & extras**: If you need QSPI XIP, external SDRAM, or camera interfaces, ensure the part supports FMC/OSPI/DSI.

- **I/O & package**: Count real usable GPIO/AFs. Choose next larger package if you need flexibility.

- **Power & battery**: pick L-series for best standby/quiescent numbers.

- **Security**: look for TrustZone, hardware crypto, TRNG, secure boot features if product needs to be hardened.

- **Lifecycle & sourcing**: check distributors, lead times, and second-source options.

- **Prototype vs production**: start with Nucleo/Discovery for prototyping, then pick a production MCU with the same family/peripherals.

---

2) What's the difference between STM32 series (F0/F3/F4/L0/L4/H7/U5/WB/etc.)?

Short summary

- **F0**: Cortex-M0 — low-cost basic MCUs.

- **F1**: legacy mainstream — general-purpose.

- **F3**: analog-rich (opamps, comparators).

- **F4**: Cortex-M4, DSP/FPU — good for audio, control.

- **F7 / H7**: higher performance M7 cores, caches, highest throughput.

- **L0/L4/L5/U5**: low-power, L5/U5 add security and better performance.

- **WB**: dual-core (M4 app + M0 for wireless), Bluetooth integrated.

- **WL**: LoRa wireless families.

How to use that knowledge

- Choose based on CPU performance needs (F4/H7 for heavy DSP or FOC), low-power targets (L-series), or integrated wireless (WB/WL).

- Newer families add security and richer peripherals — beneficial for productization.

---

3) HAL vs LL vs Bare-metal — which should I use?

HAL (Hardware Abstraction Layer)

- **Pros**: high-level, portable across series, quick to prototype (CubeMX codegen).

- **Cons**: larger code size, some overhead, less control over timing-critical code.

LL (Low-Layer)

- **Pros**: thin wrappers over registers, faster, smaller, more control.

- **Cons**: more verbose, less cross-family portable.

Bare-metal / direct register

- **Pros**: maximum performance & minimal overhead.

- **Cons**: lots of boilerplate, error-prone, harder to maintain/port.

Practical recommendation

- Start with **HAL** for bring-up and proof of concept. For performance-critical parts (ISRs, tight loops, DMA setup) use **LL** or direct register accesses inside well-isolated drivers. Keep a hardware abstraction layer in your project so you can swap implementations. Use unit tests for logic to minimize hardware coupling.

4) How do I set up STM32CubeIDE & CubeMX to start a project?

Steps

1. Install **STM32CubeIDE** (contains CubeMX).

2. Create a new project → select your MCU or board (Nucleo, Discovery, or exact part).

3. Use **Pinout & Configuration** to assign peripherals and clocks.

4. Configure **RCC/Clocks** properly (SYSCLK, PLL, peripheral clocks like 48MHz for USB).

5. Enable middleware (USB Device, FreeRTOS, FATFS) if needed.

6. Generate code — CubeIDE produces HAL-based project and SystemClock_Config() etc.

7. Build and flash using the built-in ST-LINK.

Tips

- Start with minimal peripheral set, verify SWD and LED blink first.

- Keep generated code separate — put your app in Src/App and preserve CubeMX generated code for re-generation.

5) How should I configure clocks and PLL correctly?

Rules of thumb

- Identify required peripheral frequencies (USB needs 48MHz, SDMMC often 48MHz/24MHz clock domain).

- Use CubeMX clock configurator — it enforces valid PLL combinations and flash latency settings.

- When changing SYSCLK at runtime: set flash latency *before* increasing SysClock and check PLL lock.

Manual example (pseudo)

// 1) Configure and enable HSE/HSI

// 2) Configure PLL multipliers/dividers to reach desired SYSCLK

// 3) Set FLASH latency for target frequency

// 4) Switch SYSCLK to PLL output

Pitfalls

- Wrong flash latency → hard faults at high clock.

- Forgetting to enable peripheral clocks (RCC_*).

- Not restoring clocks after STOP (STOP often leaves system on HSI/MSI).

---

6) How do I debug with ST-LINK, SWD and use SWO/ITM?

Basic SWD

- Connect SWDIO, SWCLK, GND, VTref, and NRST/SWO if needed. Use short wires.

- Use **STM32CubeIDE** or **OpenOCD + GDB** for debugging.

SWO / ITM

- Useful for low-overhead debug printing. Enable ITM stimulus port in IDE and implement _write() to send bytes to ITM->PORT[0].

- SWO must be enabled at the correct baud (set in debug configuration) and supported by MCU (ARM DWT/ITM).

Troubleshooting

- If ST-LINK cannot connect: try "Connect under reset", lower SWD clock, check BOOT0 pin (bootloader might disable debug pins), ensure VTref present.

- For intermittent connects: check power and ground continuity, check for external circuitry that holds SWD pins.

7) Why can't ST-LINK connect to my board? Common causes & fixes

Top causes

- **VTref not connected**: ST-LINK needs target voltage sense.

- **Wrong or missing GND**: missing common ground prevents communication.

- **Target not powered**: power the target board.

- **Debug pins multiplexed**: your firmware config could disable JTAG/SWD — use "connect under reset" or assert BOOT0 to start system bootloader.

- **NRST floating or tied incorrectly**: use reset wiring per ST recommendations.

- **High SWD clock**: lower SWD frequency.

Fixes

- Use ST-LINK Utility / CubeIDE with "Connect under reset". Ensure boot mode, pull BOOT0 high if needed to force system boot. Check for level shifters or series resistors on SWD lines interfering with signal.

8) How do I use DMA effectively and what are common pitfalls?

Why use DMA?

- Offloads CPU for high-throughput streams: UART, SPI, ADC, DAC, memory-to-memory copies.

Patterns

- **Peripheral → Circular DMA**: continuous receives like UART RX ring buffer.

- **Double-buffering**: ping-pong buffer for continuous streaming (use HAL_DMAEx_MultiBufferStart).

- **DMA + IRQ**: use half-transfer / transfer-complete callbacks to process streamed chunks.

Pitfalls

- **Buffer alignment & length**: ensure DMA length and alignment match peripheral expectations.

- **Cache coherency (M7/H7)**: the biggest trap — CPU cache vs DMA writes cause corruption.

  - Before DMA that reads memory written by CPU: SCB_CleanDCache_by_Addr().

  - After DMA that wrote memory: SCB_InvalidateDCache_by_Addr() before CPU uses data.

- **Incorrect DMA channel/stream mapping**: check reference manual for request mapping.

- **Peripheral peripheral/clock disabled mid-DMA**: ensure peripheral clocks enabled during DMA.

Example: UART Rx DMA circular

HAL_UART_Receive_DMA(&huart, rxBuf, RX_LEN); // circular

// use IDLE-line IRQ to determine packet length

---

9) On cacheable MCUs (M7/H7): how do I handle cache coherence with DMA?

Key idea

- CPU caches can hide changes DMA makes to memory or vice-versa. You must explicitly clean/invalidate caches for DMA buffers or place DMA buffers in non-cacheable memory (AXI SRAM, DTCM, etc).

Typical steps

- **Before DMA (CPU → peripheral)**: SCB_CleanDCache_by_Addr(addr, size) to write back dirty cache lines to memory.

- **After DMA (peripheral → CPU)**: SCB_InvalidateDCache_by_Addr(addr, size) to discard stale cache lines so CPU reads fresh data.

Alternatives

- Allocate DMA buffers in non-cacheable memory sections via linker script.

- Use MPU to mark regions non-cacheable if supported.

Pitfall example

- DMA Rx fills buffer, CPU reads stale values because D-cache contains old data — result: corrupted data.

---

10) How do NVIC priorities and interrupt preemption work in STM32?

Basics

- Interrupt lines have priority levels (numerical; lower number = higher priority in ARM convention).

- ARM Cortex-M splits priority into **preemption priority** and **subpriority** depending on PRIGROUP.

Rules

- Higher-priority IRQ can preempt lower-priority IRQ, but same priority cannot preempt.

- Critical sections: disable interrupts or use __disable_irq() or taskENTER_CRITICAL() in RTOS to avoid race conditions.

- ISRs should be short: do minimal work and defer heavy processing to tasks or lower-priority handlers (via queues/semaphores).

Pitfalls

- Misconfigured priority grouping leads to unexpected preemption.

- Using HAL_Delay() inside ISR is illegal — it's blocking and may rely on SysTick.

Practical

- Leave SysTick and PendSV priorities configured properly for RTOS (SysTick low priority so interrupts can preempt it).

11) How do I implement low-power modes (Sleep/Stop/Standby) and wake sources?

Modes overview

- **Sleep**: CPU halted, peripherals continue; shortest wake latency.

- **Stop**: main clocks off, many peripherals halted; very low current, requires reconfig of clocks on wake.

- **Standby**: deepest sleep, most state lost; wake via limited sources (RTC, wakeup pins).

Steps to use Stop

1. Prepare wake sources: RTC, EXTI lines, wakeup pins.

2. Configure power regulator mode (main vs low-power).

3. Call HAL_PWR_EnterSTOPMode(...).

4. After wake, reconfigure system clock (SystemClock_Config()).

Power considerations

- Disable unused peripherals/clocks and set GPIOs to minimize leakage (pull-down/up or analog state as recommended).

- For predictable wake latencies, measure PLL lock times.

Testing

- Use precise current meter to measure µA standby consumption. Test wake-on events and verify state retention.

12) How to design a robust OTA / Secure Firmware Update (SFU)?

Core principles

- **Authenticate**: sign images (ECDSA/Ed25519). Bootloader must verify signature before commit.

- **Atomicity**: never overwrite the running image in-place. Use A/B banks or external storage.

- **Rollback protection**: monotonic counters or anti-rollback signatures.

- **Recovery path**: bootloader must be able to revert to known-good image or accept manual reflash.

Practical flow (A/B)

1. Download new image to inactive bank.

2. Verify CRC/hash and signature.

3. Mark bank pending and reboot to run new image.

4. New image validates self; on success it reports OK; bootloader marks bank active.

5. On failure bootloader rolls back to previous.

Security

- Use TLS for download, signed manifests, and possibly encryption for confidentiality.

- Store public keys in secure area or secure element. Protect private keys off-device.

Pitfalls

- Power loss during write: avoid by writing to inactive bank.

- No verification: allow attacker to install arbitrary firmware.

---

13) How do I implement a bootloader (single-bank vs A/B)?

Single-bank bootloader

- Simpler; writes update over existing image — risk of bricking on power loss.

A/B (dual-bank) bootloader

- Safer: keep two separate application slots, download to inactive slot, verify, then flip a flag. Use a small immutable bootloader region that can always run.

Implementation details

- Place bootloader at fixed vector (start of flash) and set application's vector table accordingly (VTOR).

- Use metadata region to store image status (valid/pending/invalid), CRC, version.

- On jump to app: set MSP and PC from app vector table.

Jump to application (example)

```
void Boot_JumpToApp(uint32_t appAddress) {

  uint32_t jumpAddr = *(__IO uint32_t*)(appAddress + 4);

  __set_MSP(*(__IO uint32_t*)appAddress);

  ((void(*)(void))jumpAddr)();

}
```

Testing

- Thoroughly test update flows and simulated power loss.

---

14) Flash programming: erase/program constraints, endurance & wear-leveling

Flash basics

- Flash erase is by sector/page (size depends on MCU) and sets bits to 1; programming can set bits to 0 in smaller granularity (half-word/word/doubleword).

- Erasing frequently wears flash (typical 10k–100k cycles per sector).

Best practices

- Minimize erase cycles: group writes, use buffered logging, or external FRAM/EEPROM for high-frequency writes.

- Use wear-leveling (EEPROM emulation libraries) for frequent small writes.

- Always verify writes (readback and CRC).

- Respect program granularity (do not program partial halfword on parts requiring 64-bit writes).

Pitfalls

- Erasing wrong sector — design linker script to reserve bootloader or config areas.

- Long erase times: flash erase can block CPU for ms — plan critical timing.

---

15) How can I emulate EEPROM in flash safely?

Approaches

- **Append-only log with garbage collection**: append new key-value records, when page fills compact latest entries to new page and erase old page.

- **Double-page scheme**: two pages alternate roles (active/receive) and copy valid data during compaction.

- **Use ST-provided EEPROM emulation libraries**: they implement wear-leveling and atomicity.

Important design choices

- Use CRC or sequence counters per record for integrity and latest-value resolution.

- Write metadata and final flags in an order that ensures atomic commit (write data first, then set valid flag).

When to use external FRAM

- FRAM simplifies frequent writes (high endurance) at cost of hardware.

---

16) How do I interface external memory (QSPI NOR, OSPI XIP, SDRAM) and run code in XIP?

QSPI / OctoSPI (OSPI)

- Useful for large non-volatile storage; many NOR chips support memory-mapped XIP for code/data execution.

- Booting from external NOR often requires bootloader to init QSPI and enable memory mapping.

SDRAM via FMC

- Good for large volatile buffers (framebuffers). SDRAM requires initialization sequence, refresh rates, and careful PCB routing.

Key considerations

- For XIP: set cache & MPU attributes properly and ensure timing stable before mapping.

- For SDRAM: follow datasheet timing and length-match address/data lines on PCB.

- For NAND: handle ECC, bad block management, wear-leveling (prefer managed eMMC if possible).

Pitfalls

- Blue screen or crash if memory not initialized before use.

- Cache coherency issues when sharing DMA and external RAM — treat as non-cacheable or manage caches.

---

17) How to use ADC correctly: sampling times, calibration and DMA?

General advice

- Choose ADC sampling time based on input source impedance — higher source impedance needs longer sampling time to settle.

- Use an external op-amp buffer for high-impedance sources.

- Calibrate ADC (if supported, use hardware calibration) after power-up and temperature changes.

DMA

- For continuous acquisition, use ADC with DMA in circular mode and process half/full-transfer interrupts.

Example

HAL_ADC_Start_DMA(&hadc1, (uint32_t*)adcBuf, ADC_BUF_LEN);

Pitfalls

- Not setting right sampling time → noisy/incorrect readings.

- Not handling ADC clock/oversampling and calibration.

- ADC and DMA buffers on cacheable RAM without cache maintenance.

---

18) I²C common pitfalls: pull-ups, addressing, clock stretching

Hardware

- I²C lines are open-drain; you must include pull-up resistors (value based on bus capacitance and speed — common 4.7k for 100kHz, 2.2k–3.3k for 400kHz).

Addressing

- Be careful: some datasheets show 7-bit vs 8-bit address formats. HAL functions generally expect 7-bit address shifted left addr<<1 sometimes; check API docs and examples.

Clock stretching

- Slower slaves can stretch SCL — masters must support it. Some high-speed masters or bit-banged masters may fail; prefer hardware I²C.

Bus stuck

- If SDA stuck low, toggle SCL up to 9 cycles to clock out stray bits, then generate STOP.

Timeouts

- Implement bus timeouts and recovery (reinit peripheral) if stuck.

---

19) SPI pitfalls: CPOL/CPHA, NSS handling, full/half duplex

CPOL/CPHA

- Mismatched mode (0..3) causes shifted/misaligned data — use oscilloscope or logic analyzer to verify.

NSS/CS

- Using hardware NSS may be problematic for multi-slave setups; often manage CS manually as GPIO ensuring CS asserted before clocks and deasserted after whole frame plus required hold times.

Full-duplex vs half-duplex

- SPI is full-duplex; if your device expects write-then-read with repeated-start like I²C, implement properly (chip-specific).

FIFO & DMA

- For high rates, use DMA for TX and RX concurrently.

Pitfalls

- Forgetting to deassert CS yields corrupted packets.

- Wrong data frame size (8 vs 16-bit) mismatches peripheral expectations.

---

20) UART: DMA receive patterns, IDLE detection and RS-485

Efficient UART RX

- Use DMA in circular mode into a ring buffer. Use **IDLE-line detection** interrupt to determine end of packet:

    o On IDLE IRQ calculate len = BUFSIZE - DMA_CNDTR.

- Advantages: CPU only processes full messages.

RS-485

- RS-485 half-duplex needs driver enable (DE) pin. Prefer hardware DE if USART supports it (avoids toggling DE in software causing timing issues).

- Use T/C or DMA-complete to deassert DE only after last bit transmitted.

21) CAN and automotive/industrial networks: what should I know?

CAN basics

- Message-based, priority by ID (lower id -> higher priority). Use 11-bit or 29-bit IDs.

- Requires external transceiver and 120Ω terminations.

STM32 specifics

- Configure bit timings (prescaler, TSEG1, TSEG2, SJW) for correct sample point and tolerance. CubeMX can compute values.

Filters

- Use hardware acceptance filters to reduce CPU load.

CAN-FD

- Not all STM32 CAN controllers support FD — check datasheet.

Pitfalls

- No termination or wrong transceiver polarity leads to bus errors.

- Incorrect bit timing causes CRC errors and bus off states.

---

22) USB Device implementation (CDC, HID, MSC) — common issues & tips

Use CubeMX to enable USB device middleware — it generates descriptors and class handlers.

Common pitfalls

- Wrong endpoint sizes or wrong buffer allocation; check peripheral's dedicated USB SRAM or PMA settings (varies by family).

- For USB FS device, correct pull-up resistor or PHY configuration must be present.

- MCU must maintain 48 MHz clock domain if using USB; verify PLL settings.

DFU

- USB DFU (Device Firmware Update) can be used for OTA or factory flashing; implement signed firmware for production security.

---

23) How do I integrate an RTOS (FreeRTOS) safely with ISRs and peripherals?

Principles

- Keep ISRs short; signal tasks using semaphores, queues, or direct-to-task notifications.

- Use FromISR API variants in ISR context (e.g., xSemaphoreGiveFromISR).

- Avoid blocking calls in ISRs.

- If using HAL inside ISRs, be mindful of reentrancy and priority inversion — ensure HAL functions used from ISRs are safe.

Priority considerations

- Map ISR priorities so that RTOS critical interrupts (SysTick, PendSV) have appropriate priorities. In FreeRTOS, lowest numeric priority must be used for kernel interrupts per config.

Watchdog / Safety

- Have a high-priority watchdog refresh mechanism that validates system health (tasks reporting in).

---

24) Security: RDP, option bytes, secure boot — what should I consider?

Protecting IP & firmware

- **RDP (Read Protection)**: prevents flash readout via SWD/JTAG. Be aware: raising RDP often requires a full chip erase for recovery (depends on level). Test on non-production devices first.

- **Option bytes**: configure BOR, nBOOT, RDP, and other settings — changing them can brick/debug difficulties if misused.

- **Secure Boot**: store public verification key in secure area and verify signatures in bootloader before booting app.

Best practices

- Use secure elements for key storage if you need high assurance.

- Maintain documented recovery process for forced RDP/option byte changes during manufacturing.

- Protect SWD in production or provide secure provisioning that disables debug interfaces.

---

25) Production: programming, test fixtures, CI and long-term maintenance — how to start?

Programming & testing

- Use gang/flasher programmers or in-circuit SWD fixtures with pogo pins. Keep a small immutable bootloader for network/USB programming if using bootloader-based manufacturing.

- Create functional test firmware (smoke tests) executed by production rigs: check LEDs, UART, sensors, radio, power rails.

- Include unique device ID, firmware version, and calibration data written during test.

CI & dev workflow

- Automate builds, unit tests (host-run where possible), static analysis, and artifact storage.

- Sign firmware images and store signed artifacts with build metadata (git hash, build number).

Long-term

- Plan for component availability (alternate parts) and keep a supply buffer for critical parts.

- Maintain a secure vulnerability/patch process and an OTA update system with rollback protection.

Glossary of Terms

Glossary of Terms – Letter A

Term	Definition	Relevance to STM32 & Embedded	Practical notes / Examples
ADC (Analog-to-Digital Converter)	Peripheral that converts an analog voltage into a digital numeric value. Parameters include resolution (bits), sample rate, input channels, sampling time and reference voltage.	Essential for reading sensors (temperature, light, battery sense). Most STM32 families include one or several ADCs (with differing resolution and performance).	Use HAL/LL HAL_ADC_Start_DMA() for continuous acquisition. Choose sampling time based on source impedance. Remember calibration and ADC clock limits.
ADC Calibration	Procedure (hardware/firmware) to measure and correct ADC offset/gain errors before accurate measurement. Some STM32 parts provide hardware calibration routine.	Improves measurement accuracy—important after power-up or temperature changes. Some devices (e.g., certain L4/F4 parts) have built-in calibration registers.	Run calibration at startup; for high accuracy, re-calibrate after significant temperature change. ADC calibration API: HAL_ADCEx_Calibration_Start() (device-dependent).
ADC Channel	One selectable analog input of an ADC.	Multiplexed channels let one ADC convert	For multi-channel DMA, configure

	Channels map to specific MCU pins or internal sources (temperature sensor, Vrefint).	many signals sequentially. Channel selection affects sampling time and sequence length.	regular sequence (sConfig.Rank) and use appropriate DMA buffer size. Beware of channel switching settling time—add sample time for high-Z sources.
Analog Watchdog (AWD)	ADC feature that raises an interrupt when the converted value goes outside a configured high/low threshold.	Useful for hardware-level threshold detection without software polling — low-power wake or safety triggers.	Configure AWD thresholds per ADC channel group. Use AWD in combination with low-power mode to wake MCU on out-of-range events.
Analog Front-End (AFE)	Circuitry (amplifiers, filters, multiplexers) between sensor and ADC that conditions signals (gain, impedance matching, anti-aliasing).	Good AFE design is critical for accurate ADC results — especially for small sensors or high-resolution ADCs on STM32.	Use op-amp buffers for high-impedance sensors, low-pass RC filters for anti-aliasing, and place VDDA/ADC decoupling close to MCU. Layout matters (guard traces, short analog traces).
AF (Alternate Function)	MCU pin mode that assigns a pin to a peripheral function (USART TX, SPI SCK, TIM CH1, I²C SCL, etc.) instead of GPIO.	STM32 pins are multi-function — correct AF selection is required to enable peripherals on desired pins. CubeMX helps map AFs, but manual mapping must use correct GPIO_InitTypeDef.Alternate.	Check the datasheet AF mapping table. Many conflicts exist: avoid assigning two peripherals to same AF on same pin. For STM32 HAL: GPIO_InitStruct.Alternate = GPIO_AF7_USART1;

AFR (Alternate Function Register)	GPIO register (GPIOx_AFR[0/1]) that configures alternate functions for each pin (low/high half of port).	Low-level way to set AF when using register-level code or when CubeMX/HAL doesn't suffice. Important for advanced pin control and boot-time init.	When manipulating AFR directly, ensure proper locked/unlocked state and configure moder/pupdr appropriately. Use LL macros or MODIFY_REG for safe updates.
AFIO (Alternate Function I/O)	Legacy STM32 peripheral (prominent in F1 family) for remapping peripheral pins (e.g., remap USART, TIM).	Relevant when working with older STM32F1 designs — modern families use AFR registers and SYSCFG for remapping.	On F1, AFIO_MAPR controls remap. For new designs prefer newer families with richer AF mapping.
AHB (Advanced High-performance Bus)	High-speed AMBA bus family used inside ARM SoCs to connect CPU, DMA, and high-bandwidth peripherals.	STM32 internal bus for high-throughput peripherals (DMA, FMC, QSPI, SRAM, core interconnect). AHB clocking affects peripheral speeds and timing.	AHB prescalers and bus configuration influence timer/clock domains. E.g., on many parts timers are driven by AHB-derived clocks (or APB ×2 behavior).
AHB-Lite	Simplified single-master variant of AHB for microcontrollers (no multi-master arbitration).	Most STM32 families use AMBA/AHB-Lite for internal interconnect— understanding it helps reason about bus contention and DMA throughput.	Heavy DMA + CPU memory traffic can create contention— profile with instrumentation (DWT cycle counters) if performance issues arise.
AHB Matrix	On multi-master STM32 parts, an	Present on higher-end STM32 (H7, some F7)	Bus matrix mis-configuration or heavy

	interconnect that connects multiple bus masters and slaves, arbitrates accesses.	— important for performance and understanding which masters (CPU, DMA, GPU) access which slaves (SRAM, peripherals).	masters can starve peripherals — use priority settings and isolate timing-critical buffers into dedicated SRAM blocks.
AMBA (Advanced Microcontroller Bus Architecture)	ARM's family of open-standard on-chip interconnect protocols (AHB, APB, AXI).	The bus architecture used by STM32 internals; explains why peripherals are grouped into AHB/APB domains and how bridges work.	When reading RM (reference manual), AMBA terms show up in clock and interconnect sections—use them to trace latency and throughput.
APB (Advanced Peripheral Bus)	Lower-speed AMBA bus optimized for simple peripherals (UART, I²C, SPI). Typically split into APB1/APB2 with different clock domains.	Many STM32 peripherals live on APB buses; APB prescalers affect peripheral clocks and timer multiplier rules.	`Timers on APB often run at different clock (APB * 1 or *2) — check RM: if APB prescaler ≠ 1, timer clock may be doubled. Configure timer prescalers accordingly.`
APB1 / APB2	Two APB domains on many STM32 parts (APB1 usually lower-speed/peripheral set; APB2 handles higher-speed/peripherals).	Important to know which peripheral is on which APB to set correct clock and enable RCC clock.	Example: on STM32F4, TIM2 on APB1 may have clock = PCLK1 * (APB1 prescaler == 1 ? 1 : 2). Consult HAL_RCC_GetPCLK1Freq() and TIMx->PSC calculations.

ADVANCED STM32 MICROCONTROLLERS

API (Application Programming Interface)	Set of functions/types that a library exposes to be used by application code. In embedded, usually HAL/LL/CMSIS APIs.	Choosing a stable API improves portability: Cube HAL, LL, or custom BSP APIs let you swap MCU families with less code change.	Keep driver APIs small, well-documented and side-effect free. Example: a bme280_read() API returns a struct rather than rely on global state. Version and backward compatibility matter in production.
ABI (Application Binary Interface)	Binary-level contract (calling conventions, data sizes/alignments, register usage) between compiled modules.	For mixed-language or precompiled libs (e.g., linking DSP libs) the ABI must match (ARM EABI variants). Using wrong ABI causes crashes.	For ARM-GCC use -mabi=aapcs compatible flags. When calling assembly from C or linking prebuilt libs, ensure ABI match (-mfloat-abi=hard/soft).
ARM (Advanced RISC Machine)	Company/architecture that designs the Cortex-M cores used in STM32 (ARM Ltd.). ARM provides ISA and core designs (Cortex-M0/M3/M4/M7/M33...).	STM32 MCUs implement ARM Cortex-M cores — architecture knowledge (exception model, NVIC, system control) is essential for low-level firmware.	Read ARMv7-M/v8-M docs for exception return sequence, stack frame on interrupt, and privilege modes (PSP/MSP, IPSR, PRIMASK). Use CMSIS for portability.
ARM Cortex-M	Family of ARM microcontroller cores (M0/M0+ low-power, M3, M4 DSP, M7 high-performance, M33 TrustZone capable).	STM32 parts use different Cortex-M cores; M4/M7 include DSP/FPU units affecting performance, instruction set, and cache behavior.	Be mindful of differences: M7 has caches (manage DMA cache coherency); M33 may support TrustZone (secure/non-secure contexts). Compile with correct -mcpu/-mfpu flags.

ARR (Auto-Reload Register)	Timer register that sets the period of timer counting (the value at which timer resets/overflows).	Central to PWM frequency, timer period, and timebase generation on STM32 TIM peripherals.	For PWM: Period = $(ARR + 1) \times (PSC + 1)$ / TimerClock. If you change ARR at runtime, consider ARPE/preload to avoid glitches. Example: htim.Instance->ARR = new_val;
ARPE (Auto-Reload Preload Enable)	Timer setting that enables buffering of ARR so updates take effect at the next update event rather than immediately.	Prevents transient glitches when changing timer period (useful for live frequency changes).	Set TIM_CR1_ARPE (CubeMX can enable). When ARPE=1, writing ARR updates shadow register and becomes active on next update (UG) event.
AES (Advanced Encryption Standard)	Block cipher used for symmetric encryption. Some STM32 devices include hardware AES accelerators.	Hardware AES accelerators greatly speed up cryptographic operations and lower CPU load for secure communication, secure boot, and encrypted storage.	Use hardware crypto driver (if available) via HAL/STM32Cryptolib or mbedTLS HW engine. Remember key storage and side-channel mitigation (constant-time where possible).
Authentication	Cryptographic process to verify identity or integrity (e.g., signature verification, HMAC).	Central to Secure Firmware Update (SFU), secure boot, device attestation. STM32 secure features (TRNG, crypto engines) support authentication flows.	Use ECDSA / Ed25519 for signatures; verify in bootloader before accepting firmware. Store public key in secure area or secure element.

Atomic Operation	Operation that completes indivisibly (no observable intermediate state) — used to avoid race conditions in concurrency.	MCU register writes may be atomic for word-sized transfers; multi-step updates (e.g., 64-bit on 32-bit MCU) require protection.	Use CMSIS __LDREX/__STREX for lock-free atomics (on some cores), or disable interrupts / use mutexes for critical sections. Avoid long critical sections.
ACK (Acknowledge)	Small signal/message indicating successful receipt of a frame (used in protocols like I²C/I²S/UART flow control, and network stacks).	I²C ACK bit is central to device addressing. Many communications and protocol state machines depend on ACK/NACK handling.	For I²C, a NACK might indicate wrong address or no device — implement retries and timeouts. For TCP/MQTT, ACKs ensure QoS semantics.
ASIC (Application-Specific Integrated Circuit)	Custom silicon designed for a particular application (opposite of general-purpose MCU).	Relevant when scaling product volumes: migrating from STM32 prototype to ASIC custom SoC is a common path for high-volume, cost/power-optimized products.	For most products STM32 or modules suffice. ASICs have high NRE costs — consider second-source and long-term support before moving away from COTS MCUs.
Asynchronous (communication)	Communication where sender and receiver do not share a clock (UART is asynchronous using start/stop bits); contrasts with synchronous (SPI, I²S).	UART/USART is asynchronous serial widely used for logging and low-speed comms in STM32 designs.	Configure correct baud, parity, stop bits. Use hardware FIFO + DMA to avoid overruns. For robust protocols use checksums and timeouts.
Active mode	Power/run state where CPU and most peripherals are powered	Understanding active vs low-power states is key for battery life	Optimize active-mode time by batching work, using DMA and

	and executing code (opposite of Sleep/Stop/Standby low-power modes).	budgeting for STM32-based devices.	peripheral offloads, and returning to low-power modes quickly. Measure with a current meter.
Alternate-function mapping	Assignment of a pin's alternate function (which peripheral function is connected to the physical pin).	Critical for board design — wrong mapping causes peripherals to not appear on chosen pins.	Use CubeMX pinout and datasheet AF tables. Example: PA9 can be AF7 for USART1_TX on many parts. Verify package/pin differences across variants.
API Documentation	Reference docs describing functions, parameters, return values, error cases (e.g., HAL/LL/CMSIS docs).	Good docs speed development and prevent misuse of APIs (e.g., correct HAL init ordering).	Keep a local copy of relevant RM, DS, and HAL guides. Auto-generate docs (Doxygen) for your BSP so team members can discover interfaces quickly.

Glossary of Terms – Letter B

Term	Definition	Context in STM32	Additional Notes
Baud Rate	The number of signal changes (symbols) per second in a communication channel. For serial communication, it	STM32 USART/UART peripherals require setting the baud rate (e.g., 9600, 115200 bps) to match external devices.	Baud rate mismatch between devices causes framing errors and corrupted data.

refers to bits per second.

Term	Definition	STM32 Implementation	Notes
Bootloader	A small program that runs at startup and determines how to load and execute firmware.	STM32 devices include a built-in system bootloader that supports programming via UART, USB, CAN, or SPI.	Developers can create custom bootloaders for firmware upgrade (FOTA, OTA).
Brown-Out Reset (BOR)	A reset mechanism triggered when supply voltage falls below a threshold to prevent erratic MCU operation.	STM32 integrates BOR circuitry to reset safely during unstable VDD levels.	Critical in battery-powered designs to avoid flash corruption during low voltage.
Bus Matrix	A hardware interconnect that manages data transfer between CPU, memories, and peripherals.	In STM32, the AHB/APB bus matrix ensures high-speed access to flash, SRAM, and peripherals.	Some STM32 series feature multi-layer bus matrices to avoid bottlenecks.
Buffer	A temporary storage area for data before processing or transfer.	STM32 UART, SPI, and I2C use transmit/receive buffers to handle streaming data.	Circular DMA buffers help manage continuous data flows without CPU load.
Boot Modes	The different system startup configurations determining execution source (main flash, system memory, or SRAM).	STM32 boot mode pins (BOOT0/BOOT1) define if the system boots from flash, SRAM, or system bootloader.	Useful for debugging, in-field programming, and recovery.

Breakpoint	A debugging feature that halts program execution at a specific line of code or instruction.	STM32 supports hardware and software breakpoints via SWD/JTAG using ST-LINK or other debuggers.	Essential for step-by-step debugging and real-time variable inspection.
Bit-Banding	A memory-mapped technique allowing individual bits to be accessed as separate words.	Available in STM32 Cortex-M3/M4 devices for atomic bit manipulation in SRAM and peripheral registers.	Provides efficient way to toggle GPIOs or manage flags without bitwise operations.
Boot Pin (BOOT0/BOOT1)	Hardware pins that select the STM32 boot mode.	BOOT0 is commonly exposed for selecting flash/system memory/SRAM at startup.	Often pulled low via resistor to ensure booting from main flash by default.
Bus Fault	An exception generated when illegal memory access occurs on the system bus.	STM32 NVIC/Fault Handler raises a BusFault if invalid addresses or access violations occur.	Debugging bus faults helps identify stack corruption, invalid pointers, or memory misconfigurations.
Binary Image	A compiled firmware file containing machine code instructions for the MCU.	STM32 toolchains generate .bin or .hex files that can be flashed into MCU memory.	ST-LINK Utility and STM32CubeProgramm er support direct programming of binary images.
Bit Rate	Number of bits transmitted per unit time in communication systems.	STM32 communication interfaces (UART, CAN, SPI, I2C) require	Often confused with baud rate; in some cases, bit rate = baud rate × bits per symbol.

precise bit rate configuration.

Boot Configuration	The setup that determines which memory region the CPU executes after reset.	STM32 boot configuration is controlled by BOOT pins and option bytes in flash.	Developers can lock boot settings for secure deployment.
Bus Arbitration	A process to control access when multiple masters compete for the system bus.	In STM32 with DMA and multiple bus masters, arbitration ensures fair and deterministic memory access.	Critical in real-time systems to prevent latency issues.
Bitwise Operations	Logical operations (AND, OR, XOR, NOT, shift) performed at the bit level.	Used in STM32 firmware to configure registers and manipulate GPIO pins.	Mastering bitwise operations is fundamental in embedded C programming.
Block Diagram	A graphical representation of system components and their interconnections.	STM32 datasheets and reference manuals provide block diagrams of clock, power, and peripheral systems.	Essential for understanding MCU architecture before firmware development.
Boot Time	The duration required for a microcontroller to initialize and start executing firmware.	STM32 typically boots within microseconds depending on clock source and initialization sequence.	Optimizing boot time is important for real-time or safety-critical systems.

Bus Width	The number of bits transferred simultaneously across a bus.	STM32 internal buses include 8-bit, 16-bit, and 32-bit widths depending on memory/peripheral interface.	Wider bus width improves throughput but increases power and silicon cost.

Glossary of Terms – Letter C

Term	Definition	Context in STM32	Additional Notes
Cache	A small, high-speed memory used to store frequently accessed instructions or data.	STM32 Cortex-M7 MCUs include instruction and data caches to speed up flash and SRAM access.	Improves performance but requires careful management during DMA or self-modifying code.
CAN (Controller Area Network)	A robust serial communication protocol designed for automotive and industrial systems.	Many STM32 devices include bxCAN or FDCAN peripherals for real-time networking.	Used in robotics, vehicles, and industrial control.
CAPTURE/COMPARE	A timer feature to capture an event timestamp or compare counter value to generate output.	STM32 timers support input capture (for measuring pulse widths) and output compare (for PWM generation).	Widely used in motor control, signal measurement, and servo driving.
Clock Tree	A hierarchical structure that distributes clock	STM32 devices include configurable clock trees	Managed using STM32CubeMX for low-power and

	signals to CPU, buses, and peripherals.	with PLLs, oscillators (HSI, HSE, LSI, LSE).	performance optimization.
CMSIS (Cortex Microcontroller Software Interface Standard)	A vendor-independent hardware abstraction layer for ARM Cortex-M microcontrollers.	STM32 firmware development relies on CMSIS for register definitions, startup code, and DSP functions.	Standardized API reduces porting effort across Cortex-M families.
CRC (Cyclic Redundancy Check)	An error-detecting code used to verify data integrity.	STM32 includes hardware CRC units to accelerate checksum calculations.	Useful in communication protocols, flash memory integrity checks, and bootloaders.
Calibration	The process of adjusting hardware/software parameters for accurate measurement.	STM32 ADCs and internal sensors (e.g., temperature) require calibration for precision.	Calibration values are stored in MCU system memory during production.
Clock Gating	A power-saving technique where clock signals are disabled to unused peripherals.	STM32 RCC (Reset and Clock Control) allows enabling/disabling clocks to peripherals.	Reduces dynamic power consumption in low-power designs.
Compiler	A tool that converts human-readable source code into machine code executable by the MCU.	STM32 development uses GCC (arm-none-eabi-gcc), Keil, or IAR compilers.	Optimization levels (-O0 to -O3) affect speed, size, and debugging ease.

Configuration Register	Special-purpose register used to configure peripherals.	STM32 peripherals (USART, GPIO, TIM, etc.) are controlled via configuration registers.	Direct register access offers fine control beyond HAL libraries.
Core	The central processing unit inside a microcontroller.	STM32 devices use ARM Cortex-M0, M3, M4, M7, and M33 cores depending on performance needs.	Determines instruction set, performance, and available features.
Cortex-M	A family of ARM processor cores optimized for embedded applications.	STM32 is built on ARM Cortex-M architectures.	Each sub-family balances performance, cost, and power consumption.
Current Consumption	The amount of electrical current drawn by the MCU and peripherals during operation.	STM32 supports multiple low-power modes (STOP, STANDBY, SLEEP) to reduce current draw.	Key metric in battery-powered IoT applications.
Crystal Oscillator	An external timing source that provides accurate clock signals.	STM32 supports HSE (High-Speed External) crystals and LSE (Low-Speed External) for RTC.	External crystals improve timing accuracy compared to internal oscillators.
Clock Domain	A region of the system operating under the same clock signal.	STM32 peripherals (APB1, APB2, AHB) belong to different clock domains.	Crossing clock domains requires synchronization to prevent data corruption.

Checksum	A simple mathematical sum or hash used to detect errors in data.	STM32 bootloaders often use checksums to verify firmware integrity.	Less robust than CRC but simpler to compute.
Crossbar Switch	A digital switching fabric for connecting cores, memories, and peripherals.	Some STM32 high-performance MCUs (Cortex-M7) use crossbar interconnects to reduce bus contention.	Improves throughput when multiple masters (CPU, DMA) access memory.
Chip Select (CS)	A control signal used to enable or disable external devices on a bus.	STM32 SPI peripherals often require GPIO-based CS lines for selecting external devices.	Active-low CS signals are most common.
Code Density	A measure of how compactly code fits into memory.	STM32 Cortex-M instruction set supports Thumb-2 for high code density.	Higher code density means lower flash usage and faster fetches.
Cycle Count	The number of clock cycles taken to execute an instruction or task.	STM32 DWT (Data Watchpoint and Trace) unit can measure cycle counts.	Useful for performance profiling and real-time system tuning.
Circular Buffer	A fixed-size buffer that wraps around when the end is reached.	STM32 DMA can operate in circular mode for continuous data acquisition.	Common in UART RX, ADC sampling, and real-time audio capture.

Glossary of Terms – Letter D

Term	Definition	Context in STM32	Additional Notes
DAC (Digital-to-Analog Converter)	A peripheral that converts digital values into analog voltages.	Many STM32 MCUs include DACs for audio output, waveform generation, or motor control.	Often used with DMA for continuous waveform synthesis (e.g., sine waves).
Debugging	The process of finding and fixing errors in firmware or hardware.	STM32 debugging is supported via SWD (Serial Wire Debug), JTAG, and ST-LINK.	Debuggers allow breakpoints, step execution, and peripheral inspection.
Device ID	A unique identifier embedded in microcontrollers for identification.	STM32 includes device ID registers for recognizing MCU models and families.	Useful in bootloaders and firmware targeting multiple MCU series.
DMA (Direct Memory Access)	A controller that transfers data between peripherals and memory without CPU intervention.	STM32 uses DMA for high-speed data transfer in UART, SPI, ADC, DAC, etc.	Reduces CPU load, critical in real-time applications.
Driver	Software that controls and interfaces with a specific hardware peripheral.	STM32Cube HAL provides drivers for UART, GPIO, ADC, SPI, etc.	Custom drivers can be written for optimized or low-level control.
DFU (Device Firmware Upgrade)	A USB protocol that allows firmware updates over USB	Many STM32 MCUs support DFU mode via	Enables field upgrades without external programmers.

	without special hardware.	the built-in system bootloader.	
DSP (Digital Signal Processing)	Mathematical operations on signals to analyze or modify them.	Cortex-M4 and M7 STM32 MCUs include DSP extensions (MAC instructions, SIMD).	Used in audio, communications, and control systems.
DWT (Data Watchpoint and Trace)	A hardware unit that provides cycle counting, watchpoints, and trace functionality.	STM32 Cortex-M cores include DWT for performance profiling.	Helpful for debugging timing-critical systems.
Dead Time	A short delay inserted between switching signals to prevent overlap.	STM32 advanced timers (TIM1, TIM8) support dead-time insertion for motor drivers.	Essential in half-bridge and full-bridge circuits to prevent short-circuits.
Duty Cycle	The percentage of time a signal is active (ON) compared to its period.	STM32 timers generate PWM with configurable duty cycles.	Critical for motor speed control, LED dimming, and signal modulation.
Dual-Bank Flash	A memory architecture that splits flash into two banks for flexibility.	Some STM32 MCUs allow executing from one bank while programming the other.	Enables firmware upgrades without halting execution (firmware-over-the-air).
Debugger Probe	A hardware interface between PC and MCU for debugging.	Common tools: ST-LINK, J-Link, and CMSIS-DAP.	Provides flashing, debugging, and real-time variable inspection.

Dynamic Power Consumption	Power consumed by switching transistors in a microcontroller.	STM32 uses dynamic power scaling and clock gating to minimize consumption.	Major factor in battery-powered IoT devices.
Development Board	A ready-made board that simplifies testing and prototyping of MCUs.	STM32 Nucleo and Discovery boards provide quick start for developers.	Includes debug probe, headers, and pre-wired peripherals.
Digital Filter	A circuit or algorithm that processes digital signals to reduce noise.	STM32 timers and comparators support built-in digital filters for inputs.	Useful in noisy environments, e.g., mechanical button debouncing.
Driver Strength	The ability of a GPIO pin to source or sink current.	STM32 GPIOs have configurable output drive strength.	Important for driving LEDs or external circuits directly.
Debugging Information File (.elf, .map)	Files generated by compilers containing symbol and memory usage information.	STM32 developers use .elf and .map files for debugging firmware.	Helps track memory usage and optimize code size.
Device Tree	A data structure that describes hardware resources for an OS.	In STM32 Linux-based SoCs, device trees define peripheral mappings.	Mostly used in higher-end STM32MP1 series.
Dynamic Voltage Scaling (DVS)	Adjusting supply voltage dynamically to save power.	Some STM32 devices implement DVS in conjunction with clock scaling.	Extends battery life in portable devices.

Domain Crossing	Transfer of data between different clock or power domains.	STM32 APB/AHB buses require synchronization for domain crossings.	Critical to avoid metastability and data corruption.
Download Speed	The rate at which firmware is flashed onto the microcontroller.	STM32 supports high-speed flashing over SWD, JTAG, or USB DFU.	Influenced by programmer type and flash wait states.

Glossary of Terms – Letter E

Term	Definition	Context in STM32	Additional Notes
EEPROM (Electrically Erasable Programmable Read-Only Memory)	A type of non-volatile memory that can be erased and reprogrammed electrically.	Most STM32 MCUs don't have dedicated EEPROM but emulate it using Flash.	Used for storing configuration parameters and calibration data.
EMC (Electromagnetic Compatibility)	The ability of a device to operate correctly in an electromagnetic environment.	STM32 boards need proper PCB layout, shielding, and filtering to pass EMC tests.	Certification (CE, FCC) often requires EMC compliance.
EMI (Electromagnetic Interference)	Unwanted disturbance generated by electronic devices that affects other devices.	STM32 circuits may produce EMI from clocks, switching regulators, and GPIO toggling.	Mitigated using shielding, ferrite beads, and spread-spectrum clocking.

Embedded System	A computer system dedicated to performing specific functions, often with real-time constraints.	STM32 MCUs are commonly used in embedded systems for IoT, robotics, and automation.	Differ from general-purpose computers by low power and specific tasks.
Encryption	The process of converting data into an unreadable format to protect it from unauthorized access.	STM32 MCUs (especially STM32L4, STM32F7, STM32H7) include AES hardware accelerators.	Essential for secure IoT communication and firmware protection.
Endianness	The order in which bytes are stored in memory (Little Endian vs. Big Endian).	STM32 uses Little Endian format like most ARM Cortex-M processors.	Important in communication protocols and data storage.
Erasable Sector	A block of flash memory that can be erased as a unit.	STM32 flash memory is organized into pages or sectors for erasing and writing.	Erase operations are slower and require careful planning in firmware updates.
Error Detection and Correction (EDAC / ECC)	Mechanisms to detect and correct data corruption in memory.	STM32H7 series includes ECC for SRAM and Flash memory protection.	Enhances reliability in safety-critical applications.
ESD (Electrostatic Discharge)	Sudden discharge of static electricity that can damage components.	STM32 designs use ESD diodes, TVS protection, and grounding techniques.	ESD protection is critical for USB, GPIO, and power pins.

Ethernet	A networking technology for wired communication.	STM32F4, STM32F7, and STM32H7 families include Ethernet MAC controllers.	Often combined with LwIP stack for TCP/IP networking.
External Interrupt (EXTI)	A mechanism to trigger an interrupt from an external GPIO pin.	STM32 provides EXTI lines for event-driven designs (e.g., button presses, sensor triggers).	Configurable for rising, falling, or both edges.
Event	A hardware or software signal indicating that something has occurred.	STM32 event system allows timers, ADC, and DMA to be triggered by events.	Improves real-time responsiveness without CPU intervention.
Energy Harvesting	Capturing energy from the environment (solar, vibration, RF) to power devices.	Low-power STM32 MCUs (STM32L series) are suitable for energy-harvesting IoT devices.	Often combined with supercapacitors or small batteries.
Execution Time	The time taken for a program or instruction to run.	STM32 developers use cycle counters (DWT) to measure execution time.	Critical in optimizing real-time applications.
Embedded AI	AI or ML models deployed directly on microcontrollers.	STM32Cube.AI enables running neural networks on STM32 devices.	Used in IoT, wearables, predictive maintenance, and smart sensors.

Term	Definition	Context in STM32	Additional Notes
External Oscillator (HSE, LSE)	A clock source provided by an external crystal or resonator.	STM32 uses HSE for system clock and LSE for Real-Time Clock (RTC).	Provides better stability and accuracy than internal RC oscillators.
Edge Computing	Processing data near the source rather than in the cloud.	STM32-based IoT nodes perform preprocessing before sending data via Wi-Fi/MQTT.	Reduces latency, bandwidth use, and improves privacy.
Expansion Board (Shield)	Add-on hardware that extends MCU board functionality.	STM32 Nucleo supports Arduino-compatible shields for sensors, motors, and displays.	Speeds up prototyping and hardware integration.
Embedded Bootloader	A small program preloaded in MCU ROM that enables firmware loading.	STM32 has built-in system bootloaders supporting UART, USB DFU, CAN, etc.	Useful for production and field updates.
External Memory Interface (EMI/FSMC)	A bus interface for connecting external memories.	STM32F4/F7/H7 include FSMC or FMC to interface with SDRAM, SRAM, and NOR/NAND Flash.	Expands system memory for complex applications.

Glossary of Terms – Letter F

Term	Definition	Context in STM32	Additional Notes

Factory Calibration	Pre-programmed calibration values stored during MCU manufacturing.	STM32 devices store calibration constants for ADC, temperature sensors, and oscillators.	Improves accuracy without user calibration.
Fail-Safe	A design approach where the system defaults to a safe state during faults.	STM32 uses watchdogs, brown-out reset, and redundant systems for fail-safe operation.	Critical in automotive, medical, and aerospace.
Fault Handler	An exception routine that handles CPU errors.	STM32 Cortex-M provides HardFault, BusFault, UsageFault, and MemManage handlers.	Helps debug invalid memory access or illegal instructions.
Fast I/O (GPIO Speed)	Ability of MCU pins to toggle at high frequencies.	STM32 GPIOs can be configured for different speed modes (Low, Medium, High, Very High).	Important in high-speed communication and PWM outputs.
Firmware	Low-level software that controls hardware directly.	STM32 firmware is often written in C using HAL, LL, or bare-metal drivers.	Stored in Flash memory, updated via bootloader or SFU.
Firmware Over-The-Air (FOTA)	Remote update of firmware using wireless communication.	STM32 IoT devices use FOTA via Wi-Fi, LoRa, or Bluetooth.	Secure updates require cryptographic verification.

319

Flash Memory	Non-volatile memory that retains data without power.	STM32 MCUs use on-chip Flash for storing code and constants.	Organized in pages/sectors with limited write cycles.
Floating-Point Unit (FPU)	Hardware that accelerates floating-point arithmetic.	Present in STM32F4, F7, H7, and L4 MCUs with Cortex-M4/M7 cores.	Improves DSP, AI, and control system performance.
Frequency Scaling	Adjusting CPU clock frequency to save power.	STM32 can lower system clock or enter low-power modes.	Balances performance vs. energy efficiency.
Finite State Machine (FSM)	A computation model with defined states and transitions.	Used in STM32 applications for motor control, UI navigation, and communication protocols.	Improves code readability and maintainability.
Functional Safety (FuSa)	Standards ensuring safety in electronic systems (e.g., ISO 26262).	STM32 MCUs support ECC, dual-core lockstep, and diagnostic features.	Required in automotive, industrial, and medical fields.
Frame Check Sequence (FCS)	Error-detection code in communication frames.	STM32 peripherals like Ethernet, CAN, and UART use CRC/FCS for error detection.	Ensures reliable data transfer.
FreeRTOS	A lightweight real-time operating system for embedded devices.	STM32CubeMX integrates FreeRTOS for task scheduling and multitasking.	Widely used in IoT and industrial systems.

Frequency Modulation (FM)	Varying frequency of a carrier signal to encode data.	STM32 timers and DACs can generate modulated signals for RF/IR communication.	Used in wireless transmission and motor drives.
Firmware Update (SFU)	Secure replacement of firmware in flash memory.	STM32 provides Secure Firmware Update (SFU) solutions with authentication and encryption.	Prevents malicious firmware injection.
Flash Wait States	CPU cycles inserted while accessing Flash memory at high speeds.	STM32 adjusts wait states automatically based on system clock frequency.	Too few wait states can cause read errors.
Filter (Digital)	A signal processing technique that removes noise or unwanted components.	STM32 DSP instructions and CMSIS libraries enable FIR/IIR filters.	Used in audio, biomedical, and sensor data processing.
Frequency Division	Dividing an input clock to generate lower frequencies.	STM32 timers and prescalers divide clocks for PWM and communication protocols.	Saves power and meets timing requirements.
Frame Buffer	A memory area storing image/video data before display.	STM32 MCUs with LTDC (e.g., STM32F7/H7) use frame buffers for LCD/TFT displays.	Stored in internal SRAM or external SDRAM.

Term	Definition	Context in STM32	Additional Notes
Flash Loader	A utility or hardware tool for programming MCU flash memory.	ST provides **STM32CubeProgrammer** for Flash loading via USB/UART/SWD.	Used in production and debugging.
Firmware Integrity Check	Ensuring firmware is not corrupted or tampered with.	STM32 uses CRC, AES, and SHA hashing to verify integrity.	Often combined with secure boot.

Glossary of Terms – Letter G

Term	Definition	Context in STM32	Additional Notes
Gain	The amplification factor applied to a signal.	STM32 MCUs often interface with external amplifiers (e.g., for sensors, ADC inputs). Some STM32 op-amp peripherals also support configurable gain.	Critical in analog signal conditioning before ADC sampling.
Galvanic Isolation	Separation between circuits to prevent current flow while allowing signal transfer.	STM32-based industrial systems use isolation for UART, CAN, or SPI communication via isolators.	Protects MCU from high-voltage surges.
Garbage Collection	Automatic memory cleanup in higher-level languages.	Not native in STM32 C/C++ development, but relevant in STM32 running MicroPython or .NET nanoFramework.	Helps manage memory-constrained environments.

Gate Driver	A circuit that controls power transistors (MOSFET/IGBT).	STM32 controls external gate drivers in motor control, robotics, and power electronics.	Ensures efficient switching and protection.
Gateway	A device that connects two different networks or protocols.	STM32 IoT nodes can serve as gateways (e.g., Modbus-to-MQTT, CAN-to-Ethernet).	Enables industrial and IoT interoperability.
General-Purpose Input/Output (GPIO)	Configurable digital pins used for input or output.	STM32 MCUs provide fast GPIOs for buttons, LEDs, communication, and external control.	One of the most fundamental MCU peripherals.
General-Purpose Timer	A versatile hardware timer for counting, PWM, or event timing.	STM32 timers support input capture, output compare, PWM, and encoder interfaces.	Used in motor control, signal measurement, and scheduling.
Geolocation	Determining device location using GPS or network data.	STM32-based IoT devices integrate with GPS modules or Wi-Fi geolocation services.	Often used in asset tracking and smart mobility.
Gigabit Ethernet	A high-speed wired networking standard (1 Gbps).	STM32H7 MCUs support advanced Ethernet features but typically not full gigabit speeds.	Often paired with external PHY for faster networking.
Glitch Filter	A hardware or software filter that ignores short signal pulses.	STM32 input capture and external interrupt	Prevents false triggering from noise.

		lines can use digital filtering.	
Global Interrupt Enable (GIE)	A CPU instruction that enables/disables all maskable interrupts.	STM32 uses __enable_irq() and __disable_irq() in Cortex-M cores.	Used during critical sections to prevent unexpected interruptions.
Graphical User Interface (GUI)	A visual interface with buttons, icons, and graphics.	STM32 MCUs with TFT/LCD controllers (e.g., STM32F7, H7) support GUIs using TouchGFX or LVGL.	Enhances user experience in embedded devices.
Green Energy Applications	Low-power or renewable energy systems.	STM32 MCUs are widely used in solar charge controllers, smart meters, and battery management systems.	Leveraging ultra-low-power STM32L series.
Ground (GND)	The common electrical reference point in a circuit.	STM32 boards use ground for return paths of signals and power.	Proper grounding is critical to avoid EMI and noise issues.
Group Priority (Interrupts)	A hierarchy system for handling multiple interrupts.	STM32 NVIC supports interrupt priority grouping (preemption and subpriority levels).	Ensures critical tasks are handled before less important ones.
Guard Band	A reserved frequency range to prevent interference between signals.	STM32-based RF systems (e.g., LoRa, Wi-Fi) must account for guard bands.	Helps ensure compliance with FCC/CE regulations.

Term	Definition	Context in STM32	Additional Notes
Gyroscope	A sensor that measures angular velocity.	STM32 interfaces with gyroscopes (via I²C/SPI) in robotics, drones, and wearables.	Often used together with accelerometers for IMU systems.
GPIO Expander	External chip that increases number of available GPIOs.	STM32 communicates with expanders like MCP23017 (I²C) or MCP23S17 (SPI).	Useful when more I/O is required than the MCU provides.
Grid Tie	Method of connecting renewable energy systems to the main power grid.	STM32 MCUs are used in solar inverters and smart grid controllers.	Requires compliance with power electronics standards.
Guard Ring	A PCB design technique using a grounded trace around sensitive analog circuits.	STM32 ADC circuits often use guard rings to reduce leakage and noise.	Improves signal integrity in precision applications.

Glossary of Terms – Letter H

Term	Definition	Context in STM32	Additional Notes
Half-Duplex Communication	A communication method where data transmission occurs in both directions but not simultaneously.	STM32 UART and RS-485 interfaces can be configured for half-duplex operation.	Saves I/O pins but limits simultaneous data exchange.

Hall Sensor	A magnetic sensor that detects magnetic fields and generates a voltage.	STM32 motor control applications use Hall sensors for rotor position detection.	Widely used in BLDC motors and speed detection.
Handler	A function that executes when an interrupt occurs.	In STM32, each interrupt vector corresponds to an **IRQ handler** (e.g., USART1_IRQHandler).	Critical for real-time response in embedded systems.
Hardware Abstraction Layer (HAL)	A software layer that abstracts hardware details and provides standardized APIs.	STM32Cube HAL library allows easier peripheral access without direct register programming.	Simplifies development but may reduce efficiency.
Hardware Acceleration	Use of specialized hardware to perform tasks faster than software.	STM32 MCUs with **crypto accelerators**, **graphics accelerators**, or **floating-point units (FPU)**.	Improves performance and lowers CPU load.
Hardware Debugging	Using external tools to analyze and debug microcontrollers.	STM32 supports **SWD (Serial Wire Debug)** and **JTAG** interfaces for debugging.	Essential in firmware development and testing.
Hardware Security Module (HSM)	A dedicated component for secure key storage and cryptographic operations.	STM32 TrustZone-enabled devices can integrate HSM-like functionality.	Enhances protection against key theft.

Hash Function	A one-way mathematical function that generates a fixed-size digest from input data.	STM32 MCUs with crypto accelerators can compute **SHA-1/SHA-256 hashes**.	Used in firmware integrity checks and authentication.
Header File	A file in C/C++ containing definitions, macros, and function declarations.	STM32 projects include headers like stm32f4xx_hal.h for peripheral definitions.	Promotes modular code organization.
Heat Sink	A device used to dissipate heat from electronic components.	STM32 itself usually doesn't require heat sinks, but high-power drivers controlled by STM32 do.	Critical in power electronics and motor drives.
Heterogeneous Multicore	A processor system with different types of cores.	Some STM32 devices (e.g., STM32MP1) combine Cortex-A and Cortex-M cores.	Supports running Linux (A-core) alongside real-time control (M-core).
High-Speed External (HSE) Clock	An external oscillator source for precise MCU timing.	STM32 uses HSE for stable system clocks and accurate USB/Ethernet operation.	Typically crystal-based (8–25 MHz).
High-Speed Internal (HSI) Clock	An internal RC oscillator providing a clock source.	STM32 MCUs feature HSI as a fallback clock source.	Less accurate than HSE but requires no external components.

High-Speed USB (USB HS)	USB interface supporting up to 480 Mbps.	STM32F4, F7, and H7 series include USB HS peripherals with PHY support.	Often used in data logging, communication, and mass storage devices.
Host Controller	The controller responsible for managing USB communication from the host side.	STM32 USB OTG (On-The-Go) allows devices to act as **host or peripheral**.	Useful in USB hubs, flash readers, or embedded host devices.
Hot Plugging	Adding or removing a device without powering down the system.	STM32 USB and SD card interfaces support hot plugging.	Requires robust software handling to avoid corruption.
H-Bridge	A circuit for driving motors forward or backward by reversing current.	STM32 motor control boards often use H-bridges to control DC/BLDC motors.	Essential for robotics and automation.
Human-Machine Interface (HMI)	Interface allowing interaction between humans and machines.	STM32 with TFT/LCD + touch panels enables advanced HMIs (using TouchGFX, LVGL).	Common in appliances, kiosks, and automotive dashboards.
Hybrid Power Systems	Systems combining multiple energy sources (e.g., solar + grid).	STM32 is widely used in hybrid inverters and smart energy controllers.	Focused on efficiency and renewable integration.
HyperBus Interface	A high-speed memory interface for external RAM/flash.	STM32 MCUs (e.g., STM32H7) support	Provides low latency and high throughput.

HyperBus for external
memory expansion.

Glossary of Terms – Letter I

Term	Definition	Context in STM32	Additional Notes
I²C (Inter-Integrated Circuit)	A multi-master, multi-slave serial communication bus using two lines (SDA, SCL).	STM32 supports I²C for sensors, EEPROMs, displays, and inter-device communication.	Widely used in low-speed peripheral integration.
I²S (Inter-IC Sound)	A serial bus interface standard for digital audio data transfer.	STM32 MCUs include I²S peripherals for connecting to DACs, audio codecs, and microphones.	Common in audio playback and voice processing.
IC (Integrated Circuit)	A semiconductor device that integrates multiple electronic components.	STM32 itself is an IC that integrates CPU, memory, and peripherals.	Comes in various packages like LQFP, BGA, QFN.
IDE (Integrated Development Environment)	A software suite for writing, compiling, debugging, and flashing firmware.	Examples: STM32CubeIDE, Keil uVision, IAR Embedded Workbench.	Essential for STM32 development workflow.
Idle Mode	A low-power mode where CPU is stopped	STM32 low-power management allows idle	Useful in battery-powered designs.

	but peripherals continue running.	mode for energy savings.	
IEC Standards	International Electrotechnical Commission standards governing electronics and safety.	STM32-based products must comply with **IEC 61508 (functional safety)** or **IEC 60730 (appliances)**.	Ensures safety, quality, and reliability.
IEC 60730 Class B	A safety standard for household appliances requiring self-test features in MCUs.	STM32 includes **Class B libraries** for compliance in washing machines, ovens, HVAC systems.	Tests RAM, flash, clock, and interrupts.
IEEE 802.15.4	A standard for low-rate wireless personal area networks.	STM32WB series supports IEEE 802.15.4 for **Zigbee and Thread protocols**.	Widely used in IoT networks.
IEEE 802.11 (Wi-Fi)	Wireless communication standard for LANs.	Some STM32 IoT modules integrate Wi-Fi (e.g., STM32WL with external modules).	Used for smart homes, industrial IoT, and consumer devices.
Impedance Matching	Technique to maximize power transfer and reduce signal reflections in circuits.	Critical in STM32 designs with **high-speed USB, RF, and Ethernet**.	Achieved by designing correct PCB trace widths.
In-Circuit Debugging (ICD)	Debugging microcontrollers while they are running inside the circuit.	STM32 supports ICD via **SWD/JTAG** interfaces.	Allows real-time code execution monitoring.

In-Circuit Emulator (ICE)	A hardware device used to emulate microcontrollers for debugging.	STM32 development often uses ST-LINK as a hardware debugging tool (ICE-like).	Helps developers test before final deployment.
In-Circuit Programming (ICP)	Programming an MCU directly while soldered in the target hardware.	STM32 can be programmed via **SWD, UART, USB, or DFU mode**.	Saves time in production environments.
Indicator LED	A light-emitting diode used for status indication.	STM32 boards (e.g., Nucleo, Discovery) include user-programmable LEDs.	Commonly used for debugging and user feedback.
Industrial Automation	Use of embedded systems for controlling industrial processes.	STM32 used in **PLCs, motor controllers, robotics, and industrial sensors**.	Requires real-time performance and robustness.
Industrial IoT (IIoT)	IoT applications applied to industrial environments.	STM32 (especially STM32MP1 and STM32H7) powers IIoT gateways and smart factory solutions.	Demands secure, reliable, long-term support.
Information Security	Protection of data from unauthorized access and manipulation.	STM32 provides **AES encryption, secure boot, and TrustZone** features.	Vital in IoT and connected devices.
Inrush Current	The initial surge of current when a circuit is powered on.	STM32 systems with power supplies must	Solved using capacitors, current

		manage inrush currents to avoid resets.	limiters, or soft-start regulators.
Input Capture	A timer feature that records the time when an external event occurs.	STM32 timers use input capture for **frequency, duty cycle, and pulse width measurement**.	Essential in motor control and sensor applications.
Instruction Cache (I-Cache)	A memory cache that stores recently fetched instructions to speed up execution.	STM32 Cortex-M7 and Cortex-M33 feature I-Cache for higher performance.	Reduces wait states in flash memory access.
Interrupt	A signal that temporarily halts CPU execution to handle events.	STM32 supports **nested vectored interrupt controller (NVIC)**.	Enables real-time responsiveness.
Interrupt Service Routine (ISR)	A function executed when an interrupt occurs.	Example: EXTI0_IRQHandler() runs when an external pin interrupt triggers.	Must be fast and efficient to avoid delays.
IoT (Internet of Things)	Network of devices connected to collect and exchange data.	STM32 IoT nodes use **LoRa, BLE, Wi-Fi, Zigbee, Thread** for connectivity.	Key market for STM32 development.
Isolation	Separation between circuits for safety or noise reduction.	STM32 often uses **opto-isolators** in industrial motor drivers and communication interfaces.	Protects MCU from high voltages.

Glossary of Terms – Letter J

Term	Definition	Context in STM32	Additional Notes
JTAG (Joint Test Action Group)	A standard (IEEE 1149.1) for debugging, boundary-scan testing, and programming MCUs.	STM32 supports JTAG for programming and debugging, though SWD is more commonly used.	Requires 4–5 pins (TCK, TMS, TDI, TDO, TRST).
Jitter	Small variations in signal timing that can affect system performance.	STM32 timers, ADC sampling, and communication interfaces must minimize jitter for accuracy.	Important in motor control, real-time audio, and clock generation.
JSON (JavaScript Object Notation)	A lightweight data-interchange format.	STM32 IoT applications often use JSON for sending/receiving data via MQTT, HTTP, or REST APIs.	Human-readable and widely supported in cloud services.
Joule (J)	A unit of energy (1 Joule = 1 Watt-second).	Used to measure power consumption in STM32 low-power applications.	Power efficiency is critical in embedded systems.
Jump Instruction	An assembly-level instruction that transfers program execution to another location.	STM32 uses jump instructions in **bootloaders and ISRs**.	Example: BX LR instruction in ARM Cortex-M.

Jump to Bootloader	Process of forcing STM32 to run its system bootloader.	STM32 supports jumping to **DFU mode via USART, USB, or I2C**.	Useful for firmware upgrades.
Just-In-Time Compilation (JIT)	Technique of compiling code at runtime instead of ahead of time.	While not native to STM32, interpreted languages (e.g., MicroPython on STM32) can use JIT for optimization.	Helps in scripting environments on embedded devices.
Junction Temperature (Tj)	The temperature at the semiconductor junction of an IC.	STM32 datasheets specify maximum Tj (usually 125–150°C).	Exceeding Tj reduces reliability and lifespan.
Jumper	A small connector used to manually set hardware configurations.	STM32 Nucleo boards use jumpers for **boot configuration, power source selection, and debugging options**.	Replaced by solder bridges on some boards.
Java	A high-level, platform-independent programming language.	STM32 does not natively run Java but can interact with **Java-based IoT platforms (e.g., Eclipse IoT, Android Things)**.	Java is more common on higher-end processors (like STM32MP1 running Linux).
JavaScript	A scripting language mainly used in web development.	In STM32 IoT projects, JavaScript may be used in **Node.js gateways** to process STM32 sensor data.	Not directly run on STM32 but works with cloud/edge integration.

| Junction Leakage Current | A small unwanted current flowing through a transistor junction even when off. | STM32 datasheets provide leakage current specifications for pins and peripherals. | Increases with temperature. |

Glossary of Terms – Letter K

Term	Definition	Context in STM32	Additional Notes
Karnaugh Map (K-Map)	A diagram used for simplifying Boolean algebra expressions.	Helps optimize STM32 digital logic in FPGA/MCU mixed designs or when designing efficient state machines.	Useful for reducing power and gate count in hardware logic.
Kernel	The core component of an operating system (OS) responsible for task scheduling, memory, and process management.	STM32 often runs **RTOS kernels** (e.g., FreeRTOS, CMSIS-RTOS) for multitasking.	Provides thread scheduling, IPC, and resource allocation.
Kernel Mode	A privileged execution mode in which the processor can access all system resources.	STM32 Cortex-M cores have **privileged and unprivileged modes** controlled by the MPU.	Ensures security and task isolation.
Kilo (k)	Metric prefix representing 10^3 **(1000)**.	Used in STM32 datasheets for memory sizes (e.g., 128 KB Flash, 64 KB SRAM).	Distinguish between kB (1000 bytes) and KiB (1024 bytes).

KiloByte (KB)	Unit of data storage (1 KB = 1024 bytes in computing).	STM32 Flash and SRAM are commonly specified in KB.	Some documents use 1 KB = 1000 bytes (SI standard).
Kinetics (System Dynamics)	Study of forces and motion in physical systems.	Relevant in STM32-based robotics and motor control where feedback loops manage kinetics.	Requires IMU sensors for closed-loop control.
Key Matrix	An arrangement of switches (like a keyboard) in rows and columns to reduce GPIO usage.	STM32 scans key matrices using GPIO and timers for debounce handling.	Used in **custom keypads, keyboards, and control panels**.
Keil MDK (Microcontroller Development Kit)	A popular IDE and compiler suite for ARM Cortex-M microcontrollers.	Widely used for STM32 development with debugging, simulation, and RTOS support.	Uses ARM Compiler and integrates with CMSIS.
Kilohertz (kHz)	Frequency unit equal to **1000 cycles per second**.	STM32 timers, PWM, and ADC sampling rates are often expressed in kHz.	Higher frequencies affect power consumption.
Kinematic Equations	Equations used to describe motion (position, velocity, acceleration).	STM32 applies kinematic equations in **robotics and drone flight controllers**.	IMUs provide data for real-time calculations.

Key Derivation Function (KDF)	A cryptographic algorithm to derive keys from a master key.	STM32 cryptographic libraries use KDFs for secure communication.	Ensures unique session keys for encryption.
Kernel Tick (SysTick)	A periodic interrupt generated by a system timer.	STM32 uses SysTick for **RTOS task scheduling and delays**.	Configurable to different tick frequencies.
Knowledge Base (KB)	A structured collection of information or troubleshooting solutions.	Developers use STM32 knowledge bases (ST forums, app notes) to solve issues.	Helpful for debugging and best practices.

Glossary of Terms – Letter L

Term	Definition	Context in STM32	Additional Notes
Ladder Logic	A graphical programming language used in industrial automation.	STM32 can interface with PLCs or emulate ladder logic for automation tasks.	Often used in **industrial STM32-based controllers**.
LAN (Local Area Network)	A network connecting devices within a limited area.	STM32 with Ethernet MAC/PHY or external modules (ENC28J60, W5500) connects to LAN.	Used in IoT gateways and industrial automation.
Latch	A basic memory element that holds a state (0 or 1).	STM32 GPIO outputs can drive external	Different from flip-flops, as latches are level-triggered.

		latches for signal retention.	
Latency	The delay between an input signal and the corresponding output response.	STM32 interrupt latency is critical in **real-time control systems**.	Cortex-M cores have deterministic low latency.
LCD (Liquid Crystal Display)	A display technology based on liquid crystal alignment.	STM32 drives **alphanumeric and graphic LCDs** using GPIO, SPI, or FSMC.	Widely used in **embedded HMIs**.
LDO (Low Dropout Regulator)	A power regulator that maintains stable output with a small difference between input and output voltage.	STM32-based boards often use LDOs for stable **3.3V or 1.8V power supply**.	Efficiency is lower than switching regulators.
LED (Light Emitting Diode)	A semiconductor device that emits light when current flows.	STM32 controls LEDs for indication, status, and displays (LED matrix, RGB).	Commonly used in **blinking LED tutorials**.
Library	A collection of reusable software functions.	STM32 developers use **HAL, LL, CMSIS, or third-party libraries**.	Improves code reusability and maintainability.
Linker Script	A file that defines memory layout for code and data placement.	STM32 firmware projects include .ld files specifying Flash, RAM, stack, and heap.	Critical for **bootloaders and memory optimization**.

Little-Endian	A memory storage format where the least significant byte is stored first.	STM32 Cortex-M cores use **little-endian architecture**.	Must be considered when exchanging binary data.
Load Cell	A sensor that measures force or weight.	STM32 reads load cell data via **ADC or external HX711 modules**.	Used in **weighing scales and robotics**.
Logic Analyzer	A debugging tool that captures and analyzes digital signals.	STM32 developers use logic analyzers for **protocol debugging (SPI, I²C, UART)**.	Complements oscilloscopes for firmware debugging.
Low-Power Modes	Energy-saving states of the microcontroller.	STM32 supports **Sleep, Stop, and Standby modes**.	Essential for **battery-powered IoT devices**.
LSE (Low-Speed External Oscillator)	A 32.768 kHz crystal used for real-time clock accuracy.	STM32 uses LSE for **RTC timekeeping** and low-power applications.	Provides long-term stability.
LSI (Low-Speed Internal Oscillator)	An internal ~32 kHz RC oscillator.	STM32 uses LSI for watchdog and RTC when low precision is acceptable.	Saves cost by avoiding external crystals.
LVD (Low Voltage Detector)	A circuit that monitors power supply voltage levels.	STM32 includes LVD to prevent unpredictable behavior during brownouts.	Triggers reset when voltage falls below threshold.

Term	Definition	Context in STM32	Additional Notes
LVTTL (Low-Voltage TTL)	A signaling standard with lower voltage levels than TTL.	STM32 I/O pins support LVTTL for interfacing with **modern logic circuits**.	Helps reduce power consumption.

Glossary of Terms – Letter M

Term	Definition	Context in STM32	Additional Notes
MAC (Media Access Control)	A hardware address unique to each network device.	STM32 microcontrollers with Ethernet (e.g., STM32F107, STM32H7) use a MAC for communication over LAN.	Required for **TCP/IP networking**.
Machine Cycle	The basic time unit in which a microcontroller executes an instruction.	STM32 cores (Cortex-M) execute instructions in a few cycles depending on instruction complexity.	Performance depends on **clock speed and pipeline**.
Main Stack Pointer (MSP)	The default stack pointer used by Cortex-M processors.	STM32 uses MSP during system startup and exceptions.	Works alongside **Process Stack Pointer (PSP)**.
MCU (Microcontroller Unit)	A small computer on a single chip, integrating CPU, memory, and peripherals.	STM32 is a family of 32-bit ARM Cortex-M-based MCUs.	Used in **embedded systems, robotics, IoT**.

Memory Protection Unit (MPU)	Hardware that enforces access rules on memory regions.	STM32 with Cortex-M3/M4/M7/A cores use MPU for safety and security.	Prevents **illegal memory access and malware attacks**.
Memory-Mapped I/O	Technique where peripheral registers are accessed like memory locations.	STM32 peripherals (GPIO, UART, ADC, etc.) are controlled via memory-mapped registers.	Simplifies **peripheral programming**.
MISO (Master In Slave Out)	SPI signal line where the slave sends data to the master.	STM32 SPI peripheral reads data from external sensors or memory via MISO.	Works with **MOSI, SCK, CS**.
MOSI (Master Out Slave In)	SPI signal line where the master sends data to the slave.	STM32 sends data to SPI devices (displays, SD cards) via MOSI.	Must be synchronized with **SCK**.
MQTT (Message Queuing Telemetry Transport)	A lightweight publish-subscribe messaging protocol for IoT.	STM32 with Wi-Fi or Ethernet can act as an MQTT client node.	Used in **IoT applications and cloud integration**.
MSP430 (for comparison)	A low-power MCU family by Texas Instruments.	Compared with STM32 in **embedded system selection**.	STM32 usually offers more performance and peripherals.
MSP Debugging Interface	Debug protocol for ARM Cortex-M microcontrollers.	STM32 supports **SWD (Serial Wire Debug)** for debugging firmware.	Provides faster debugging than JTAG in some cases.

MTD (Memory Technology Device)	Abstraction layer for accessing flash memory.	STM32 external flash memories use MTD drivers in RTOS/Linux-based systems.	Important in **data logging and firmware updates**.
Multithreading	Running multiple tasks simultaneously.	STM32 achieves multithreading using **RTOS (FreeRTOS, RTX, Zephyr)**.	Enables **real-time multitasking applications**.
Multiplexer (MUX)	A device that selects one of many inputs to be sent to an output.	STM32 uses multiplexers internally for peripheral pin remapping.	Controlled via **alternate function registers**.
MVB (Microcontroller Voltage Bandgap)	A reference voltage used for calibration.	STM32 ADCs use bandgap reference for stable measurements.	Improves **ADC accuracy**.
Machine Learning (ML)	A branch of AI where models learn from data.	STM32 integrates ML via **TensorFlow Lite Micro, Edge Impulse, STM32Cube.AI**.	Used in **voice recognition, anomaly detection, predictive maintenance**.
Memory Footprint	The amount of Flash and RAM consumed by firmware.	STM32 developers optimize memory footprint for small MCUs (e.g., STM32F0).	Critical in **low-cost designs**.
Microampere (μA)	A unit of current, 10^{-6} Amperes.	STM32 ultra-low-power series (STM32L0/L4) operate in μA sleep currents.	Important for **battery-powered devices**.

Micropython	A Python 3 implementation for microcontrollers.	STM32 Nucleo and Pyboard support MicroPython.	Enables **rapid prototyping with high-level scripting**.
Middleware	Software layer between the OS/firmware and application.	STM32Cube provides middleware like USB stacks, file systems, and TCP/IP.	Simplifies **application development**.
Millisecond (ms)	A unit of time equal to 10^{-3} seconds.	STM32 SysTick timer often operates with a 1ms tick for RTOS scheduling.	Used in **delays and time-based tasks**.
Motor Driver	A circuit that controls motors from microcontrollers.	STM32 interfaces with L293D, DRV8833, or custom H-bridges for robotics.	Used in **mini robots, drones, automation**.

Glossary of Terms – Letter N

Term	Definition	Context in STM32	Additional Notes
NAND Flash	A type of non-volatile memory used for mass storage.	STM32 interfaces with external NAND Flash for file systems or firmware updates.	Offers **high density** but requires error correction.
Nanoampere (nA)	A unit of electric current (10^{-9} Amperes).	STM32 ultra-low-power (L0, L4, U5) can	Crucial for **wearables, IoT, medical sensors**.

		achieve **nA-range shutdown currents**.	
NMI (Non-Maskable Interrupt)	A high-priority interrupt that cannot be disabled.	STM32 uses NMI for **critical faults** like clock failure or watchdog reset.	Ensures **system stability and recovery**.
Node	A device or endpoint in a network system.	STM32 acts as a **sensor/actuator node** in CAN, IoT, or MQTT networks.	Fundamental in **distributed embedded systems**.
Non-Volatile Memory (NVM)	Memory that retains data after power is removed.	STM32 internal Flash and external EEPROM are NVM.	Used for **firmware storage and calibration data**.
NVIC (Nested Vectored Interrupt Controller)	Hardware that manages and prioritizes interrupts in ARM Cortex-M.	STM32 NVIC supports nested interrupts with programmable priority levels.	Enables **real-time responsiveness**.
NVRAM (Non-Volatile RAM)	RAM that preserves data without power (battery-backed).	STM32 with external NVRAM can retain variables across power cycles.	Used in **RTC modules and logging systems**.
Neural Network (NN)	A machine learning model inspired by the human brain.	STM32 runs NNs using **STM32Cube.AI, TensorFlow Lite Micro**.	Used in **speech recognition, predictive maintenance**.

Noise Margin	The tolerance of a digital circuit to electrical noise.	STM32 I/O voltage thresholds define safe noise margins.	Important in **signal integrity and EMC design**.
Network Stack	Layers of protocols enabling device communication.	STM32Cube provides **TCP/IP, UDP, HTTP, MQTT stacks**.	Essential for **IoT and Ethernet applications**.
Notch Filter	A filter that removes a specific frequency band.	STM32 DSP (CMSIS-DSP library) uses notch filters for signal processing.	Used in **audio, vibration, ECG signal filtering**.
Nyquist Rate	The minimum sampling rate required to avoid aliasing ($2\times$ signal frequency).	STM32 ADC sampling must respect the Nyquist rate for accuracy.	Used in **digital signal processing applications**.
Namespace	A scope for organizing variables, functions, or libraries.	STM32 firmware in **C++ and MicroPython** uses namespaces.	Prevents **naming conflicts in large projects**.
Network-on-Chip (NoC)	An interconnect architecture for high-speed cores.	Advanced STM32H7/A series use NoC concepts for bus optimization.	Improves **memory/peripheral throughput**.
Nonlinear Control	Control systems that are not proportional or linear.	STM32 controls motors and robotics with nonlinear algorithms (e.g., PID + nonlinear compensation).	Applied in **autonomous vehicles and drones**.

Term	Definition	Context in STM32	Additional Notes
Normalized Frequency	Frequency expressed relative to sampling rate.	STM32 DSP computations use normalized frequency for filter design.	Used in **digital filter and FFT analysis**.
Numerically Controlled Oscillator (NCO)	A digital oscillator used for waveform generation.	STM32 implements NCO via timers and DAC for signal synthesis.	Used in **communications, modulation, motor control**.
Network Time Protocol (NTP)	Protocol for synchronizing time across systems.	STM32 with Ethernet/Wi-Fi syncs RTC using NTP.	Essential in **IoT timestamping and logging**.
Near-Field Communication (NFC)	A short-range wireless technology (13.56 MHz).	STM32 connects to external NFC chips/modules for secure access.	Used in **payments, authentication, IoT sensors**.
Numerical Methods	Mathematical algorithms for approximations.	STM32 uses numerical methods for **control systems, simulations**.	Implemented via **CMSIS-DSP**.

Glossary of Terms – Letter O

Term	Definition	Context in STM32	Additional Notes
Octet	A unit of digital information equal to 8 bits.	STM32 memory, buffers, and communication	Equivalent to a **byte**, but emphasizes 8-bit definition.

		protocols use octets for data representation.	
OLED (Organic Light Emitting Diode)	A display technology with self-illuminating pixels.	STM32 drives OLED displays using **I²C/SPI** for GUIs.	Used in **wearables, IoT dashboards, handheld devices**.
On-Chip Debugger (OCD)	Hardware/debug interface integrated into microcontrollers.	STM32 supports OCD via **SWD/JTAG** for programming and debugging.	Enables **breakpoints, memory inspection, and trace**.
One-Time Programmable (OTP) Memory	A type of memory that can be written once and cannot be erased.	STM32 includes OTP regions for **device IDs, security keys, calibration data**.	Enhances **tamper resistance and device security**.
Open-Drain	An output configuration where the pin is either driven low or left floating.	STM32 GPIO pins can be set to open-drain mode for **I²C communication, LED driving**.	Requires **external pull-up resistors**.
Open-Loop Control	A control method without feedback.	STM32 timers generate PWM in open-loop motor control applications.	Simpler but less accurate than **closed-loop control**.
Operating System (OS)	Software that manages hardware and software resources.	STM32 supports **FreeRTOS, Zephyr, ThreadX** for multitasking.	Used in **IoT, robotics, industrial automation**.

Operating Voltage	The recommended voltage range for reliable MCU operation.	STM32 operates typically at **1.7V–3.6V**, with some series supporting 1.8V low-power domains.	Critical for **power supply and regulator design**.
Operational Amplifier (Op-Amp)	An analog device for amplification and signal conditioning.	Some STM32 MCUs (e.g., STM32G4, STM32L4+) have **integrated Op-Amps**.	Used in **sensor interfacing, signal processing, motor drivers**.
Optimization Level	Compiler setting that balances execution speed, size, and debugging ease.	STM32CubeIDE allows **-O0 to -O3 optimizations** for C code.	Affects **code performance, power consumption, and debug visibility**.
Oscillator (OSC)	A circuit that generates a periodic clock signal.	STM32 uses **internal RC oscillators (HSI, LSI)** and **external crystal oscillators (HSE, LSE)**.	Provides **timing, synchronization, and peripheral clocking**.
Overclocking	Running the MCU at a higher frequency than specified.	STM32H7 and STM32F7 can be overclocked for performance experiments.	Can cause **instability, heat, and reduced reliability**.
Overcurrent Protection (OCP)	A safeguard to prevent damage from excess current.	STM32-based power systems use OCP in **motor drivers, power supplies**.	Often implemented with **external MOSFETs and sense resistors**.

Overflow	A condition when data exceeds the maximum representable value.	STM32 timers, counters, and arithmetic operations must handle overflow conditions.	Managed with **interrupts or software checks**.
Over-the-Air (OTA) Update	Wireless firmware upgrade mechanism.	STM32 with Wi-Fi, BLE, or LoRa supports **OTA firmware updates**.	Crucial for **IoT devices, remote sensors, and maintenance-free systems**.
Oversampling	A technique to improve ADC/DAC accuracy by sampling above Nyquist rate.	STM32 ADC supports **hardware oversampling** to reduce noise.	Enhances **signal resolution and stability**.
Overtemperature Protection (OTP)	A mechanism that prevents overheating damage.	STM32 integrates temperature sensors to trigger protective shutdowns.	Used in **motor drivers, battery systems, and industrial MCUs**.
Open-Source	Software with freely available source code.	STM32 ecosystem leverages **open-source RTOS, drivers, and AI frameworks**.	Encourages **collaboration and rapid development**.
Output Compare (OC)	Timer feature that toggles an output at a specific counter value.	STM32 timers use OC for **PWM, event triggering, and waveform generation**.	Enables **precise timing and synchronization**.
Out-of-Band (OOB)	Communication outside the main data channel.	STM32 debugging or management functions may use OOB signaling.	Common in **secure communication and control systems**.

Glossary of Terms – Letter P

Term	Definition	Context in STM32	Additional Notes
Parity Bit	An error-detection bit added to data in communication.	STM32 USART/UART supports **even, odd, or no parity** in data transmission.	Improves reliability in **RS232, RS485, Modbus protocols**.
Peripheral	A hardware module inside or external to the MCU that provides additional functionality.	STM32 peripherals include **USART, SPI, I²C, ADC, DAC, timers, CAN, USB**.	Each STM32 series differs in **number and type of peripherals**.
Peripheral Clock (PCLK)	The clock signal provided to MCU peripherals.	STM32 divides the main system clock into **APB1 and APB2 peripheral clocks**.	Critical for ensuring **timing accuracy**.
Phase-Locked Loop (PLL)	A circuit that generates stable high-frequency clocks from lower frequency sources.	STM32 uses PLL to derive system clock from **HSE or HSI** oscillators.	Ensures **flexibility in clock management**.
Pin Multiplexing	The ability of a pin to perform multiple functions.	STM32 pins may act as **GPIO, USART Tx/Rx, I²C SDA/SCL, or SPI MOSI/MISO** depending on configuration.	Managed through **STM32CubeMX or datasheets**.

Pinout	The arrangement of pins on a microcontroller package.	Each STM32 MCU has unique **pinout diagrams** for power, GPIO, communication, and debug pins.	Important for **PCB design and prototyping**.
Pipeline	A sequence of instruction stages executed in parallel to improve performance.	STM32 Cortex-M cores use **3-stage (M0), 5-stage (M3/M4), or 6-stage (M7/H7) pipelines**.	Reduces instruction execution time.
Polling	Method of checking peripheral status in a loop without interrupts.	STM32 HAL drivers allow **polling mode for UART, ADC, I²C**.	Simpler than interrupts but wastes CPU cycles.
Port	A group of GPIO pins controlled together.	STM32 organizes pins into **GPIOA, GPIOB, ..., GPIOK**.	Ports are managed with **ODR (output data register) and IDR (input data register)**.
Power Consumption	The amount of current drawn by the MCU during operation.	STM32 supports **Run, Sleep, Stop, and Standby** modes to optimize power usage.	Crucial in **IoT, battery-powered devices, and wearables**.
Power Management Unit (PMU)	Circuit that manages MCU power domains.	STM32 PMU controls **voltage regulators, low-power modes, and wake-up sources**.	Enhances **energy efficiency**.
Power-On Reset (POR)	A reset that occurs when the MCU is powered up.	STM32 automatically initializes to a known state after POR.	Protects against **undefined startup states**.

Preemption	The ability of a higher-priority task/interrupt to interrupt a lower-priority one.	STM32 NVIC allows **nested interrupt preemption**.	Enables **real-time responsiveness**.
Prescaler	A divider used to slow down clock signals.	STM32 timers use prescalers to adjust **PWM frequency, baud rates, and sampling rates**.	Allows precise timing adjustments.
Programming Interface	The method used to load code into MCU flash memory.	STM32 supports **SWD, JTAG, UART bootloader, USB DFU**.	SWD is most commonly used for **debugging and flashing**.
Programming Voltage (Vpp)	The voltage required to program memory.	STM32 flash programming works at **operating voltage (no external Vpp required)**.	Simpler than older MCUs that required high-voltage programming.
Project Configuration	Setup of clock, peripherals, pins, and middleware for an application.	STM32CubeMX and STM32CubeIDE automate project configuration.	Saves development time.
Protocol	A set of rules for communication between devices.	STM32 implements **I²C, SPI, UART, USB, CAN, Ethernet, LoRa, BLE**.	Essential for **IoT and embedded connectivity**.

Pulse-Width Modulation (PWM)	A method of controlling power by varying pulse duty cycle.	STM32 timers generate PWM for **motor control, LED dimming, audio output**.	Duty cycle controls **speed, brightness, or volume**.
Pull-Up Resistor	Resistor connecting a pin to Vcc to ensure a default logic HIGH.	STM32 GPIOs support **internal pull-up resistors**.	Useful in **buttons, I²C, and open-drain configurations**.
Pull-Down Resistor	Resistor connecting a pin to GND to ensure a default logic LOW.	STM32 GPIOs support **internal pull-down resistors**.	Prevents **floating inputs**.
Push-Pull Output	A GPIO output mode where the pin drives both high and low states actively.	STM32 GPIO defaults to push-pull mode for digital outputs.	Stronger drive capability than open-drain.
PVD (Programmable Voltage Detector)	Monitors supply voltage to detect brown-out conditions.	STM32 PVD can trigger interrupts when voltage drops below threshold.	Prevents **data corruption and system instability**.
Package	The physical casing of the MCU (e.g., LQFP, BGA, QFN).	STM32 MCUs are available in **different packages** depending on pin count and size.	Affects **PCB design, soldering, and cost**.
Peripheral DMA Request	Signal from a peripheral requesting DMA service.	STM32 DMA controller moves data between peripherals and memory without CPU load.	Boosts **performance in ADC, USART, SPI transfers**.

Glossary of Terms – Letter Q

Term	Definition	Context in STM32	Additional Notes
QFN (Quad Flat No-Lead)	A surface-mount MCU package with pads underneath.	Some STM32 MCUs are available in **QFN packages** (small footprint, low cost).	Suitable for **compact PCB designs** but harder to solder by hand.
QSPI (Quad Serial Peripheral Interface)	An enhanced SPI that transfers **4 bits per clock cycle**.	STM32 supports **QSPI Flash memory interface** for high-speed code execution (XIP) and data storage.	Used in **graphics, audio, and external memory expansion**.
Quadrature Encoder	A sensor that outputs two signals (A and B) to indicate rotation and direction.	STM32 timers can be configured in **encoder mode** to read quadrature signals.	Common in **motor control, robotics, CNC machines**.
Queue (RTOS)	A data structure used for inter-task communication.	In **FreeRTOS with STM32**, queues allow tasks to send/receive messages safely.	Ensures **synchronization and decoupling of tasks**.
Quasi-Bidirectional I/O	A GPIO mode where the pin can act as input or output without strong driving.	Some older MCUs use this, but STM32 uses **push-pull and open-drain modes** instead.	Mentioned for **historical comparison**.

Quiescent Current (IQ)	The current consumed by a device in idle state (no switching).	STM32 datasheets specify **IQ in standby and sleep modes**.	Important for **battery-powered and IoT applications**.
Quality of Service (QoS)	A mechanism to prioritize certain data transfers.	STM32 **AXI bus and DMA** support QoS levels for memory and peripheral access.	Improves **real-time performance in multimedia and AI tasks**.
Quasi-Resonant Converter	A type of SMPS power supply circuit optimized for efficiency.	STM32 is often used as a **controller in quasi-resonant power supplies** for appliances and chargers.	Enables **energy-efficient embedded power solutions**.
Quantization	Converting continuous values into discrete digital steps.	STM32 **ADC and DSP libraries** perform quantization when sampling analog signals.	Critical for **signal processing, audio, and ML on MCU**.
Quadrant Selection (Memory Mapping)	Dividing flash/ROM into sections for access.	STM32 bootloaders and memory controllers may partition flash into **banks or quadrants**.	Useful for **dual-bank flash and secure boot**.

Glossary of Terms – Letter R

Term	Definition	Context in STM32	Additional Notes

RAM (Random Access Memory)	Volatile memory used for data storage and stack/heap operations.	STM32 MCUs have **SRAM (internal RAM)** ranging from a few KB to several MB in high-end models.	Crucial for **variable storage, buffers, and RTOS execution**.
RCC (Reset and Clock Control)	A subsystem that manages MCU clock sources and resets.	STM32 developers configure **RCC registers** to select HSE, HSI, PLL, etc.	Essential for **system performance tuning and low-power modes**.
Register	A small storage location in the CPU or peripheral used for control or data.	STM32 peripherals are configured by writing to **memory-mapped registers**.	Registers are the **lowest-level programming interface** of the MCU.
Reset Vector	The memory address where execution begins after reset.	STM32 reset vector typically points to the **startup code in flash memory**.	Defined in the **vector table** of CMSIS/firmware.
RTC (Real-Time Clock)	A peripheral that keeps track of time, even in low-power mode.	STM32 RTC can run off a **32.768 kHz LSE crystal** or internal clock.	Used in **time-stamping, alarms, and calendar functions**.
ROM (Read-Only Memory)	Non-volatile memory that stores firmware permanently.	In STM32, flash memory acts as ROM for storing the **program code**.	Can be updated by **firmware flashing or OTA updates**.
RTOS (Real-Time Operating System)	Software that schedules tasks with precise timing.	STM32 often uses **FreeRTOS, Zephyr,**	Ensures **deterministic execution in real-time systems**.

	or **CMSIS-RTOS** for multitasking.	
RNG (Random Number Generator)	Hardware module that generates random numbers.	STM32 MCUs include **true RNG hardware** for cryptography.	Essential for **secure communications and encryption**.
Reset Pin (NRST)	A dedicated hardware pin to reset the MCU.	Pulling **NRST low resets STM32** to default state.	Used in **debugging, watchdog reset, and external reset circuits**.
Readout Protection (RDP)	A security feature to prevent unauthorized code access.	STM32 supports **RDP levels 0, 1, 2** (increasing restrictions).	Ensures **firmware IP protection and anti-cloning**.
Reference Manual	Official technical documentation describing MCU registers.	Each STM32 series has a **detailed reference manual (RMxxxx)**.	More detailed than the **datasheet**, intended for developers.
ROM Table (Debug)	A table that provides access to debug components.	STM32 Cortex-M cores expose debug information via **ROM tables**.	Used by **SWD/JTAG tools for chip introspection**.
Reset Source Identification	Mechanism to determine the cause of reset.	STM32 has **RCC_CSR register** to identify resets (power-on, watchdog, software, etc.).	Useful for **fault recovery and diagnostics**.

Term	Definition	Context in STM32	Additional Notes
RAM Parity Check	A hardware feature that detects memory errors.	High-end STM32 MCUs support **RAM ECC/parity checking**.	Improves **system reliability and fault tolerance**.
Read-Modify-Write (RMW)	A CPU operation where a register is read, modified, and written back.	STM32 peripherals may be affected by **RMW timing issues** in concurrent access.	Requires use of **atomic operations or CMSIS functions**.
Resource Sharing	Using a peripheral by multiple tasks or cores.	In STM32 dual-core MCUs (Cortex-M7 + M4), **resource sharing must be synchronized**.	Requires **mutexes, semaphores, or hardware exclusion mechanisms**.
Reset Handler	The function that runs immediately after reset.	In STM32, defined in **startup.s** and initializes stack/variables.	Jumps to **main() function** afterward.
Ring Buffer	A circular buffer for efficient data storage.	Commonly used in STM32 **UART, DMA, and streaming data applications**.	Supports **non-blocking communication**.

Glossary of Terms – Letter S

Term	Definition	Context in STM32	Additional Notes
SRAM (Static Random Access Memory)	On-chip volatile memory used for variables, stack, and runtime data.	STM32 devices have SRAM sizes ranging from **2 KB to 1 MB**, depending on series.	Faster than Flash, critical for **RTOS task stacks, buffers, and dynamic data**.

SWD (Serial Wire Debug)	A two-pin debugging protocol defined by ARM.	STM32 supports **SWD via SWCLK and SWDIO pins**, replacing JTAG in many cases.	Essential for **firmware flashing, breakpoints, and debugging**.
SPI (Serial Peripheral Interface)	A high-speed synchronous serial communication protocol.	STM32 integrates multiple **SPI peripherals**, often supporting master/slave modes.	Used for **sensors, displays, memory chips, and communication modules**.
Systick Timer	A 24-bit timer included in ARM Cortex-M cores.	STM32 uses Systick for **OS tick generation** in RTOS or periodic interrupts.	Fundamental for **FreeRTOS and CMSIS-RTOS** task scheduling.
STM32Cube	STMicroelectronics' ecosystem of initialization code, drivers, and middleware.	Developers use **STM32CubeMX and STM32CubeIDE** for code generation.	Speeds up **project setup and peripheral configuration**.
Sleep Mode	A low-power mode where the CPU is stopped, but peripherals can run.	STM32 can enter **Sleep, Stop, or Standby modes** depending on use case.	Important for **IoT and battery-powered applications**.
Startup Code	Assembly/C code executed before main().	STM32 startup code initializes **stack pointer, vector table, and data sections**.	Generated automatically by **STM32CubeIDE or toolchains**.

Stack	Memory region used for local variables, function calls, and return addresses.	Each STM32 core has its **Main Stack Pointer (MSP)** and optionally **Process Stack Pointer (PSP)**.	Stack size must be carefully managed to **prevent overflow**.
Supply Voltage (VDD)	The voltage powering the MCU core and I/O.	STM32 typically runs at **1.8V–3.6V**, with some supporting **dual voltage domains**.	Impacts **performance, power consumption, and peripheral compatibility**.
SPP (Samples Per Point)	Number of samples collected per measurement cycle.	In STM32 ADC/DSP processing, **SPP defines resolution in signal analysis**.	Critical in **audio and motor-control applications**.
Sensor Fusion	Combining data from multiple sensors for better accuracy.	STM32 often integrates **IMU + Magnetometer** fusion via DSP libraries.	Used in **drones, robotics, wearables, and automotive systems**.
Secure Boot	A process ensuring only authenticated firmware runs.	STM32 with **TrustZone or crypto hardware** supports secure boot.	Protects against **malware and unauthorized firmware**.
Signal Integrity	Quality of digital/analog signals under transmission.	STM32 board design requires **good PCB layout, decoupling, and impedance control**.	Critical for **high-speed buses like USB, SPI, and SDIO**.

ADVANCED STM32 MICROCONTROLLERS

Serial Bootloader	Bootloader that communicates via UART, USB, or CAN.	STM32 MCUs ship with a **ROM bootloader** for in-field programming.	Enables **programming without dedicated hardware programmer**.
Standard Peripheral Library (SPL)	A legacy library for STM32 peripheral programming.	Superseded by **HAL/LL drivers in STM32Cube**.	Still used in older STM32 projects.
Standby Mode	Deepest low-power mode with minimal current consumption.	STM32 retains **RTC and backup registers** in standby mode.	Used in **battery-powered IoT devices**.
Servo Control	Using PWM signals to control servo motors.	STM32 timers generate **precise PWM duty cycles** for motor control.	Essential in **robotics, drones, and automation**.
Segger J-Link	A widely used hardware debugger and programmer.	Supports STM32 debugging over **SWD/JTAG**.	Popular for **professional development and production programming**.
SVD (System View Description)	XML file describing MCU registers and peripherals.	STM32CubeIDE uses **SVD files for debugging register view**.	Enhances **debugging and low-level analysis**.
Supervisor Call (SVC)	ARM Cortex-M instruction for requesting OS services.	Used in STM32 **RTOS task management and system calls**.	Core part of **privilege separation in embedded OS**.

Simulation	Virtual execution of firmware without hardware.	STM32CubeIDE supports **limited simulation**, while Keil uVision offers detailed MCU simulation.	Useful for **testing algorithms before deployment**.
Soft Reset	Reset triggered by software command.	STM32 can trigger soft reset via **NVIC_SystemReset()**.	Useful for **firmware recovery and watchdog resets**.
Step-Down Regulator	A power regulator that lowers input voltage.	STM32 boards often integrate **buck converters** for efficient power supply.	Essential for **battery-powered systems**.
Soldering	The process of attaching MCU/package to PCB.	STM32 comes in packages like **QFP, BGA, LQFP, and WLCSP**.	Impacts **manufacturability and debugging accessibility**.

Glossary of Terms – Letter T

Term	Definition	Context in STM32	Additional Notes
Timer (TIM)	A hardware peripheral for counting, measuring, or generating events.	STM32 integrates multiple **general-purpose, advanced, and basic timers**.	Used for **PWM, input capture, event timing, and motor control**.
TrustZone	ARM Cortex-M33/M23 feature for hardware-	STM32L5 and STM32U5 series	Separates **secure and non-secure firmware**

	based security partitioning.	include **TrustZone technology**.	to improve system integrity.
TWI (Two-Wire Interface)	Another name for **I²C communication protocol**.	STM32 supports **multi-master and slave modes** via I²C hardware.	Widely used for **sensors, EEPROMs, and low-speed comms**.
TDP (Thermal Design Power)	Maximum amount of heat a device must dissipate under typical load.	STM32 MCUs have very low TDP due to efficient design.	Important in **industrial and automotive environments**.
TCK (Test Clock)	Clock signal in JTAG interface.	STM32 supports **JTAG debugging** with TCK as synchronization clock.	Often replaced with **SWD for efficiency**.
TRST (Test Reset)	Reset signal for JTAG debugging interface.	Present on STM32 JTAG-compatible devices.	Not used in **SWD-only configurations**.
TFT (Thin Film Transistor) Display	A type of LCD display with active matrix addressing.	STM32 MCUs with **LTDC (LCD-TFT Controller)** can drive TFT displays.	Used in **HMIs, dashboards, and smart devices**.
Trace Port Interface Unit (TPIU)	Provides real-time program execution trace.	STM32 supports **SWO trace via TPIU**.	Enables **advanced debugging and profiling**.

TRNG (True Random Number Generator)	Hardware-based random number generator.	Available in STM32 devices with **crypto hardware accelerators**.	Used in **encryption, authentication, and secure boot**.
Transistor-Transistor Logic (TTL)	A logic family based on 5V operation.	STM32 I/O pins are **not 5V tolerant** in some series.	Requires **level shifting when interfacing with TTL devices**.
TAP (Test Access Port)	Part of JTAG standard for test/debug.	STM32 implements TAP for boundary scan and debug.	Essential in **board testing and programming**.
Thread	A lightweight execution unit within an OS.	STM32 RTOS (FreeRTOS, CMSIS-RTOS) uses **threads for multitasking**.	Allows **concurrent processing of multiple tasks**.
Throughput	Amount of data processed per unit time.	STM32 throughput depends on **clock speed, DMA, and bus efficiency**.	Critical in **real-time comms and DSP**.
Toggle	Repeated switching of a digital pin state.	STM32 GPIOs support fast toggling using **BSRR register**.	Used in **LED blinking, clock generation, and debug signaling**.
TFTP (Trivial File Transfer Protocol)	Lightweight file transfer protocol.	STM32 with Ethernet/Wi-Fi can implement **TFTP bootloading or OTA update**.	Often used for **firmware updates**.

TSC (Touch Sensing Controller)	Peripheral for capacitive touch detection.	Some STM32 devices include **TSC hardware**.	Used in **touch buttons, sliders, and user interfaces**.
Timer Capture/Compare (CCR)	Timer feature for input signal capture and PWM output compare.	STM32 timers have **CCR registers** for this purpose.	Used in **frequency measurement, PWM control, and event timing**.
Task Scheduler	RTOS component that manages thread execution.	STM32 FreeRTOS uses a **preemptive or cooperative scheduler**.	Provides **deterministic multitasking**.
TDP (Total Dissipated Power)	The power consumed by the MCU during operation.	STM32 typically consumes **low mW range in active mode**.	Optimized with **low-power modes**.
Test Bench	Hardware/software environment for testing designs.	STM32 projects use **test benches for firmware validation**.	Essential in **production and certification**.
Timeout	Event triggered when a timer or process exceeds set duration.	STM32 peripherals use **timeout detection for comms protocols**.	Prevents **infinite wait in I²C, UART, or SPI transfers**.
Transceiver	Device that can transmit and receive data.	STM32 interfaces with **CAN, RS485, and RF transceivers**.	Used in **industrial and IoT comms**.
Topology	Structure of power distribution or	STM32 can operate in **star, bus, or mesh networks**.	Important in **IoT and distributed control systems**.

Term	Definition	Context in STM32	Additional Notes
	communication network.		
TSP (Touch Sensing Pin)	Pin configured for capacitive sensing.	STM32 maps **specific GPIOs as TSPs** when TSC is enabled.	Used for **touch buttons, sliders, and wheel sensors**.
Through-Hole Technology (THT)	PCB mounting technique with pin-in-hole soldering.	STM32 development boards sometimes mix THT and SMT.	More robust for **prototyping and mechanical stress**.

Glossary of Terms – Letter U

Term	Definition	Context in STM32	Additional Notes
UART (Universal Asynchronous Receiver/Transmitter)	A hardware module for asynchronous serial communication.	STM32 MCUs include multiple **UART/USART peripherals**.	Commonly used for **debugging, GPS modules, and serial comms**.
USART (Universal Synchronous/Asynchronous Receiver/Transmitter)	Communication module supporting both synchronous and asynchronous modes.	STM32 USART can function as **UART, SPI-like sync, or IrDA**.	Offers **greater flexibility than UART**.
USB (Universal Serial Bus)	Industry-standard interface for data transfer and peripherals.	STM32F, STM32H, and STM32L series feature **USB FS/HS device, host, and OTG**.	Supports **HID, MSC, CDC, DFU, and custom classes**.

USB OTG (On-The-Go)	USB feature allowing a device to act as both **host and device**.	STM32 supports **OTG FS/HS** with role switching.	Used in **USB flash drive connections and device-to-device comms**.
ULP (Ultra-Low Power)	Power-saving operation mode in microcontrollers.	STM32L series is optimized for **ultra-low-power operation**.	Extends **battery life in IoT, wearables, and medical devices**.
Update Event	An event generated when a timer counter overflows or resets.	STM32 timers trigger **update events for interrupts and DMA**.	Often used in **periodic interrupts and PWM refresh**.
Unaligned Access	Memory access where the address is not aligned to data size.	Some STM32 MCUs support **unaligned access**, others raise faults.	Critical for **ARM Cortex-M programming efficiency**.
Unified Power Format (UPF)	A format for defining power intent in designs.	STM32 does not use UPF directly but **power domains and scaling** relate.	Mostly relevant in **ASIC/SoC design**, but concept applies to MCU power mgmt.
User Button	Hardware push button provided on dev boards.	STM32 Nucleo and Discovery boards have **USER or RESET buttons**.	Used for **reset, boot, or user input** in demos.
USART DMA Mode	USART feature using DMA to transfer data without CPU intervention.	STM32 supports **DMA-based USART communication**.	Enables **high-speed serial transfers** with low CPU load.

Term	Definition	STM32 Context	Importance
UCPD (USB Type-C / USB Power Delivery Controller)	Hardware peripheral for managing USB-C and PD.	STM32G0/G4 and STM32L5 series integrate **UCPD block**.	Used for **USB-C charging, role detection, and power negotiation**.
Unified Debug Model (UDM)	Standardized debug architecture in ARM Cortex-M.	STM32 follows ARM's **CoreSight debug model**.	Ensures **compatibility across tools**.
Undefined Instruction Exception	Exception triggered by unrecognized opcode.	STM32 Cortex-M cores handle **undefined instructions via exception vector**.	Useful for **fault detection and debugging**.
User Mode	Privileged level of execution with restricted access.	STM32 Cortex-M cores support **privileged and unprivileged (user) modes**.	Essential for **RTOS security and memory protection**.
Unsigned Integer	An integer data type with only non-negative values.	Used in STM32 C code as uint8_t, uint16_t, uint32_t.	Optimized for **bitwise operations and registers**.
Update Request Source (URS)	Timer setting controlling update events.	STM32 TIMx_CR1 register has URS bit.	Ensures **precise timing event control**.
Unlock Sequence	Specific write sequence required to unlock a register.	STM32 FLASH and WDT registers need **unlock sequences**.	Prevents **accidental writes to critical registers**.

Upcounter Mode	Timer mode where the counter increments until overflow.	STM32 timers default to **upcounter operation**.	Can be combined with **interrupts, PWM, and capture modes**.
Unbuffered Mode	Mode where data is transferred directly without intermediate buffer.	STM32 ADC/DAC/USART may use unbuffered settings.	Trades **performance for simplicity**.
USB DFU (Device Firmware Upgrade)	USB protocol for firmware updates.	Many STM32 devices support **DFU bootloader mode**.	Allows **firmware update via USB without external programmer**.
Unsigned Saturation	Operation where values clamp at maximum instead of wrapping.	STM32 DSP instructions include **saturation arithmetic**.	Useful in **signal processing**.
Unclocked Peripheral	Peripheral disabled by turning off its clock in RCC.	STM32 RCC allows **peripheral clock gating** for power saving.	Prevents **unnecessary power consumption**.
User Stack Pointer (PSP/MSP)	ARM Cortex-M has two stack pointers: Main (MSP) and Process (PSP).	STM32 allows switching between **MSP and PSP**.	Important in **RTOS thread management**.
USB HID (Human Interface Device)	USB class for keyboards, mice, joysticks.	STM32 USB stack supports **HID device implementation**.	Common in **consumer and industrial applications**.

Glossary of Terms – Letter V

Term	Definition	Context in STM32	Additional Notes
VDD	Main supply voltage pin for the MCU.	STM32 MCUs usually operate at **1.8V – 3.6V** depending on the family.	Must be properly decoupled with **capacitors near pins**.
VSS	Ground reference for MCU (0V).	All STM32 packages have multiple **VSS pins**.	Always connect all **VSS pins to ground plane** for stability.
VDDA	Analog supply voltage pin.	Required for **ADC, DAC, comparators, and analog peripherals**.	Should be filtered separately from VDD for **noise reduction**.
VSSA	Analog ground pin.	Used with **VDDA** to isolate analog and digital grounds.	Connect to system ground at a **single point (star grounding)**.
VREF+ (Voltage Reference Positive)	Positive reference for ADC/DAC conversion.	Can be tied to **VDDA or external reference source**.	Higher accuracy if external **precision reference** is used.
VREF- (Voltage Reference Negative)	Negative reference for ADC.	Normally tied to **ground (VSSA)**.	Some STM32s allow flexible routing.
VREFINT (Internal Reference Voltage)	Internal stable reference (~1.2V).	Used by ADC for **calibration and temperature sensing**.	Accessible through **ADC channels**.

Voltage Regulator	Regulates input voltage to stable internal core voltage.	STM32 MCUs have **embedded LDO or SMPS regulators**.	Core usually runs at **1.2V or 1.8V**, even if VDD = 3.3V.
VBAT	Backup battery supply pin.	Powers the **RTC, backup registers, and LSE oscillator**.	Keeps **time and data retention** when main VDD is off.
Vector Table	Memory table storing exception and interrupt vectors.	Located at start of **Flash or RAM** in STM32.	Can be **relocated using SCB->VTOR register**.
Vector Table Offset (VTOR)	Register holding base address of interrupt vector table.	Allows **dynamic relocation** of vector table in STM32.	Useful in **bootloaders and RTOS systems**.
Voltage Detector (PVD)	Peripheral that monitors supply voltage levels.	STM32 PVD can trigger **interrupt or reset** when VDD drops below threshold.	Protects system from **brown-out conditions**.
VECTACTIVE	Field in the Interrupt Control and State Register (ICSR).	Indicates the **currently active exception number**.	Useful in **RTOS and debugging**.
Virtual COM Port (VCP)	USB feature that emulates a COM serial port.	STM32 USB CDC class implements **VCP for serial comms**.	Commonly used for **debugging via USB**.
Voltage Scaling	Power management technique to reduce core voltage.	STM32L and STM32H series support **dynamic voltage scaling**.	Balances **performance and power consumption**.

Variable	A named data object in software.	STM32 firmware uses **C/C++ variables stored in SRAM or Flash**.	Important for **embedded memory optimization**.
Volatile Keyword	C keyword telling compiler not to optimize access to a variable.	Used for **hardware registers and shared RTOS variables**.	Essential in **embedded programming**.
VECTRESET	Bit in the Application Interrupt and Reset Control Register (AIRCR).	Performs a **system reset** when set.	Alternative to **NVIC_SystemReset()**.
Vector Interrupt Controller (VIC/NVIC)	Handles prioritization and dispatching of interrupts.	STM32 uses **Nested Vectored Interrupt Controller (NVIC)**.	Provides **fast interrupt response**.
Voltage Drop (Vdrop)	Loss of voltage across a regulator or conductor.	Must be minimized in **PCB power traces**.	Important in **high-current STM32 designs**.
Variable Clock Domain	A subsystem clock that can be scaled independently.	STM32 RCC supports **different clock domains (AHB, APB, etc.)**.	Useful for **performance tuning**.
VECTPENDING	Field in the ICSR register showing pending interrupt number.	STM32 uses it for **debug and system diagnostics**.	Allows monitoring of **interrupt queue**.

Voltage Reference Buffer	Internal amplifier that drives reference voltages.	STM32H7 has dedicated **VREFBUF peripheral**.	Can be used instead of external **precision references**.
Variable Frequency Timer	Timer that can change frequency dynamically.	STM32 general-purpose timers allow **on-the-fly frequency adjustment**.	Used in **motor control and PWM applications**.
VDDIO2	Separate supply for I/O pins in some STM32 packages.	Enables **dual-voltage domains for GPIO** (e.g., 1.8V and 3.3V).	Ensures compatibility with **mixed-voltage systems**.
Voltage Comparator	Compares two input voltages and outputs logic signal.	STM32G4, STM32L4 have **on-chip comparators**.	Useful in **signal conditioning and protection circuits**.
Vectoring	The process of redirecting CPU to correct ISR address.	Managed by **NVIC using vector table**.	Critical for **real-time responsiveness**.

Glossary of Terms – Letter W

Term	Definition	Context in STM32	Additional Notes
Watchdog Timer (WDT)	Hardware timer that resets the system if not refreshed.	STM32 has **Independent Watchdog (IWDG)** and **Window Watchdog (WWDG)**.	Essential for **system safety and fault recovery**.

Window Watchdog (WWDG)	Watchdog with configurable open/closed refresh window.	Used in STM32 for **timing-critical fault detection**.	Prevents accidental refreshes outside the allowed window.
Independent Watchdog (IWDG)	Standalone watchdog running on its own clock (LSI).	Continues to run even in **low-power modes**.	Crucial for **safety-critical embedded designs**.
Word (32-bit)	A data unit typically 4 bytes (32 bits) on Cortex-M.	STM32 CPUs handle data in **words, halfwords, and bytes**.	Important for **memory alignment and efficiency**.
Word Alignment	Arranging data in memory at natural word boundaries.	STM32 requires aligned access for **efficient memory operations**.	Misalignment may cause **BusFaults** in some series.
Word Swap (Endianness)	Changing byte order within a word.	STM32 is **little-endian** by default.	Endianness is relevant in **networking and external peripherals**.
Wait State	Extra clock cycle inserted during memory access.	STM32 Flash requires **wait states at high clock speeds**.	Configured via **FLASH_ACR register**.
Write Protection	Mechanism preventing modification of memory or registers.	STM32 supports **Flash write protection, option bytes, and WPR registers**.	Protects against **accidental overwrites**.

Word of Data	The standard data size for CPU operations (32 bits in Cortex-M).	STM32 load/store instructions operate on **bytes, halfwords, and words**.	Optimizing data size improves **performance and memory usage**.
Write Buffer	Temporary storage before data is committed to memory.	STM32 bus interfaces use **write buffers for efficiency**.	Improves performance in **DMA and peripheral writes**.
Warm Reset	A reset that preserves some system state.	STM32 warm reset occurs during **system reset without full power loss**.	Different from **cold reset** which clears everything.
Write Cycle	Operation of writing data to Flash or EEPROM.	STM32 Flash has defined **write cycle times**.	Exceeding limits reduces **Flash endurance**.
Wait-for-Interrupt (WFI)	CPU instruction that halts until an interrupt occurs.	Used in STM32 low-power modes.	Saves **power while idle**.
Wait-for-Event (WFE)	CPU instruction that halts until an event or interrupt occurs.	STM32 supports **event-driven synchronization**.	Useful in **multi-core and RTOS systems**.
Word Access	Memory access in word-size chunks (32-bit).	STM32 peripherals often require **word writes for configuration registers**.	Misaligned access can cause **fault exceptions**.

Write-Through Cache	Cache policy where data is written to both cache and memory.	STM32 Cortex-M7 implements **write-through/write-back cache**.	Ensures **data consistency**.
Write-Back Cache	Cache policy where writes are delayed until necessary.	STM32H7 uses **write-back cache** for performance.	Risk of **data loss if cache not flushed before shutdown**.
Window Mode (ADC)	ADC feature that triggers interrupt if result falls inside/outside a threshold.	STM32 ADC supports **analog watchdog (AWD)** window comparison.	Useful for **signal monitoring**.
Word Stack Alignment	Ensuring stack frames align to word boundaries.	Required in STM32 Cortex-M for **efficient exception handling**.	Misalignment may break **function calls**.
Write Lock	Protection mechanism to lock write access to registers or memory.	STM32 has **GPIOx_LCKR, FLASH_WRP, and RTC write-protection bits**.	Used in **secure applications**.
Waveform Generator	Module to create digital or analog waveforms.	STM32 DAC and timers generate **sine, square, PWM, etc.**	Used in **signal processing and motor control**.
Word Instruction	CPU instruction occupying 32 bits.	STM32 Cortex-M supports **Thumb-2 ISA with 16-bit and 32-bit instructions**.	Balances **code density and performance**.

Write Pending Flag	Status bit indicating ongoing write operation.	STM32 Flash memory sets **BSY flag during write/erase**.	Must be cleared before issuing next command.
Window Comparator (Analog)	Compares signal against upper/lower thresholds.	Implemented in STM32 **ADC watchdog**.	Useful for **overvoltage/undervoltage detection**.

Glossary of Terms – Letter X

Term	Definition	Context in STM32	Additional Notes
XOR (Exclusive OR)	A logical operation that outputs true only if inputs differ.	Used in STM32 for **bitwise register operations, checksum, encryption, and parity checks**.	Instruction available in Cortex-M cores for **fast bit manipulation**.
XTAL (Crystal Oscillator)	External quartz crystal providing stable clock source.	STM32 uses **HSE (High-Speed External) crystal** for precise system clock.	Frequency range usually **4–26 MHz**, depending on device.
XIP (Execute in Place)	Technique to run code directly from external memory without copying to RAM.	STM32 with **QSPI or Octo-SPI** can execute firmware directly from external Flash.	Saves RAM but may be slower than internal Flash.
XBAR (Crossbar Switch)	Hardware interconnect for managing bus	Present in advanced STM32 families (e.g., STM32H7, STM32F7).	Allows **parallel bus transactions for performance**.

	access between CPU and peripherals.		
X Coordinate (GUI/Display)	The horizontal position in a graphical system.	STM32 with **TFT, LTDC, or graphics libraries** use X coordinates for rendering.	Paired with **Y coordinate** for full graphics control.
XML (Extensible Markup Language)	Markup language for data representation.	STM32CubeMX generates **project configurations in XML format**.	Useful for **toolchain interoperability**.
XBee Module	A wireless communication module based on ZigBee protocol.	Often interfaced with STM32 via **UART or SPI**.	Popular in **IoT and embedded wireless projects**.
XIP Cache	Cache mechanism for execute-in-place memory.	STM32 Octo-SPI supports **XIP with instruction/data caching**.	Greatly improves performance when running from external Flash.
Xfer (Transfer)	Abbreviation for data transfer in drivers and APIs.	STM32 HAL/LL libraries often use "xfer" in DMA, SPI, and I2C functions.	Example: HAL_SPI_TransmitReceive_DMA manages SPI xfers.
XON/XOFF	Software flow control using special characters.	STM32 UART supports **XON/XOFF protocol** in serial communication.	Alternative to **hardware RTS/CTS flow control**.

Term	Definition	Details	Application
XREG (Extended Register)	Extended or special-purpose CPU register.	STM32 Cortex-M uses **special registers like xPSR, PRIMASK, BASEPRI**.	Useful for **interrupt and system control**.
X-CUBE (STM32 Software Pack)	STM32Cube expansion packages with middleware and examples.	Examples: **X-CUBE-AI (AI on STM32), X-CUBE-USB, X-CUBE-BLE**.	Extends functionality of STM32 ecosystem.
X-CUBE-AI	STM32Cube expansion pack for Artificial Intelligence.	Allows deploying **deep learning models on STM32 MCUs**.	Converts trained neural networks to run on STM32 hardware.
X-Y Plotting	Representing data on X-Y axes.	STM32 used in **oscilloscopes, data loggers, signal visualization**.	Implemented with **TFT LCD or PC plotting tools**.
X Direction (Motion Control)	Axis in robotic and motor control systems.	STM32 timers and encoders manage **multi-axis motion (X, Y, Z)**.	Critical for **CNC, robotics, and 3D printing**.
XIL (X-in-the-Loop)	Simulation methodology (HIL, SIL, PIL).	STM32 is often tested using **SIL/PIL with CubeIDE and MATLAB/Simulink**.	Enhances **verification of embedded systems**.
X-cube-MEMS	STM32 software package for motion and environmental sensors.	Provides drivers for **accelerometers, gyroscopes, magnetometers, barometers**.	Used in **IoT, wearables, and robotics**.

| XBUS (External Bus Interface) | External interface bus for peripherals/memory. | STM32 with **FSMC/FMC** supports XBUS for external SRAM, SDRAM, LCD. | Used for **expanding memory and display connectivity**. |

Glossary of Terms – Letter Y

Term	Definition	Context in STM32	Additional Notes
Y-Axis (Coordinate System)	Vertical axis in a 2D coordinate system.	STM32 graphics libraries (e.g., **TouchGFX, LVGL**) use Y-axis with X for rendering images and UI elements.	Essential for **TFT/LCD screen drawing**.
Y-Cable	A cable that splits one connection into two.	Used with STM32 boards to provide **both power and data via USB**.	Common in debugging or powering external devices.
Yaw (Rotation around Vertical Axis)	Angular rotation around the Z-axis (yaw in 3D motion).	STM32 motion-sensing projects use **gyroscopes and IMUs** to measure yaw.	Crucial in **drones, robotics, and navigation systems**.
Ymodem Protocol	File transfer protocol based on packets.	STM32 bootloaders and firmware updaters use **Ymodem for UART/serial updates**.	Supports error detection and **chunked data transfer**.

YUV (Color Encoding)	Color format separating luminance (Y) and chrominance (U, V).	STM32 with **camera interface (DCMI)** supports YUV for video input.	Used in **image processing, machine vision, and video apps**.
Yield (Task Switching)	Voluntary task handover in multitasking systems.	STM32 running **RTOS (FreeRTOS/ThreadX)** uses yield to let other tasks execute.	Prevents CPU hogging by a single process.
Y-Capacitor	Capacitor used in EMI/EMC filtering between line and ground.	STM32 power supply design may include Y-capacitors for **safety and noise reduction**.	Ensures **compliance with EMC standards**.
Yttrium-Aluminum-Garnet (YAG) Crystal	A laser crystal sometimes used in optical electronics.	Indirectly linked to STM32 in **laser control or optical sensing applications**.	Example: medical or industrial laser controllers.
Y2K38 Problem (Year 2038 Bug)	Integer overflow problem in 32-bit time systems.	STM32 using **32-bit signed timestamps** may face issues beyond year 2038.	Mitigated by **64-bit time representations**.
Y-Signal (Video Signal)	Luminance component of a video signal.	STM32 video processing (with **LTDC + DCMI**) uses Y-signal in **grayscale and YUV color models**.	Crucial for **image clarity and brightness control**.
Y-Branch (PCB Routing)	A branching structure in circuit design.	STM32 PCB layouts use Y-branches for	Must be carefully designed to **avoid reflections/noise**.

		signal splitting (e.g., clock lines, buses).	
Y-Buffer	Memory buffer for Y (luminance) channel in video frames.	STM32 DMA transfers video data into **separate Y, U, and V buffers**.	Optimizes **real-time image processing**.
Yagi Antenna	Directional antenna for wireless communication.	STM32-based IoT systems may use Yagi antennas with **LoRa, Zigbee, or Sub-GHz radios**.	Provides **long-range communication**.
Yellow Wire (Ground/Power Reference)	Conventionally used in wiring to denote power signals.	STM32 prototyping often uses **yellow wires in breadboards** for consistent mapping.	Helps **visual wiring discipline**.
Yield Instruction (Assembly)	Assembly-level instruction hint for power-efficient waiting.	Cortex-M cores in STM32 support **WFE (Wait For Event) / WFI (Wait For Interrupt)** for yielding CPU.	Reduces **power consumption in low-power apps**.
YUV422	Specific YUV color format with chroma subsampling.	STM32 camera and display interfaces often use **YUV422** for efficient video compression.	Balances **color quality and memory usage**.
Yaw Rate Sensor	A sensor that measures angular velocity around vertical axis.	STM32 projects with **MPU6050, L3G4200D,**	Important in **vehicle stability, drones, and robotics**.

		or other IMUs capture yaw rate.	
YML (YAML)	Human-readable data serialization format.	STM32 developers sometimes use **YAML configs** in CI/CD pipelines or build systems.	Easier alternative to **JSON/XML**.
Yoke (Magnetic/Electrical)	Magnetic or structural part in motors and displays.	STM32 used in **motor drivers and old CRT display control** may involve yokes.	Still relevant in **BLDC motor control systems**.

Glossary of Terms – Letter Z

Term	Definition	Context in STM32	Additional Notes
Zener Diode	Semiconductor diode that allows current to flow in reverse when voltage exceeds its breakdown voltage.	Used in STM32 **power regulation, reset circuits, and ESD protection**.	Helps prevent **over-voltage damage**.
Zero Crossing	The point where an AC waveform crosses the zero voltage line.	STM32 in **AC motor control, dimmers, and power electronics** uses zero-cross detection.	Enables **synchronization with AC mains**.

Zigbee	Wireless communication protocol based on IEEE 802.15.4.	STM32 supports Zigbee through **external RF modules or STM32WB series (with integrated wireless)**.	Used in **IoT, smart homes, and industrial automation**.
Z-Buffer (Depth Buffer)	A buffer that stores depth information in 3D graphics.	STM32 with **GPU-accelerated GUIs (Chrom-ART, TouchGFX)** may simulate depth handling.	Ensures **proper rendering of overlapping objects**.
Zero Latency Interrupt (ZLI)	Interrupt with the highest priority, bypassing normal latency.	STM32 Cortex-M cores allow **NVIC priority configuration** to achieve near-zero latency.	Useful in **critical control systems**.
Zener Clamp	A circuit that uses a Zener diode to limit voltage spikes.	Common in **STM32 I/O pin protection** against surges.	Prevents **damage to GPIOs**.
Zero-Drift Amplifier	Op-amp with minimal offset drift over temperature.	Used with STM32 in **precision sensor applications**.	Ensures **stable ADC readings**.
Zigzag Routing	PCB trace routing pattern to match signal lengths.	STM32 PCBs use zigzag routing for **high-speed buses (USB, SDRAM, QSPI)**.	Helps in **signal timing synchronization**.

Zero-Padding	Adding extra zeros to data for alignment or processing.	STM32 **DSP and FFT operations** use zero-padding for efficiency.	Improves **accuracy of signal analysis**.
Zettabyte (ZB)	Unit of digital information = 10^{21} bytes.	STM32 itself cannot handle ZB, but relevant in **cloud + IoT big data storage**.	Highlights **IoT data growth**.
ZIF Socket (Zero Insertion Force)	Socket that allows IC insertion without pressure.	Used in STM32 prototyping boards for **swappable MCU testing**.	Useful in **development and debugging labs**.
Zero-Wait State Memory	Memory access without added delay cycles.	STM32 internal flash often supports **zero-wait execution** at low clock speeds.	Boosts **performance at lower frequencies**.
Zener Breakdown	Breakdown of diode due to reverse bias exceeding voltage threshold.	Considered in STM32 **power supply and surge protection** circuits.	Must be managed to **avoid unwanted failures**.
Z-Index (GUI Layering)	Ordering property of overlapping graphical objects.	STM32 GUI frameworks (e.g., **TouchGFX, emWin**) use Z-index for screen layering.	Essential for **multi-layer displays**.
Zigzag Antenna	Special antenna shape used in compact RF designs.	Used in STM32 IoT boards for **LoRa, Zigbee, or BLE modules**.	Saves space while **maintaining good RF performance**.

Zero-Knowledge Proof (ZKP)	Cryptographic method to prove knowledge without revealing the information itself.	STM32 with **secure elements** may implement ZKPs in **IoT security**.	Important for **future cryptographic IoT devices**.
Zener Voltage	Voltage at which a Zener diode conducts in reverse.	STM32 circuits use it for **voltage reference and regulation**.	Typical values: 3.3V, 5.1V, 12V.
Zsh (Z Shell)	Advanced command-line shell environment.	STM32 developers often use **Zsh with ARM toolchains**.	Provides **better scripting in embedded development**.
Zero-Bias Diode	Diode that can operate with no external bias voltage.	Sometimes used in STM32 **RF front-end circuits**.	Provides **low-noise detection** in radio receivers.
Zooming (UI)	Scaling operation in GUIs and graphics.	STM32-based **touchscreen UIs** support zooming using TouchGFX or LVGL.	Common in **maps, medical imaging, and dashboards**.

Made in the USA
Monee, IL
08 September 2025

25232175R00214